Flickering Shadows

This series of publications on Africa, Latin America, Southeast Asia, and Global and Comparative Studies is designed to present significant research, translation, and opinion to area specialists and to a wide community of persons interested in world affairs. The editor seeks manuscripts of quality on any subject and can usually make a decision regarding publication within three months of receipt of the original work. Production methods generally permit a work to appear within one year of acceptance. The editor works closely with authors to produce a high quality book. The series appears in a paperback format and is distributed worldwide. For more information, contact the executive editor at Ohio University Press, Scott Quadrangle, University Terrace, Athens, Ohio 45701.

Executive editor: Gillian Berchowitz
AREA CONSULTANTS
Africa: Diane Ciekawy
Latin America: Thomas Walker
Southeast Asia: William H. Frederick

The Ohio University Research in International Studies series is published for the Center for International Studies by the Ohio University Press. The views expressed in individual volumes are those of the authors and should not be considered to represent the policies or beliefs of the Center for International Studies, the Ohio University Press, or Ohio University.

# Flickering Shadows

## CINEMA AND IDENTITY
## IN COLONIAL ZIMBABWE

J. M. Burns

Foreword by Peter Davis

*Ohio University Center for International Studies*
Research in International Studies
Africa Series No. 77
Ohio University Press
Athens

*Library of Congress Cataloging-in-Publication Data*

Burns, James McDonald.
Flickering shadows : cinema and identity in colonial Zimbabwe / J.M.
    Burns ; foreword by Peter Davis.
        p. cm. — (Research in international studies. Africa series ; no. 77)
    Includes bibliographical references (p. ) and index.
    ISBN 0-89680-224-8 (pbk. : alk. paper)
        1. Motion pictures—Zimbabwe—History. I. Title. II. Series.

PN1993.5.Z55 B87 2002

2002019548

# Contents

# Illustrations

# Foreword

Cinema was the greatest propaganda tool ever fashioned. Many of the most accomplished early films, from a technical and aesthetic point of view, were also consummate propaganda, from *Birth of a Nation*, through the work of Eisenstein in postrevolution Russia, to Milestone's *All Quiet on the Western Front* and beyond. Sometimes the cause was good, as in Chaplin's attack on Hitler in *The Great Dictator*; sometimes it was supportive of evil, as in Leni Riefenstahl's *Triumph of the Will*. These were accomplished practitioners of the art of persuasion. But where the propaganda element was effective, it is probably fair to say that this was due to a combination of skill in storytelling and ability to manipulate the emotions. This was true also of the positive social propaganda produced by great documentarians like John Grierson. Whatever the message, it was sculpted by superb craftsmanship. Whether in documentary or fiction, entertainment values were paramount.

Often the most effective propaganda was produced by men who did not even know they were doing it. Blatant propaganda supporting the British Empire was churned out by both British and Hollywood studios in the form of adventure dramas like *Sanders of the River, The Four Feathers, Charge of the Light Brigade, King Solomon's Mines, Soldiers Three, Stanley and Livingstone.* . . . It is a long list. There can be no doubt that the images of these films supported the ethos of white superiority, molding the minds of all people who saw them.

Each portion of the British Empire reflected a different relationship to film. Under the tight rein of censorship, countries like India and Egypt developed their own industries; these countries were wealthy enough to make their own films, and large urban centers gave them ready audiences. Sub-Saharan Africa was different. The preconditions for the creation of an indigenous cinema simply did not exist. Most of the population was poor and scattered in rural areas, with no access to cinemas, which, where they did exist, were largely for Whites Only. If Africans were to see films, the effort had to be made to bring films to them. Cinema for Africans was virgin territory, and with full control over production and distribution the colonial power could cultivate it at will.

Those Europeans who during the nineteenth century invaded African lands not only wanted to exploit the land but also needed the labor of the inhabitants. To turn Africans into submissive servants required persuading them to accept colonial rule. For the colonizer, the perpetual challenge was to control the mind of the colonized. This was implemented through the law, the education system, the churches, control of the press, and, as James Burns so masterfully demonstrates, motion pictures. In some areas, the colonizers became film producers. There was a genuine desire "to improve the lot of the native," so instructional films on health and agriculture were made and disseminated. But the films left no doubt that all benefits to Africans flowed from the fount of white beneficence.

Burns's exploration of the records and films still extant adds massively to our knowledge of the process of colonial rule, revealing very clearly the kinds of debate that took place around films for Africans. The films themselves offer an idealized representation of the colonial mission in Africa, while at the same time confirming the rigid hegemonic nature of the relationship between white and black. These films invite close analysis, for they expose the kinesis of colonization. The poses of whites, their movements, the military neatness of the clothes they wear, the dominance of their figures within the frame, their command of technology, their clear presentation as decision takers, are contrasted with the deference and respectful gestures of blacks, who are shown as "primitives," as primarily manual laborers, as subservients who receive and carry out orders, as grateful re-cipients of largesse. One film carries the title *We Were Primitive:* unashamedly, by using "We," white script-writers have appro-priated the black voice. No Africans were consulted for the scripts or trained as technicians. But while even the newsreels should be seen as constructs and not as slices of "reality," there are nevertheless glimpses of actuality to be caught for the dis-cerning viewer. These are not great works of art, but they do tell us a lot about relations between black and white and about the nature of power. Burns has turned us on to a treasure trove of material.

In his dedication to finding out the impact on Africans of the films that were produced for their consumption, Burns is a pio-neer. His research suggests that results were far different from the hopes and expectations of the colonizers, who firmly and ar-rogantly believed that they knew what was best for Africans and consistently misread "the African mind." Above all, these earnest colonial filmmakers ignored what every advertiser knows: you persuade most effectively when you also entertain.

PETER DAVIS

# Preface

In the fall of 1952, a frustrated official of the Rhodesian Information Service filed a report that captured something crucial about the cultural project of colonialism. J. Stakesby-Lewis, an officer in a mobile cinema unit that showed government-produced films to rural people in the British colony of Southern Rhodesia, had begun to despair about their value as a medium that could influence African audiences: "For the more primitive Africans the film as an aid to education is still of negligible value," he lamented after five years of field experience. "They fail to organize perception on a higher plane, everything familiar is greeted with laughs of recognition until the show becomes more than anything else just a 'source of innocent merriment.'"[1]

Stakesby-Lewis's report expressed both the hopes and fears of a generation of colonial officials. Since motion pictures first appeared in Africa in the waning years of the nineteenth century, Europeans had expected the medium to exert a powerful sway over the indigenous peoples of Africa. Whites believed the cinema would prove to be a potent vehicle of social change, one that would help assimilate Africans into a new cultural, economic, and political order. However, the unpredictable behavior of audiences frequently frustrated these lofty aspirations. Officials like Stakesby-Lewis were mystified when Africans appeared to misunderstand or misinterpret films. They also feared that the purported "imitative" tendencies of Africans made them peculiarly vulnerable to "antisocial" images. These concerns made film an unpredictable medium, capable of both "civilizing" and "unsettling" African audiences. In rendering his pessimistic assessment, Stakesby-Lewis was merely one of dozens of colonial observers who, over a span of seven decades, concluded that Africans were doomed never to master this complicated, modern media completely.

This book is a study of the relationship between cinema and society in colonial Africa. It focuses on the experience of one particular region, now known as Zimbabwe, which from 1896 to 1964 was the colonial settler state of Southern Rhodesia and thereafter, until 1980, was known simply as Rhodesia. As a colony, this region was home to two of the most ambitious state-sponsored film production units in Africa, the Central African Film Unit (CAFU), and the Rhodesian Information Services' Film Unit (RIS). The story of these film units is a remarkable, and largely unknown, chapter in the history of colonialism. Over three decades these units produced hundreds of films that were seen by millions of people throughout colonial Africa. Shown primarily in rural areas, these films provided many Africans with their first contact with the world outside of the village.

This book began as a study of the policies and productions of these two film units, which operated for a relatively brief span in one region of Africa. However, the focus widened as it became apparent that the history of colonial filmmaking developed over a much wider geographical region and had roots in a much broader cultural and political context. It became a study of a colonial state's attempt to use film as an instrument of social and cultural hegemony and the ways in which that state rapidly lost control over this powerful medium. It focuses on the experience of colonial Zimbabwe, but considers that colony's experience within a much broader context. The book examines several aspects of the motion-picture industry in colonial Africa, including production, distribution, censorship, and audience reception. It also analyzes seventy years of public discussion regarding the appropriate role of motion pictures in colonial society and reveals the ways in which this discourse was rooted in racist assumptions of African "difference."

Chapter 1 demonstrates that, from the moment film arrived in British Central Africa, the medium inspired tremendous anxiety in colonial society. Settler communities throughout Southern Africa feared that motion pictures would inspire anti-social behavior in Africans and pressured their governments to circumscribe the exposure of "natives" to films. In Southern Rhodesia the state responded with stringent censorship and eventually investigated the possibilities of producing films exclusively for African audiences. Thus the subsequent creation of a state-sponsored cinema in the region stemmed from two impulses: on the one hand, it represented an attempt to educate Africans through a medium that was believed to exercise an almost hypnotic influence over them; on the other, it was a defensive effort to shield Africans from the "dangerous" images of the commercial cinema.

Chapter 2 examines the history of "colonial cinema," motion pictures made for Africans, in the era leading up to World War II. It focuses on a new approach to filmmaking that was pioneered in British Africa during the 1920s and 1930s.[2] Several officials developed this style while working on behalf of the British government and the International Missionary Society. This approach assumed that Africans were unable to comprehend screen images as quickly and thoroughly as audiences in Europe and North America; it therefore featured an extremely simplified style that offered a marked contrast to the techniques found in commercial films. Though the work of several anthropologists discredited the premises of this theory during the 1950s, filmmakers in Southern Africa remained reliant upon it until 1980.

Chapters 3 and 4 examine the career of CAFU, the film-production unit organized by the governments of Northern Rhodesia, Southern Rhodesia, and Nyasaland in 1948. Chapter 3 considers the context within which this organization produced and distributed films for Africans. It demonstrates that its use of the "colonial cinema" style, which it inherited from earlier experiments, rendered many of the unit's productions dull, unconvincing, and ultimately ineffective. It also suggests that audiences found many of the films' images alienating. In keeping with this argument, chapter 4 examines the responses of audiences to CAFU films and confirms that the work of the unit was often ineffective, and frequently counterproductive. The chapter evaluates the fleeting evidence of resistant and alternative readings of films and concludes that audiences were capable of ascribing meanings to motion pictures that diverged dramatically from those intended by the creators.

Chapter 5 examines the public debate regarding the cinema and its influence on Africans that paralleled the career of CAFU. In the late 1940s, settlers in Southern Rhodesia revived their calls for stringent censorship of films shown to Africans. This time, unlike in the 1920s, when there was a similar movement, educated Africans joined ranks with white critics in calling for greater governmental control of cinema images. The debate over film censorship lasted for a decade and culminated in a series of government hearings that exhaustively considered the influence of cinema on Africans in the region. This public discussion and the government investigation it inspired reveal that the settler community's lingering fear of African cinema audiences had not abated by the end of the Rhodesian Federation in 1963.

Chapter 6 briefly outlines the history of state-sponsored motion-picture production and distribution in Rhodesia after it became an independent state in 1965. It demonstrates the continuities in technique and personnel between the federal era of 1953–63 and the later work of the more notorious Rhodesian Information Service during the 1960s and 1970s. It also illuminates the growing resistance of Africans to state-sponsored propaganda during the last two decades of colonial rule.

This study draws on a variety of sources. During my ten-month stay in Zimbabwe I examined the extensive holdings of official and unofficial papers relating to film production and censorship at the National Archives in Harare. These documents included official correspondence of the governments of both Southern Rhodesia and the federation of the Rhodesias and Nyasaland. In the archive's audio-visual library I viewed scores of films produced by CAFU, the RIS, and other official and unofficial film-production organizations. I also examined the extensive discussions of the cinema that appeared in the region's many colonial and African newspapers.

Of all of the challenges posed by this project, the thorniest problem was assessing audience reactions to these films. The difficulty lay not in a lack of evidence: the files of the colonial government contain voluminous reports produced by agents of the state describing African responses to the films. However, the objectivity of such documents was patently questionable, and some secondary source of information was clearly necessary. Originally, I attempted to conduct interviews with older rural Zimbabweans who remembered the showings. Not surprisingly this proved unsatisfactory, as the original screenings had been organized more than five decades before. Thus many informants had at best vague memories of their initial responses. As an alternative, I located and interviewed many of the African cinema officers who had been in attendance at these early shows and whose responsibility it had been to assess crowd reactions. I understood that several impediments hindered their abilities to produce objective assessments of audience responses. These

included their status as outsiders, their position as representatives of the colonial state, and the communications problems
inherent in interviewing people in a language other than one's
mother tongue. Despite these problems, the interviews elicited
a wealth of information and detail that had not found its way
into their official reports. In general, these informants provided
me with an invaluable complement to the official story and significantly amplified the African voice in the project.[3]

Despite this important resource, ultimately a large part of the
picture seemed destined to remain a part of a "hidden transcript"—
an unrecorded voice lost to the archivist.[4] However, I have attempted to tease out a more complete picture by reading official
documents, press coverage, and the oral histories I accumulated
"against the grain." This has allowed me to detect the faint
echoes of African agency and African resistance.

The history of the cinema in British Central and Southern
Africa has implications far beyond the borders of colonial Zimbabwe. Colonial film units were active in Portuguese, French,
and Belgian colonies. Although many textbooks mention their
existence,[5] no monograph has evaluated the origins or impact
of their efforts. The histories of the African press and broadcasting are well documented, but the story of the cinema during
the colonial era, one of the most significant modes of communication between ruler and ruled, has been largely ignored. This
book explores the important role played by the cinema in shap-
ing the ways the colonized viewed the colonizers throughout
Africa, but particularly in Zimbabwe.

Within the relatively uncharted territory of colonial film
studies, this book attempts to refine and expand upon the work
of the handful of scholars who have directed their attention toward state-sponsored cinema. The British scholar Rosaleen
Smyth has made the greatest contribution to the field through
a series of path-breaking articles on British filmmaking in

Africa, published in the late 1970s and 1980s.[6] Dr. Smyth's body of work, though invaluable as a departure point for further research, provides a primarily descriptive outline of the development of colonial cinema. This book offers a more comprehensive and analytical overview of the subject. Regarding the history of CAFU itself, the few scholarly examinations of the unit's work in existence contain a number of misconceptions.[7] These faults stem not, I believe, from a willful misrepresentation of the unit's work, but rather from the scholars' choice of sources. Virtually all of the historians who have written about CAFU and the RIS Film Unit have relied on interviews with white veterans of the units as their primary sources of information.[8] While the white veterans' views have provided an important resource for this study, too, this vision of the CAFU and RIS units' histories and activities was limited by a number of logistical and cultural impediments. By contrasting these views with those of African witnesses, this manuscript offers a corrective to those earlier studies. It aspires to integrate both sides of the dialogue into a larger narrative that highlights the continuities and discontinuities of colonial filmmaking over a half century.

In exploring the relationship between cinema and society, this study provides insight into the nature of colonial rule in Southern Rhodesia and the way in which Africans negotiated the colonial experience. Rhodesian film policy—production, distribution, and censorship—reflected the blend of anxiety and condescension that characterized settler views of Africans. For seventy years, the Rhodesian government based its censorship policy on the assumption that Africans were intellectually different from, and inferior to, Europeans. Therefore they produced films for Africans that were remarkable for their simplistic style, demeaning images, and paternalistic messages. When these films elicited angry responses, colonial observers ascribed these criticisms to the inability of their audiences to comprehend a sophisticated medium. This settler arrogance allowed the state to continue to produce inflammatory motion pictures for increasingly hostile audiences during the liberation struggle of the 1970s. This heavy-handed film propaganda appears to have driven some members of these audiences to support the nationalist cause. Relying on extensive interviews and documents from the colonial archives, this book reveals the role of Rhodesian propaganda in eroding support for the minority white regime.

This study also demonstrates that Rhodesian propaganda during the 1940s and 1950s differed little from that of the later Rhodesian Front period of the 1960s and 1970s. Historians of the Rhodesian Front have drawn a distinction between the regime's notorious use of the media and the more benign work of its predecessor.[9] However, a study of film production under both regimes reveals strong similarities in personnel, approach, and content. In highlighting these continuities, this study illuminates the hazards posed by projecting artificial categorizations and reading fine distinctions into the nature of colonial rule in Africa.[10]

My analysis of the construction of images of Africans in colonial film draws on the thinking of Edward Said, particularly his work *Orientalism*. Said's important contribution lies in his insight into the way Western efforts to represent the colonial "other" reflect the fantasies and aspirations of the colonizer. Put simply, Western novels, paintings, and motion pictures that purport to represent the non-Western world provide more insight into the mind-set of the artist than the subject. So it was with specifically colonial films—remarkable documents that constitute the colonizer's effort to represent the colonized to themselves. The films of CAFU were demonstrably Orientalist, in Said's sense, in that their representations of Africans did not reflect the experiences of their audiences but rather the fantasies and aspirations of the state that produced them. As a result, African audiences failed to identify with these films because they did not recognize themselves on the screen. Such an interpretation is borne out by an analysis of the filmmakers' approach to their craft as well as by the empirical evidence of audience resistance to these images.

Overall, this book draws attention to one colonial state's efforts to influence Africans through the cinema. By examining the goals and the assumptions of those who expected film to transform African behavior, we can achieve a richer understanding of the aspirations of the colonial state. By exploring the preconceptions and assumptions that guided film production and censorship, we can begin to recognize a broader pattern of imperial self-deception that casts light on the ultimate failure of white rule in Zimbabwe. And finally, by listening to the faint voices of these African audiences, and appreciating the autonomy and agency they exercised in developing their own cinema tastes, we can catch glimpses of a range of subtle, though resolute, acts of resistance that characterized the colonial relationship.

Today an artistically vibrant, politicized African cinema attests to the continued faith of many Africans in the power of the medium to effect social and cultural change. The aesthetic and political aspirations of today's African cinema are in part a reaction to a little-known though highly significant chapter in the history of colonialism. African directors today remain engaged in a heated dialogue with a somewhat obscure colonial past.[11] This study seeks to cast a spotlight on that past of flickering shadows.

# Acknowledgments

In the course of researching and writing this book I have bene-
fited from the kindness of many individuals and institutions. I
would like to thank the USIA Fulbright Program for gener-
ously supporting my research in Zimbabwe. My study in the
United Kingdom was made possible by a grant from the Department of History at the University of California, Santa
Barbara. I also received significant support from UCSB's
Graduate Division and from the Interdisciplinary Humanities
Center, as well as the College of Arts, Architecture, and Humanities at Clemson University.

Many individuals cooperated to make this project possible.
Several former members of the Central African Film Unit
graciously offered their assistance, especially Stephen Peet,
Anker Atkinson, Geoffrey Mangin, Alan Izod, Richard Raynor,
and Louis Nell. Mr. Nell provided an invaluable service by
helping me contact his retired colleagues, and I am particularly grateful for his support. Both he and Mr. Mangin also allowed me to read unpublished manuscripts. Many retired
officers of the Federal Information Services and the Rhodesian Information Services assisted me as well, among them
Edward Chiranga, Anthony Kadyevu, Mr. Garwe, David Hlazo,
Lovermore Mhlala, Ben Musoni, and Lawrence Moringay. I

also appreciate the efforts of Sylvester Timuri, who helped me contact several former employees of the Rhodesian Information Service, and Lawrence Vambe, who made time to speak with me about the early days of the cinema in Harare. Though they are too many to mention, I would also like to thank the dozens of Zimbabweans who sacrificed time to sit and reminisce about the early days of the cinema. Special thanks is owed also to the staff of the National Archives in Harare, Zimbabwe, particularly to Elizabeth Chifamba, who made an invaluable contribution to this book as an archivist, interpreter, and friend throughout the course of my stay in her country.

Several scholars have aided me along the way, particularly Andrew Roberts, Timothy Burke, Merrick Posnansky, Kedmon Hungwe, Rosaleen Smyth, Guy Thompson, and David Giltrow. Their selfless assistance is greatly appreciated. I would also like to acknowledge the invaluable assistance provided by the readers at the Ohio University Press, whose suggestions and guidance inform every aspect of the book.

My scholarly debts to the University of California, Santa Barbara (UCSB), are large. This work would not have been possible without the guidance and unstinting support of Professors Nancy Gallagher and Alfred Gollin. Their encouragement and rigorous critiques gave the project focus and momentum. Several colleagues from UCSB also influenced this study. Monica Orozco contributed moral and logistical support throughout the course of the project, while Daniel Siegel provided invaluable assistance by reading the entire manuscript in draft form. His influence is to be found on every page. I owe my greatest intellectual debt to Robert O. Collins, a scholar, teacher, and gentleman of the highest caliber. His demanding standards and unwavering support had a formative influence on the finished manuscript.

I would also like to thank my parents for instilling in me a love of books, my siblings, who have provided me with moral and material support over the last five years, and my children Megan and Andrew, who patiently waited (and waited . . . ) for the manuscript's completion. Finally, but most importantly, I would like to thank my wife, Renee, who sacrificed so greatly to make a dream come true. Her enthusiasm for this story and her faith in its author brought this book to life.

# THE EMPIRE

## Palace of Varieties.

Lessees   ·   ·   Messrs. Alexander & Hyman.
Acting Manager   ·   · Mr. Edgar M. Hyman.

## TO-NIGHT, MONDAY, MARCH 11TH
### (For Six Nights Only)
## THE PHOTO-ELECTRIC
## SENSATION OF THE DAY !

First production of the Great London
Sensation,

# CINEMATOGRAPHE.

Introduced by CARL HERTZ.

The latest invention in Photography, the
most startling scientific marvel of the age.
Every scene in motion reproduced as in real
life. A marvellous reproducti n of animated
nature. Impossible to realise that the figures
represented are not actually living.

This is the same performance now being
produced at the Empire and Alhambra,
London.

And full Grand Company of

# 14  LONDON TURNS.

Advertisement for one of the first cinema shows in South Africa, 1896
From Thelma Gutsche, *The History and Social Significance of Motion Pictures in Africa*
(Cape Town: Timmins, 1972)

An African commentator recording narration for the Bantu Educational Kinema Experiment. From L. A. Notcutt and G. C. Latham, *The African and the Cinema* (London: Edinburgh House, 1937)

Leslie Notcutt preparing a shot for the BEKE. From L. A. Notcutt and G. C. Latham, *The African and the Cinema* (London: Edinburgh House, 1937)

Mattaka, the star of the Central African Film Unit comedy *Mattaka Buys a Car*. Author's collection

Southern Rhodesian authorities rolling out a new fleet of Mobile Cinema vans. From *Rhodesia and Nyasaland News*

Audience at a Mobile Cinema Show in Northern Rhodesia. From Thelma Gutsche, *The History and Social Significance of Motion Pictures in Africa* (Cape Town: Timmins, 1972)

Flickering Shadows

# Chapter 1

# Cinema and Censorship in Southern Rhodesia, 1914–1940

The birthplace of the cinema is usually ascribed to Paris, where the first demonstrations, in 1895, of what was called "the bioscope" created a sensation. The new technology soon spread across the world, debuting in Africa before the advent of the new century. Initially the cinema penetrated into those regions of the continent with large European populations, such as South Africa, and it was in such colonies that Africans first came into contact with the new medium. But the cinema spread rapidly into the equatorial colonies as well, with the first film shows appearing in Senegal in 1900 and Nigeria in 1903.[1]

As it circled the globe, the cinema brought with it a challenge to colonial administrations. From India to Gold Coast, white settlers, government officials, and missionaries pondered the influence of the medium on the colonized. Anxiety about the movies was particularly acute in the white-settlement colony of Southern Rhodesia. There, from the first moments that Africans had an opportunity to watch motion pictures, settlers expressed strong reservations about allowing them

1

unrestricted access to the medium. After World War I, settler associations organized to pressure the government to monitor and regulate the motion pictures shown in the colony. In the decades preceding World War II, members of the white community besieged the British South African Police (BSAP) with demands that Africans be banned from seeing a wide variety of commercial films. Lobbying by civic organizations such as the Scouting Association and the Federated Women's Clubs of Rhodesia resulted in the passage of three separate film-censorship bills between 1912 and 1948. It also inspired the colony's Native Affairs Department and Chamber of Mines to force distributors to ruthlessly edit films shown to Africans. By the late 1930s, the concerns of these groups had crystallized into a demand for a state-sponsored film industry to produce films expressly for African audiences.

What are we to make of Southern Rhodesia's rather hysterical fear of the cinema? White alarums warning of the corrosive influence of the cinema echoed throughout the colonized world, and the concerns of Southern Rhodesians were shared from India[2] to Nigeria;[3] however, in this region of Southern Africa these fears were particularly impassioned and long-lived. The response of white Rhodesia to the movies must be understood in the context of that colony's unique history. Cinema arrived in Southern Africa at a moment when fundamental assumptions about the nature of African intellect, and the identity of white society, were undergoing a process of reformulation. In South Africa, Southern Rhodesia's neighbor to the south, the first three decades of the new century witnessed a spirited academic debate regarding the innate mentalities of Africans. Professionals in mental health in Europe and South Africa conducted a series of experiments and concluded that Africans had a peculiar, biologically based intellect that made them "permanently and eradicably different from . . . 'Western man.'"[4] This discussion was closely connected to a public debate about the merits of the enfranchisement of non-whites in the region.[5] Thus settler fears that Africans were incapable of understanding cinematic images became entangled in a broader debate about African "difference," a discussion that held a crucial relevance for white politics in Southern Africa.

Such issues had immediate resonance in Southern Rhodesia, where white settlers followed events in their southern neighbor quite closely. However, Southern Rhodesia had its own particular dynamic that shaped the colony's unique experience with the early cinema. Dane Kennedy, in his study *Islands of White*, has observed that in Southern Rhodesia, a colony governed by an isolated and self-consciously vulnerable white minority, settlers searched tirelessly for "symbolic and material boundaries" that distinguished them from their African subjects.[6] Such divisions served to legitimize white claims to power. Southern Rhodesia's settlers were a tiny minority, surrounded by a recently conquered African population. In this environment, mastery of Western technology became a key boundary separating the ruler from the ruled. In the pantheon of Western technologies, the cinema, the most modern and sophisticated of technologies, held a privileged place. By strictly controlling the motion-picture industry, the colony's whites were asserting their mastery over the most complicated of the European "Tools of Empire," and consequently their moral and political authority over their subjects.

Thus, while officials in London, Malaya, or India could retain a degree of critical distance in their discussions of the cinema's influence on the colonized, in Southern Rhodesia the stakes were much higher. There, the ability to master these tools lay at the heart of the white community's identity. It was what made them "civilized" and therefore different from the

Africans. Such views would retain their currency in Southern
Rhodesia for the final seven decades of white rule. To dispute
them—to suggest that Africans were capable of critically
viewing motion pictures—was to question the legitimacy of
settler rule.

Motion pictures first arrived in Southern Rhodesia around
the turn into the twentieth century. The first shows were
screened at the New London Bioscope in the capital of Salisbury.[7] This was very early in the history of the cinema (consider, for example, that regions of the United States remained
untouched by the cinema until the 1930s). The first record of
this peculiar settler concern with African audiences appeared
shortly before World War I. In June 1914, the Rhodesian
Criminal Investigations Department ( CID) sent an officer to
investigate the public screening of the film *Wilder Spender.* In
a "Strictly confidential memorandum," the superintendent of
the CID asked the detective to go to the Empire Theatre to
see the censored film and to

1. Note particularly who are there
2. The criticisms passed
3. The occupants of the gallery, nationality, etc.
4. Render me a strictly confidential report upon the exhibition of
   the "film" under all these circumstances[8]

The detective dutifully reported back the next day: "I should
not call the picture immoral in so far as the adult European
mind is concerned but I certainly think the pitcure [*sic*] has a
tendency to create a certain amount of lewdness in the minds
of the younger persons and natives."[9] Though the detective
did not elaborate on the nature of this "lewdness," he clearly
worried that the film might inspire immoral sexual behavior
in two potentially impressionable groups, youths and Africans. This fear of African sexuality and the threat it posed to

the women of the European settler community was the initial impetus for film censorship in the region.

Fear of "sexual immorality" among the colonized was part of a larger trend being felt throughout the British Empire in the early days of the cinema. What Brian Larkin calls a "moral panic" was a part of the early cinema history of Nigeria,[10] India,[11] and other regions of the colonial world. Closer to Southern Rhodesia, in South Africa, fear of a "Black Peril" swept the mining regions of the neighboring Transvaal in 1912, inspiring several civic organizations to agitate for stringent film censorship for Africans.[12]

When World War I broke out in 1914, many white men left the colony to fight for the empire. This left the settler community feeling particularly vulnerable to the threat of an African uprising. In 1914, Southern Rhodesia was still a very new colony. It had been established as a chartered company owned by the South African diamond magnate Cecil John Rhodes in 1890. The original settlers were "pioneers" hired by Rhodes to wrestle the country from the indigenous Shona and Ndebele peoples between 1889 and 1893. In late 1895, many white law-enforcement officers left the colony to join L. S. Jameson's ill-fated raid on the Transvaal. With the colony denuded of police, the Shona and Ndebele peoples made a bid to throw off white rule. The company government eventually put down the rebellion after suffering heavy casualties and incurring crippling expenses. In 1914, the memory of the rebellion was fresh in the minds of most settlers. Thus the exodus of white troops after 1914 left the colonists increasingly apprehensive about anything that might "unsettle" the African community.[13]

The advent of the war sparked new concerns over the content of the motion pictures being shown in the colony. With many of the settlers away, white uneasiness over the "lewdness" of films was joined by a new fear regarding screen violence, particularly when perpetrated by blacks against whites. Vulnerable settlers came to fear that Africans would imitate violent acts they witnessed on the screen. In November 1916, the administrator of the colony received a letter from a white physician who warned that screen violence posed a greater threat to white rule than "lewdness":

> There are much graver dangers than indecency. . . . I was both disgusted and alarmed the other night at the exhibition in the Salisbury theater of a film illustrating illicit drink traffic on the Randt. In this film Natives from a compound with sticks raid and sack . . . Kaffir Store and downed and maltreat a white man the owner. I felt that the mere taking of such a picture should be made impossible, as the effect of both the taking and exhibition was too dangerous.[14]

The writer went on to express his apprehension regarding a report in the *Gatooma Mail* ("at present on the Club table"), a leading provincial weekly, describing a proposal to make a film about the battle of Blood River, the Trek Boer's military triumph over the Zulus. He concluded by calling for the Southern Rhodesian government to develop stricter censorship laws in coordination with the government of South Africa.[15]

The letter was received sympathetically by the colony's administrator, who turned it over to the attorney general, Robert Tregold, writing: "I agree that great care should be taken to prevent the exhibition of pictures likely to have a bad effect on natives."[16] Tregold concurred:

> I cannot help urging that a closer censorship be exercised in regard to these exhibitions in general. My recent sojourn at an hotel led me to a more frequent attendance at bioscope entertainments and I have been surprised to note the nature of some of the productions. Pictures of criminal methods even in murders, and also of suicides have been shown. These are wholly unnecessary;

undoubtedly lead to harmful suggestion; and merely pander to a depraved taste.

Tregold concluded his letter with a summary that encapsulated the ambivalence many white Rhodesians felt about the cinema: "So much good instruction can be given by means of the cinematograph and so much innocent and pleasurable amusement afforded, that it is a grave pity that any debasing influence should be introduced and allowed."[17]

As the war dragged on, alarm over film violence spread throughout the colony. In Bulawayo in 1917 the police banned an unnamed film owing to "scenes shewing two white men being murdered by natives, and an endeavour being made by natives to secure and carry off a European woman to their kraal."[18] Over the next year, the BSAP and CID in Salisbury and Bulawayo responded to numerous complaints about films that were perceived to pose a threat to public order or white prestige. After receiving reports that Africans in the audience were laughing at a scene in the film *Zulu Town* in which a black ice skater knocked down a white woman, the Bulawayo police urged that the film be banned for African audiences: "This film taken as a whole would not appeal to the European part of the audience but would be very much appreciated by the natives, as was evident from the laughing caused in the Empire on the night of the 14th. I am of the opinion that this film should not be shown to an audience consisting of natives."[19] Shortly thereafter the government also banned the showing of the first interracial heavyweight boxing championship, won by Jack Johnson, an African American, to any but white audiences. This increasingly stringent censorship prodded the colony's only film distributor, African Films, Ltd., to write to the colony's administrator to assure him that the "sundry incidents depicting conflict between black and white people" found in two recently censored films would not be viewed by African audiences. "We are of opinion that you will see eye to eye with us—that it is competent to exhibit such a picture in Rhodesia, providing it be not screened to coloured and native audiences, a class of the community for whom we do not cater."[20]

Settler preoccupation with the cinema appears even more remarkable when it is realized how few Africans were actually attending bioscopes. Before 1918 most films were shown in the handful of theaters in the colony's major cities of Salisbury and Bulawayo. While some did permit Africans and "Coloureds" to sit in the balcony, most did not, with advertisements in the press warning that programs were "For Europeans Only." When the CID received a complaint from a "Coloured" man who had been denied admission to a movie house in Bulawayo, the officer in charge curtly informed him that the owner was well within his rights to refuse him admission.[21] But even for Africans not discouraged by racism, the high cost of theater tickets made the cinema unaffordable. Thus it was only a few score of African patrons who had the colony's security forces in a quandary.

This was soon to change. During the later stages of the war, Africans were introduced to the cinema in large numbers. African troops from Southern Rhodesia and Nyasaland were provided with cinema shows as a reward for service, and mine owners throughout Southern Africa began running their own bioscopes for African laborers. The mine shows were pioneered in South Africa by an American missionary, the Rev. Ray Phillips. Phillips had been charged by the mine owners with providing "wholesome" entertainment for miners to distract them from more antisocial activities such as drinking and fighting. Phillips had no difficulty finding entertainments such as athletics to occupy the miners during the day. But he had greater difficulty devising a form of entertainment that would occupy their evenings.[22] His first experiment showing movies proved extremely popular: "The result was immediate and gratifying. The thousand gathered around the screen and showed their appreciation by filling the compounds so full of joyful sound that outsiders often decided that a riot was going on. With amazed delight the happy crowds went off on trips on the modern magic carpet to other lands."[23] The shows pleased the mine owners as well. Not only did they seem to discourage drinking and violence, they also attracted new workers. In his evaluation of these early shows, labor historian Charles van Onselen has written: "For a largely illiterate audience, films, as a form of cheap mass entertainment, readily suggested themselves to mine managers. Not only was the cost moderate but if screened at peak drinking hours on a weekend evening they also had the beneficial effect of making inroads into the total cases of Monday morning hangover. Further, and again unlike alcohol, films were unlikely to lead directly to violence."[24]

The popularity of the shows convinced Phillips that the medium held a powerful sway over Africans. He believed that carefully chosen films would have the effect of "sublimating potential criminal tendencies" among miners.[25] He claimed that he had averted a riot during the 1922 Rand strike by beginning a cinema show, thus stopping the African employees of the Primrose Mine in their tracks.[26] When the Phelps-Stokes Commission on African education toured the region in the early 1920s, it applauded Phillips's efforts.

> It is evident that the value of these shows is not only in diverting the minds of the thousands of Natives from less helpful subjects, but also in giving to them pictures of activities and life that will influence their own actions and, through them, the actions of hundreds of villages scattered far and wide.[27]

The Transvaal Chamber of Mines and the Tea Marketing

Board in South Africa supplied him with films of an "extremely moral character."[28] In the estimation of one South African film historian, it was "probable that their showing profited the police more than the tea-growers," and overall the films generally "kept otherwise idle natives off the street."[29]

However, films of such a high morale caliber were in short supply, and Rev. Phillips supplemented his supply by editing commercial films for the shows. Initially the mine owners assumed that Africans would be captivated by the images of the cinema but would not be capable of following a narrative; therefore they assumed that they could show the same small collection of "extremely moral" and heavily edited films repeatedly. However, this proved not to be the case, as miners throughout the region began demanding new films. This left the mine owners scrambling to secure a steady supply of new films to keep their workers placated. In an effort to guarantee a regular source of movies, the chamber of mines entered into an agreement with the South African production and distribution company African Films, Ltd., which enjoyed a monopoly on the cinema business in Southern Africa.

Although African Films, Ltd., did produce some original films, a large part of their business was distributing American films, most of which were westerns, the most popular genre in Southern Africa, as indeed it was throughout the world.[30] The bulk of the films supplied by African Films were therefore grade-B American westerns. Since these films inevitably contained scenes deemed inappropriate for Africans, Rev. Phillips edited out any romance or violence before screening them in the compounds. One can only imagine the effects of this kind of censorship on a film's continuity. An account of a similarly edited western from British Malaysia provides some insight into this experience. There a European observer recounted: "I found it rather bewildering, because vital parts of every shooting scene had been cut out by the censor. It was not considered healthy for the people to see the gun fired, though they were allowed to see it aimed, then the actual 'bang' was eliminated and miraculously the victim lay dead while the villain or hero, as it might be, lowered his smoking gun."[31]

Even with such heavy editing, the mine owners became apprehensive about the kinds of films being supplied by African Films, in large part because their contract gave them no say in the selection of films to be supplied. As the manager of the Globe & Phoenix mine in Que Que complained, "We are bound hand and foot and must accept and pay for whatever they elect to send us for six years."[32] To save money, African Films simply sent to the mines copies of the same films being shown in white movie houses. Compound managers, who felt that African Films had little understanding of the susceptibilities of African audiences, were particularly exercised by the posters that advertised the films. In a letter to the Rhodesian government, a mine manager indicated his displeasure with the posters: "Some of these depict practically naked white women in various attitudes, and attract crowds of natives who gaze at them for hours on end. . . . I feel it is time that drastic action [is] taken to prevent the exhibition of posters which can only bring white women into disrepute."[33]

Pressure from the mine owners forced the colony's police to open an investigation into the question of censorship.[34] In April 1927, the chief superintendent of the CID in Bulawayo, declaring that the "whole system of censorship of these films is most unsatisfactory," wrote to several key law-enforcement officers inquiring about censorship practices in the region.[35] A BSAP detective in South Africa wrote back explaining the complicated system of censorship currently in place. He reported that a board in Cape Town initially censored all films entering South Africa and a second board reviewed "films which are intended to be displayed to native audiences" in the Transvaal. After this screening, "A native film passed by the Transvaal police may be shown at any native bioscope, but, where such bioscopes are under the control of the Chamber of Mines, a further censorship is imposed"; finally, "that section of the Chamber of mines which deals with native labour, the 'Native recruiting corporation,' exercised a further censorship over films to be shown in all compounds on the Reef." The officer justified the necessity of this complicated and rigid system by arguing: "The reason for this is that, there being hardly any films which have not some feature which would be considered [harmful] to show to natives (even the popular cowboy films, while showing the whiteman [*sic*] as a fine horseman, also shows him indulging in promiscuous pistol shooting and murder)."[36]

The report of a second respondent provides insight into the principles guiding this strict censorship. He described the film program circulating among several major mines as follows: "I am informed that the films forwarded are selected as being the most suitable for the native mind, and consist of News, Interest, Comedy, and Drama, but loves scenes, tragedy, or anything suggestive to the native mind is not permitted as far as this is possible. Kissing, for instance, has been shown, so Mr. Fraser [the compound manager] informs me, then the audience would make a similar noise."[37] Regarding a program shown the previous evening, he went on, "In one of the News Films, a Beauty Competition Prize Winner was shown, and thrills of delight went up, which I considered was not altogether proper, Mr. Fraser remarking 'that's the sort of thing I object to, white woman on the films.'"[38] On the subject of the plots of the films, he reported, "The reading on the films are in English . . . there is insufficient time for translation, so of course the natives would not be able to follow such a film (unless they can read English) where a plot is being laid . . . all they follow really is the picture itself."[39]

This correspondence between the police and the mine administrators suggests that by the late 1920s an emphasis on censoring sexually suggestive films had eclipsed the wartime obsession with screen violence. Another law officer's report to the commissioner reflects this shift: "The following are a few examples of those portions which would be cut out of a picture to be shewn to natives i.e. Scenes of almost nude women, [love scenes] in bedrooms, fighting in a bar, drunken scenes and any portion where black or coloured men are depicted on familiar terms with white women."[40]

The complaints fielded by the police in the 1920s are consistent with trends that can be seen in the early history of the cinema worldwide. Images of white women were closely circumscribed by officials in Europe and the United States, and censorship in the colonial world followed similar patterns, with colonial observers decrying the representations of "white" women on screens in Malaya, India, and throughout much of Africa. In his study of this phenomenon, the anthropologist Brian Larkin understands this anxiety as a fear of "reverse ethnography," in which white civilization is placed on display for the gaze of the colonized. Larkin found that in Indian and Nigerian movie theaters, the discomfort of white viewers was accentuated by the presence of nonwhite colonial subjects in the audience, who were presumed to be enjoying an illicit gaze on the colonizer. For Larkin, such anxieties are the product of racially integrated theaters, where the colonizer and the colonized shared a window into white society. However, in colonial Zimbabwe cinema shows were strictly segregated. Thus the "moral panic" of the colony appears to be rooted in broader settler perceptions of status and vulnerability.

Alarmed by reports of Africans snickering at "lewd" images, the BSAP continued to monitor the proliferation of "native" bioscopes closely. When disturbances flared up in the Bulawayo township in late 1929, they seized the opportunity to close down several movie houses. By this date, however, the cinema had spread and was rapidly becoming a fixture of urban life. These new bioscopes were run by white welfare officers who shared the mine owners' hope that cinema shows could provide urban audiences with a healthy form of entertainment. The police were thus faced with an immediate demand that the venues be reopened. In early January 1930, Father Escher, the clergyman who ran one of the bioscopes in Bulawayo, complained about the closure, arguing that while there had been some friction at the performances "as there is nothing objectionable in the actual Bioscope display itself it should be permitted."[41] The clergyman found an unlikely ally in the chief native commissioner, H. M. Jackson, who maintained that "there is nothing wrong in a well-conducted bioscope, any more than in a boxing match."[42] The superintendent of natives for Bulawayo acceded to Father Escher's request, conceding, "I doubt . . . whether we can stop these performances, so long as they are not inherently bad."[43]

These comments reflect not only the balance struck by the authorities between allowing film shows and maintaining public order but also the hold the cinema had attained over African audiences by the late 1920s. Then in the early 1930s settler pressure began to mount on the police as several civic organizations called for stricter film censorship. In 1931 the district commissioner for the Southern Rhodesian Scouting Association wrote to Major Brundell of the Bulawayo CID informing him: "I have been asked by several societies to call a meeting of all those interested in the matter of films shewn at matinees for children, films shown to coloured people and natives, and posters which are shewn openly in the streets."[44] These groups, which included several fraternal organizations and women's groups, agreed that the threat posed by the cinema demanded stringent censorship. After debating the matter at their annual meeting, the Federation of Women's Organizations commissioned a study by Mr. L. Thornton into the question of censorship in the colony.

Thornton's report is a curious document that casts significant light on settler attitude on the subject. It begins by proclaiming that "the scope of this report was to inquire into the position of film censorship and how it may be improved with special reference to children, British Indians, Cape Coloured, and natives."[45] Thornton established early in the report that his main interest was in making the case for a censorship code based on racial lines: "A country with a homogeneous population can best be served by an outright censorship; i.e. the censor's verdict is equally applicable to the whole adult population without distinction. Where, however, a country has a population of very mixed racial origins of varying degrees of civilization, selective censorship is bound to come into operation." Thornton argued that Southern Rhodesia and South Africa should not be bound by a recent recommendation of the Colonial Office's Colonial Films Committee, which discouraged any film censorship based on race. "The recommendation . . . is quite inapplicable to the settled territories south of the Zambesi, and is a direct negation of what should be the maxim in censorship—the greatest good for the greatest number [*with a minimum friction.*]"

Thornton's views on cinema censorship were heavily informed by the Social Darwinism of his era:

> The Audiences catered for by the film industry consist of every grade of intelligence, intellect, moral standard, education and development, and belong to a heterogeneity of civilizations from

the emergent Bantu to the highest expressions of European and Asiatic culture; it is therefore foolish to imagine that a non-selective censorship is feasible, unless it is scaled down to the Native intelligence and is based on Native psychology.

Thornton's condescension was not reserved exclusively for black audiences. He saw cinema audiences in general as "belong[ing] indeed to a stage of [lower] mental development, and the average audience is noted for having the outlook of the adolescent." In this, his views were consistent with many early critics of the cinema in Europe and America. He was not, however, advocating censorship for white audiences; instead, he argued for separate treatment of the colony's three main populations. "Coloureds and Asiatics" he recommended should not be permitted to see "any picture derogatory to the existing governmental, social or moral institutions, and [which] embraces such wide things as the successful revolt of subject races, miscegenation and 'poor white trash.'" Africans however would be treated even more rigorously. "Similar arguments apply to the Natives with even greater force; but it cannot be too strongly pointed out that there is very little, if any, similarity between their social customs and organizations and outlook and ours, and to the Native there is a wealth of opportunity for misunderstanding even in our simple domestic melodramas."

Thornton then explained the reasoning underlying his recommendations: "Incident is everything to the Native, and unless the subject deals quite definitely with an artistic development based on his own psychology, a wrong impression is bound to be created." This is a clear articulation of the prejudice motivating this trend toward greater censorship: Africans have a unique "psychology" that is particularly vulnerable to "a wrong impression" presented in film. Thornton's recommendations for censoring films to the "Coloured and Asiatic" populations were rooted in his fears of both political instability and miscegenation. With Africans, however, he focused mainly on the danger that motion pictures would encourage immoral sexual behavior. He deprecated in particular the cinema's tendency toward what he referred to as "suggestiveness." "It should be pointed out that suggestiveness is very frequently due to the actors, who make up for lack of artistry by the accentuation of their more obvious personal charms or bodily proportions. . . . For this reason censors should adopt a rigorous standard in this direction, especially for suggesting by bodily movement of posturing."

In conclusion, Thornton recommended a cinema of apartheid: "The establishment wherever possible of Location Bioscopes for the non-European population." This came to pass in the postwar era as African entrepreneurs began renting out halls in locations and townships for film shows. In the meantime, the combined weight of the law-enforcement community and private organizations like the Boy Scouts led to the introduction of a new film censorship bill in Southern Rhodesia's parliament.

The *Entertainments Control and Censorship Bill* was introduced by the government in April 1932. It had the full support of groups like the Federation of Women's Institutes of Southern Rhodesia, whose president, Mrs. L. E. Friff, informed the attorney general's department that her organization considered the bill "essential in a country in which a large section of the community has not reached the same state of civilization as the Europeans."[46] Mrs. Friff's views were embraced by the ruling party, and her letter was quoted extensively when the bill was introduced into the legislative assembly.[47]

The proposed legislation superseded a 1912 censorship act that, the bill's sponsors claimed, "contained no provision which compels producers to submit films for censorship."[48]

This meant that while the police had the authority to ban any film for African audiences, they could not do so until after it had proven unacceptable through an initial showing. The bill also restricted the screening of films outside of "static," or traditional, theaters. "Cases have occurred of persons traveling about the colony giving exhibitions to Europeans and natives and difficulty has been experienced in dealing with censorship of films held by such persons."[49] Such shows posed a particular problem because "the exhibitions given by these traveling companies are sometimes rather suggestive and as such should not be seen by natives."[50] As the acting commissioner of the BSAP explained: "The evil aimed at is in regard to pictures such as can be seen in slot machines, posters of low class traveling shows, posters being exported from Russia and elsewhere which it is desirable should not be exhibited to the Public, more especially natives."[51] A final provision reflected the mine owners' complaints over suggestive film posters: "It is the opinion of some that the exhibition of such posters in a purely European country should be prohibited; it is even more necessary to have proper control of them in this country where we have natives."[52]

When the bill was introduced in April 1932, the colonial secretary declared: "This Bill is somewhat overdue. It is now almost two years since the Commissioner of Police recommended me to introduce a Bill on these lines, which would bring our law up-to-date, as judged by our neighbors both to the west and south of us, as well as the law in other civilised countries."[53] The bill faced some parliamentary opposition, with Godfrey Huggins, the future prime minister, calling the introduction of such legislation during the depression "a typical example of Government fiddling while Rome is burning."[54] A colleague in Huggins's Rhodesia Party declared, "I should characterise this as another instance of the grandmotherly type of legislation of which we have had so many examples during the last four years." He continued, "I consider the Bill offers the possibility of interference by all the cranks and faddists who can possibly be got together and put on that Board."[55] However, neither speaker questioned the fundamental principle that African audiences needed to be shielded from certain film images: rather, they both maintained that this was being adequately accomplished under existing legislation.[56] In the event, the colonial secretary insisted that "this legislation is the absolute minimum that is needed on the subject. It has not only been asked for by the Commissioner of Police, but by practically all public bodies which have taken any interest in the matter,"[57] and the bill was passed into law.

However, the new censorship legislation meant that there were now even fewer films available for African audiences. If it were true that, as one South African police sergeant complained, there were "hardly any films which have not some feature which would be considered [harmful] to show to natives" before the act was passed, it was even more true afterward.[58] This made it increasingly difficult for mine owners and welfare officers to keep up with the demands of audiences who expected a new program each week. This proved especially problematic at the mine compounds, where twice-weekly bioscopes were a fixture by the 1930s. Demand for new films forced African Films, Ltd., to continue to supply their circuits with unedited versions of unacceptable films, which did not sit well with the compound managers. In November 1935, J. D. Morton, the secretary of the Rhodesian Chamber of Mines, complained to the general manager of African Films, "It is generally felt by members of the Chamber that there is very considerable room for improvement in the type of films at present available for use in this Colony."[59] The secretary laid out specific objections:

It is considered that the bioscopes would form a very valuable factor in native education if the right type of film were shown, but that a large number of films at present provided have the opposite effect and are such as to give the native wrong ideas and to have an adverse effect on his attitude towards Europeans. . . . There is no doubt that as the native has little else to think about the films he sees occupy his mind to a very considerable extent and have an important effect on his mentality and behaviour. It is also generally his ambition to imitate European habits, and if he is shown scenes of stealing, fighting, gambling &c., he is likely to consider that this is representative of European behavior, and adopt similar bad habits.[60]

The secretary was not only afraid that films would inspire crime or violence: "It would be better if films in which European females appear could be entirely debarred for native showing, as there are usually certain aspects of such pictures which are objectionable from the point of view of the native respect for and general attitude towards white women."[61]

The secretary's letter received a cold reception from the general manager of African Films, a Mr. Watson, who requested specific examples of what the secretary had found unacceptable in the films. Watson wondered if the views expressed in his letter represented "the considered opinion of the Compound managers who, we presume, would actually see the films which are exhibited and are in close touch with the Native and able to gauge the effects of such upon the native mind."[62] Watson's letter went on to roundly criticize the secretary's opinions on the cinema and African audiences. In doing so, he became one of the first whites to question the assumption that African audiences were particularly credulous or impressionable:

It has been our experience over many years that there is a great deal of loose thought and talk about the effect of films upon the native mind, upon children, and upon adults, all of which has proved to be fallacious, and it is also proved that these widely spread opinions are given by people who are not in close touch with the subject, and that it is mainly gathered from what they have heard from someone else, or from what they have been told. . . . Does it not seem somewhat absurd to actually take for granted that if he sees an act of stealing on a film, that the native will immediately go away and perform a similar act?[63]

Morton remained unconvinced. He sent a similar letter to Charles Bullock, the chief native commissioner (CNC) of Southern Rhodesia, where he received a more sympathetic hearing.[64] But Bullock had to report that he had no jurisdiction in the matter and could not force African Films to change their programs; the mine owners' only option, it seemed, was to find an alternative source of films.

In another letter to Watson of African Films, Morton proposed an intriguing solution to the dilemma. He observed that "the trade in films for purposes of native recreation is now sufficiently large to warrant the production of pictures specially suitable for that purpose"; he suggested that African Films consider producing such films.[65] Watson dismissed the idea as uneconomical: "You can take it for granted that the idea of special productions for natives is impracticable, owing to the very high costs involved and the very small amount of revenue which can be derived."[66] When Morton made a similar suggestion to Bullock, however, he discovered that the chief native commissioner's office had already begun considering this option. Bullock informed Morton that his office was following the progress of a group of filmmakers who had recently begun working in East Africa:

I may mention that a party of experts connected with the British Film Institute is now operating in Tanganyika Territory with a view to the introduction of Native films for Natives. . . . They are going very thoroughly into many questions connected with this problem. For example they will not only take films of Native life, but will test the response of Natives from points of view of interest, education, entertainment etc.[67]

The "experts" were Major L. A. Notcutt and Geoffrey Latham, two British citizens turned filmmakers who called themselves the Bantu Educational Kinema Experiment (BEKE). They had begun making films for African audiences in Tanganyika in 1935. BEKE, the first systematic attempt to produce motion pictures for African audiences, was sponsored by the International Missionary Society, the Carnegie Corporation, and the British Colonial Office. It represented the culmination of a decade of discussion and experimentation into the production of motion pictures for the subjects of the British Empire. In the ten years preceding its 1935 inauguration, several organizations and individuals in London had launched investigations into the future of film as a source of entertainment and tool of education in the colonies. It is worth briefly examining these efforts because they were followed very closely in Southern Rhodesia and ultimately influenced cinema policy in the colony.

The idea of producing motion pictures specifically for African audiences was first suggested at a colonial conference, convened in 1927, to investigate the future of the film in the empire. One of the members of the Colonial Films Committee, Sir Hesketh Bell, who served as a Colonial Office official in Uganda, expressed his profound enthusiasm for the future of the cinema in African education: "To the millions of unsophisticated people in Africa, who are unable to read and write, moving pictures must be a most impressive vehicle of instruction. By no other means could greater progress be made in giving them the foundation of general knowledge of the outer world upon which a more elaborate form of education may, later on, be built up."[68] The committee had concluded that if colonial governments needed educational films, there were plenty available in England. Hesketh Bell, however, feared these films would prove unsuitable for Africans: "Nearly all of them were prepared for the instruction of white adults and children. Illustrations of the life history of the mosquito or of the devastating effects of the hookworm, which might be understood by more or less civilized coloured people, who have some notions about microbes and microscopes, would be quite bewildering to unsophisticated natives who have not the faintest idea of modern science and have only a rudimentary sense of proportion."[69] He argued that special films, adapted to the perceived needs and capabilities of African audiences, were needed: "Cinema pictures, intended for the education of primitive people, must be specially produced. They must be constructed by persons who are intimately acquainted with the mentality of natives and their limits of comprehension."[70] Such films should teach lessons that would be of little interest to European audiences. "Pictures suitable for the uplift of uncivilized Africans should illustrate the advantages of cleanliness, decent living, industry, and humanity."[71] He realized that such films were unlikely to be commercially viable and argued that the governments of various African territories should finance their production.

Hesketh Bell was joined in his advocacy of the idea by Hans Vischer, secretary of the Advisory Committee on Native Education in Tropical Africa. Vischer agreed that films could "help spread general knowledge particularly about "health and economic development" in Africa. The Colonial Films Committee ultimately discounted the suggestion, citing the cost of such a project and the relative ignorance of the capabilities and potential of African film audiences.[72] The committee did however recognize the cinema's potential in the development of Britain's tropical empire. Lord Passfield, the Labour government's colonial secretary, expressed his support for the idea in a dispatch sent to each colonial governor: "The use of the cinematograph film as an instrument of culture and education merits the closest attention, especially with primitive peoples, and I am anxious that its development, not only as a means of amusement, but more particularly in the sphere of education, should be most carefully watched in the territory under your administration."[73]

In 1929 the British Institute of Adult Education and the Association of Scientific Workers appointed a commission to investigate the use of films in education. An unofficial body, the Commission on Educational and Cultural Films included representatives from several government departments, among them the Colonial Office. Its highly influential report, *The Film in National Life*, was published in 1932.[74] A section of the report, "The Cinema and the Empire," considered the report of the 1927 Colonial Films Committee and echoed many of its conclusions, reporting that "the Colonial Office is keenly interested in the possibility of making use of the cinematograph as an instrument of adolescent education in dependencies with a population representing various stages of mental development, and various kinds of culture."[75] The report's authors were convinced that film had a remarkably potent influence on colonial peoples. "The backward races within the Empire can gain more and suffer more from the film than the sophisticated European, because to them the power of the medium is intensified. The conception of white civilization which they are receiving from third-rate melodrama is an international menace, yet the film is an agent of social education which could be as powerful for good as harm."[76] Here we see the articulation of a view that was already accepted as orthodoxy among mine owners and administrators in Southern Rhodesia: for good or ill, Africans were peculiarly susceptible to the messages and images of motion pictures.

The Colonial Office's next step was to investigate what was required in making films for African audiences. In 1929 the Colonial Advisory Committee on Native Education sent Julian Huxley, the eminent biologist, to East Africa to test the response of African audiences to educational films. Huxley spent several weeks screening films in Kenya and Uganda and presented his conclusions to the Colonial Office in a report in 1930.[77] He had taken three films "deliberately chosen to represent three levels of difficulty of comprehension by the natives." The simplest was an Empire Marketing Board Film, *Cotton Growing in Nigeria;* slightly more sophisticated was *Fathoms Deep Beneath the Sea;* and the most complicated was *The Life of a Plant,* which featured "many unfamiliar details of technical structure and process" and "technical devices . . . employed to produce wholly unfamiliar kinds of results." Huxley showed the films to children at government schools. He gauged their comprehension by having them write essays about the films. The organizers of the shows assured him that 80 to 90 percent of the audiences had never seen motion pictures before. Huxley was very impressed with the results of these shows, and his report was very enthusiastic regarding the potential of African audiences to comprehend sophisticated film techniques. Huxley saw no difference between illiterate audiences in Africa and those elsewhere. He observed that "native boys and girls are capable of grasping difficult subjects such as speeded up film."[78] In general, Huxley concluded that African audiences should be treated no differently from any other group.

Encouraged by Huxley's optimistic assessment, the Colonial Office began considering plans to begin producing films for Africans. They invited Dr. A. R. Paterson, a medical officer with the Kenyan government and an amateur filmmaker, to draw up a proposal for making experimental films in East

Africa. Unfortunately, Paterson submitted his plan in the midst of the Great Depression and the government decided that it was too expensive. The Colonial Office's cinema ambitions would have to wait until funding was forthcoming from a source other than the British Treasury and the colonial governments' treasuries. It did not have to wait long. In 1932 an American missionary, J. Merle Davis, traveled to Northern Rhodesia to study the effects of industrialization on African communities in the Copperbelt, and the next year he published his observations in a book titled *Modern Industry and the African*.[79] Davis found that the mines of the Copperbelt had profoundly altered the preindustrial societies of Central Africa. He returned from the Copperbelt convinced that the cinema could play a decisive part in helping illiterate Africans adjust to urban industrial life. He convinced the Carnegie Corporation to fund a plan that was almost identical to Paterson's. When this was accepted, he had little difficulty in securing the support of the Colonial Office. The result was BEKE, Notcutt's and Latham's Bantu Educational Kinema Experiment, a short-lived, though highly influential, pioneering foray into filmmaking for African audiences.

G. K. Latham was the commissioner of native education for Northern Rhodesia; L. A. Notcutt was a supervisor on an East African sisal plantation. The two men shared Julian Huxley's enthusiasm for colonial education. They agreed with Hesketh Bell, however, that the cinema could have a pernicious influence on Africans. Notcutt wrote: "Although the cinema has a constructive potentiality of great importance, it easily lends itself to unreality and to destructive moral influence, and might do an infinite amount of harm if exploited by irresponsible persons."[80] BEKE aspired to produce a large enough number of films to allow colonial authorities to completely restrict Africans from viewing commercial productions. "The

Governments concerned may then be glad to restrict the rights of exhibiting films to natives of their territories to the Corporation which, it is hoped, may arise out of this experiment."[81] Thus the project was not merely an attempt to teach through films, but was also a form of proactive censorship.

In two years, Notcutt and Latham produced thirty-five films, several of which are stored at the National Film Archive in London. The subjects ranged from the educational—for example, teaching agricultural techniques and explaining the workings of government health and savings services—to simple entertainment. BEKE showed films over a period of two years to eighty thousand viewers. Most of their audiences had never seen a film before. They were screened in a completely self-sufficient traveling mobile cinema van that allowed Notcutt and Latham to operate in remote areas. The films were silent, but were shown with a soundtrack supplied by a record player. The topics shared a common theme that the filmmakers described as "progress vs African methods." The handful of entertainment films included a bizarre production called *White People*, which was intended to educate Africans about European life.[82]

The Carnegie endowment granted funds to the experiment to operate for two years, with the understanding that this would give the governments of the East African territories an opportunity to decide whether to finance their own film production after 1937. It turned out that the administrators in these colonies were unimpressed by the experiment's effort, and they declined the invitation to continue film production. Since there were few cinema houses in these colonies, and almost no shows for African audiences, the governments of East Africa felt that they did not need BEKE. The governor of Kenya believed a better solution to the problem of censorship was simply to prohibit Africans from seeing any films. By 1937, thanks largely to the apathy of colonial officials, BEKE ceased production.[83]

Officials in the Southern Rhodesian government watched these developments very closely. The Native Affairs Department files held at the National Archives in Zimbabwe contain an abundant collection of reports and letters from the late 1920s and 1930s attesting to the department's growing interest in filmmaking for Africans. They include Huxley's report, an extensive correspondence between the chief native commissioner and Geoffrey Latham, BEKE's official report, and sundry correspondence between the department and several organizations and individuals interested in similar schemes. For example, the Native Affairs Department cooperated with the organizers of a 1934 conference of the International Congress of Educational and Instructional Cinematography (ICEIC), held in Rome, that focused on the use of cinema in the teaching of illiterates. The government welcomed the ICEIC's request for information regarding the potential future of the cinema as a tool of education in the colony, and the heads of departments in Southern Rhodesia responsible for African affairs sent their views on the subject to the conference's secretary.[84] In one of these responses, the colony's director of education requested "films showing industrial developments in civilised communities and conditions of life among less highly developed peoples". The colony's medical director requested films "for natives . . . showing the digging of suitable latrines, appropriate scenes in hospitals including leprosy hospitals, etc, and how diseases, such as malaria, are contracted";[85] the medical director continued with a curious request: "for European adults films showing more advanced lessons in general and tropical hygiene, and also films dealing with matters pertaining to sex instruction would be appropriate."[86] The department also corresponded with the International Colonial Institute and the British Film Institute regarding the tastes and psychology of African audiences.

Of all of the department heads, it was the CNC who was most enamored of the idea of a cinema for Africans. In 1935, Bullock sent the colony's prime minister, Sir Godfrey Huggins, a memo outlining his hopes for using film in his department: "The cinematograph has immense potentialities as an instrument of instruction, as well as of wholesome entertainment, which may serve to stop undue drift to towns. Films may also have an important function in supersedenceof certain superstitions which are inimical to healthy life and progress."[87] Bullock proposed that the department send its agricultural officer, E. D. Alvord, an American, to the United States to purchase "films illustrating prevention of soil erosion, better agriculture etc.," as well as projection equipment. Bullock recommended the formation of a committee composed of himself, the medical director, and the director of native education to discuss the question. Alvord shared Bullock's enthusiasm and expressed his high expectations for the medium: "There is no question in my mind that visual instruction by means of films is a most excellent way of giving instruction to Native audiences."[88] Alvord bought several projectors in America and returned to Southern Rhodesia ready to begin teaching agricultural techniques with motion pictures. But he immediately confronted a familiar problem: "We are now fully equipped with a portable cinematograph outfit with the exception of suitable films for Native audiences."[89]

If the colony had no films that were deemed appropriate for African audiences it was not Bullock's fault. While Alvord was in America, the CNC had been investigating ways of securing appropriate films both for his department and for the mine owners. He initially hoped to get films from BEKE and had suggested to the native-affairs minister that a film commission be established in the country to coordinate with Notcutt and Latham.[90] In the event, BEKE was unable to accept an invitation to tour Southern Rhodesia. Bullock settled for having Alvord try to acquire copies of the experiment's thirty-five productions, but this, too, did not work out.

Bullock also considered other schemes for making films in the colony. For example, he encouraged the efforts of Gordon Cooper, a British filmmaker who was interested in making films for government departments. Cooper had originally contacted Prime Minister Huggins to offer his services to the government. In a letter to Huggins, Cooper explained that he had formed his company, Rhodesian Film Productions, to produce films for Africans because "at the present time the old silent films used for this purpose are exhausted, and the ordinary talkies are quite unsuitable."[91] Cooper was in the process of making two films on his own initiative and expressed confidence that "the Government would take an interest through the Native Department from an educational point of view, as there are so many ways of educating the native through the medium of the films."[92] Huggins turned the matter over to Bullock, who expressed a strong interest in the proposal: "Regarding films for Native audiences, I would suggest that the firm be informed that consideration is being given to possibilities in this connection. I have in view that inquiries might be made as to whether or not the firm has apparatus capable of producing films dealing with subjects such as the life circle of the mosquito; the growth of plants etc."[93] In the event, Cooper ignored the CNC's guidelines and instead made a film called *The Poison Ordeal*, which was inspired by a story that had appeared in *N.A.D.A.*, the magazine of the Southern Rhodesia Native Affairs Department. In Cooper's words, the film was "a Matabele romance" and "a faithful record of manners and customs of bygone days."[94] The Native Affairs Department was not impressed enough to purchase the film, and Cooper soon drifted on to other projects.[95]

The Native Affairs Department, unlike government departments in Kenya, Tanganyika, and Uganda, clearly shared the Colonial Office's growing interest in filmmaking. The department's enthusiasm was motivated in part, as we have seen, by the need to supply suitable films to mine administrators and welfare officers, whose workers had developed an insatiable appetite for new films. By 1931, however, the department was no longer interested in securing films simply for the enjoyment of proletariat audiences. As the department's correspondence indicates, it had begun investigating the potential use of the cinema in rural education. This sudden interest in films for rural peoples stemmed from developments within the colony, where the responsibilities of the Native Affairs Department were suddenly changing.

Whites in Southern Rhodesia had achieved a form of self-government in 1923. Thanks to their relative autonomy from the Colonial Office, in 1931 the white-elected legislative assembly was able to pass the Land Apportionment Act, which formalized the division of the colony's land into white and black areas. In the words of one historian, "This Act remained the centrepiece of the government's segregation policies for the next forty-six years. It stipulated that no African was entitled to hold or occupy land in white areas."[96] The results were disastrous for African peasants. Within a few years, agricultural officials found that the reserves were overcrowded and could not support a further increase in population. Land deterioration became a permanent feature of life in the reserves.[97] Thus officials in the Native Affairs Department found themselves pressed to teach European agricultural practices to rural farmers.

Unfortunately for the department, there was no simple or efficient way of imparting such lessons. The colony's settlers were loath to spend their tax dollars on African education, and therefore there were almost no state-funded schools. Most of the peasants who did attend schools in the colony were taught by missionaries. Though the government encouraged the missions, and their teachings were generally acceptable to the state, they could not be relied on to undertake the ambitious campaign required to spread the department's message to their pupils. The virtual absence of formal education meant that most Africans were illiterate. The educational policies of the colonial government left it with little contact with most of its African subjects. In the native reserves, state policy was transmitted through local leaders who had been co-opted into the colonial administration. Therefore if the department wanted to teach Africans how to adapt and survive on diminished landholdings, they would have to do so themselves, and they could not rely on written instructions. Thus the departments' interest in the many "films for Africans" schemes floated in the colony during the 1930s should be understood as a response to the pressing need for an efficient and inexpensive method of communicating with rural peoples.

By the end of the 1930s, the idea of using film as a tool of education had spread from the Native Affairs Department to several other departments of the Southern Rhodesian government. This inspired the government to form a film institute, modeled on the British Film Institute (BFI). When Oliver Bell, a founding member of the BFI, approached the high commissioner for Southern Rhodesia, Sir Lanigan O'Keefe, about creating a similar institute in the Rhodesias, his suggestion was warmly received.[98] O'Keefe placed W. D. Gale, an officer of the Southern Rhodesian Public Relations Office, in charge of coordinating the efforts of the government departments in Southern Rhodesia. Gale outlined his ambitions for the new institute in an article that he prepared for the British film journal *Sight and Sound*. In it he expressed his vision of the future role of motion pictures in Southern Rhodesian society. He began by articulating his lofty ambition for the cinema in the colony: "The greatest problem which Southern Rhodesia has to face is the problem of race relationships—the day-to-day relation between the European, with his thousand years of race development and cultural background, and the native, only a short remove from savagery, with his superstition, his primitive ways, his crude habits, his poor mental developments." Gale believed that for colonialism to succeed in the colony, Africans had to learn more about European "ways of life, ways of thought, outlook and background. And that knowledge can best be imparted by the film."[99] But Gale also recognized that film had a very practical role to play in rural education:

> Similar work needs to be done in the spheres of agriculture and public health. . . . The film would bring that knowledge to both European farmer and native pastoralist, vividly and realistically, to ensure their support of measures to conserve the soil. Similarly, in public health, the two greatest menaces are malaria and bilharzia. Here, too, film would illustrate the harm these two diseases do, why they are contracted, how they can be avoided. The result will be a healthier community, a greater chance of the colonisation experiment succeeding.[100]

The outbreak of World War II forced Gale to shelve his plans for the institute for the duration. After the war, however, he became the organizer of the largest film project ever undertaken in any British colony. Given Gale's subsequent influence on policy, it is worth examining his views on the unique requirements of a cinema for Africans, which he articulated in a 1942 letter to the BFI. Gale's thoughts are a distillation of the prejudices about the peculiarities of African film audiences that had characterized settler discourse on the subject since 1914. In 1942, Oliver Bell had written to Gale inquiring about the future of film production for Africans in the territory:

> I gather, and I hope you will correct me, that for pure entertain-ment the native must be treated as we treat a ten-year-old white child, i.e. that he must be shown films of action of the Western type, films of excitement such as CAPTAIN OF THE CLOUDS and simple cartoons of the Popeye rather than the Disney type and news, most of which last named will be misunderstood or not un-derstood at all but through which slowly an interest in ordinary types of film may develop.[101]

It is worth noting that Bell's views, though undoubtedly con-descending, anticipate that Africans will eventually learn to understand "ordinary types of film."

Gale did not agree. In his reply to Bell he offered a much less optimistic assessment of African audiences. He began, "In regard to your question about natives. You are quite right— the mental level of the average adult is about that of a 10-year-old European child. In a film he is interested in movement and action; anything subtle leaves him cold."[102] Gale's under-standing of African psychology brought him to the conclu-sion that "a native's mental perception is very limited. . . . Therefore, the films must be simple in treatment, with long shots to enable him to grasp their meaning. His sense of hu-mour is extraordinarily simple. My native servants at home shriek with mirth at the same things that amuse my young daughter."[103] Finally, he expressed the lingering sense of "moral panic" that was alive and well in Southern Rhodesia: "I am angered beyond measure by the kind of 16 m.m. films which a commercial organisation sends on the circuit of schools, locations and compounds in this country—the same films for European and native consumption. Films of bedroom scenes, with half naked women, sophisticated, unreal . . . God knows what the native must think of our white women after seeing them, or the European's general standard of morality."[104] Gale's views on African audiences were consistent with those of most of white Rhodesia in the 1940s. They were also consistent with the views of many colonial observers during the "moral panic" of the 1920s. Compare his comments with, for example, an Indian Office Report from the early 1920s: "The Native of India is astonishingly credulous, and the plays (native dramas) and stories (folk tales) he delights in would bore to death an English child of tender years by their simplicity."[105] However, by the early 1940s such views were beginning to diverge with those held by other observers in Britain and the empire and commonwealth. Though Bell appeared to be willing to defer to Gale on the question, his views reflect a different expectation of African audiences. Likewise in other parts of the empire and former empire, the "moral panic" that had characterized the 1930s had subsided.[106] In Southern Rhodesia, however, such concerns remained commonplace during and after World War II. Gale went on to play an instrumental role in postwar film production and censorship, and his views on Africans and motion pictures shaped government film policy in the colony over the next three decades.

Gale's views reflect the widely held assumption that the ability to comprehend motion pictures was an attribute unique to the settler community. It was one of a cluster of skills and abilities that enabled them to lay claim to authority over their African subjects. Cinema censorship and efforts to produce special films for Africans were predicated on the conviction that whites and blacks perceived motion pictures in fundamentally different ways. From the settlers' perspective, film was complicated, subtle, sophisticated, and modern: Africans were "conservative," "simple," and had "extraordinarily limited mental perceptions." To officials like Gale, the ability to understand a modern, complex medium like the cinema was at the heart of the distinctive identity that justified the perpetuation of white rule.

After World War II, the Colonial Office's enthusiasm for teaching Africans with motion pictures gradually waned. As Britain orchestrated the independence of much of its African empire, many stereotypes expired in the process, including the belief that the peculiar psychology of Africans made them highly susceptible to film images. But the idea died hard in Southern Rhodesia. Indeed, as we shall see, it underpinned an ambitious postwar program to produce films for Africans. It retained currency in Southern Rhodesia until the settler regime fell in 1980. The government continued to censor motion pictures and to produce and screen special films because it believed the cinema held a powerful influence over Africans. To doubt this was to question the core of white identity and the legitimacy of settler domination.

# Chapter 2

# Watching Africans Watch Films

## Theorizing Film Literacy in British Africa

The government of Southern Rhodesia's developing interest in filmmaking during the 1930s was part of a wider movement within the British Empire to study the influence of the cinema on African audiences. Beginning in the late 1920s, an army of administrators, filmmakers, academics, journalists, missionaries, marketers, and educators descended on the African continent to measure the abilities of Africans to make sense of motion pictures. Their investigations focused on several key questions: Could Africans be taught to understand the "language" of the cinema? Were Africans particularly susceptible to motion-picture images? Did African audiences inevitably accept action on the screen as a literal depiction of reality or could they be taught to distinguish between "truth" and "fiction"? These were not merely academic questions. These analysts represented groups committed to transforming African societies, and though their agendas ranged from selling soap to saving souls, they shared the common hope that motion pictures might prove an efficient and potent tool for influencing African audiences.

Colonial observers conducted dozens of experiments into the cognitive abilities of African audiences over a span of forty years. They held discussions in the press, in colonial journals, and in public debates. This chapter chronicles the history of these investigations and the evolution of a colonial discourse of film literacy. It demonstrates that until World War II conventional wisdom held that the peculiar intellect of Africans made them slow to recognize and comprehend cinematic images. After the war, this orthodoxy came under attack both from within the filmmaking community and from educated Africans. A series of more systematic experiments ultimately demonstrated that African audiences adapted quite readily to the conventions of the cinema.

Despite these conclusions, which were readily accepted by the British Colonial Office, this revised assessment made little impact on officials in the settler states of Southern Africa. In these last outposts of colonial rule, white "experts" ignored research conducted by outsiders and relied instead on studies conducted by their own Native Affairs Departments, which continued to attest to the peculiar needs and vulnerabilities of African audiences.

The history of this discourse reveals the close link between film theory and the justification of white rule in Britain's African empire. The belief that African audiences had limited capabilities and unique needs reinforced a broader colonial stereotype regarding the intellectual potential of Africans. After World War II this stereotype was challenged in those regions of Africa that the British Colonial Office was preparing for self-rule. In West Africa in particular, theories that presumed innate intellectual differences between races became increasingly untenable as independence approached. However, in

Southern Africa, where the white minority sought to cling to power indefinitely, these theories retained their currency because they served to legitimize the perpetuation of settler control. In questioning the abilities of Africans to comprehend motion pictures, white theorists in Southern Africa were able to hint at much more fundamental concerns regarding the limitations of Africans to comprehend modern media. From this assertion, it was a short step to the conclusion that Africans were incapable of participating effectively in a technologically sophisticated democratic society.

The first recorded experiment into African film literacy was conducted in the early 1920s, when William Sellers, a medical officer with the Nigerian government, began studying the reactions of Africans to British documentaries.[1] After observing audiences for three years, Sellers produced a film of his own called *Plague Operations in Lagos*, to show Nigerians how rats spread contagion.[2] This was perhaps the first motion picture created specifically for a colonial audience. Over the next seven years, Sellers made fifteen similar films. He concluded early on that African audiences inevitably were confused by the sophisticated techniques employed in most motion pictures. His own films therefore utilized a special method that he had developed by a process of trial and error over a thirteen-year period. Sellers articulated these rules in a lecture that he presented in London in 1941. He explained that he had originally begun teaching health lessons with a magic lantern but decided that his audiences were incapable of recognizing two-dimensional pictures. In his words: "It is well known that if an illiterate African is handed a photograph of himself or some scene familiar to him he will invariably turn it the wrong way up in an effort to focus his eyes on the picture."[3] Sellers therefore decided to see if Africans could recognize moving pictures.

After his first experiments, Sellers became convinced that, while audiences could comprehend motion picture images more easily than still pictures, they could not impose any logic on them. "They looked upon the films as a collection of animated photographs a few of which they could appreciate, but they were quite unable to link the scenes together to form any kind of story."[4] To Sellers, these early experiments "proved conclusively that if films were to be successful in conveying a story or teaching a lesson to these people, they would have to be specially made."[5] Therefore, when he began producing his own films, he used simple camera angles and instructed his actors to move very slowly in the hopes that these techniques would gradually teach the audiences to comprehend film structure and narrative.

Because Sellers's work influenced a generation of colonial filmmakers, it is worth examining how he arrived at these conclusions. He determined one of his rules after several members of an audience expressed an unwarranted interest in the activities of a chicken in one of his productions: Sellers did not even remember filming the creature, but when he again viewed the movie he found it, running off-camera after being startled by one of the actors. From this incident, Sellers deduced that the audience noticed the chicken because of its position at the base of the screen. African audiences, he decided, "read" the screen from bottom to top, scrutinizing it as one would read a written page, rather than focusing on the projected image as a whole.[6] "The eyes of illiterate people are not trained to see non-stereoscopic things," he concluded. "They focus their eyes on to the screen and they scan the picture and analyze it in detail. They fasten their gaze on to any movement in the scene to the exclusion of everything else in the picture."[7] Films for Africans therefore would have to rely on simple action and few characters and props.

A second incident similarly impressed Sellers's developing "grammar" of colonial cinema. In what was to become one of the most enduring and oft-told tropes of African credulity, Sellers recounted an experience from early in his career: "In a film on malaria I included some very satisfying full close-ups of mosquitoes in the act of sucking blood, but the results when the film was shown were disastrous. The people became alarmed and enquired about the country where the people had to contend with such wicked looking monsters and remarked that they themselves were very fortunate to have mosquitoes which were quite small and comparatively harmless."[8] From this incident he concluded that African audiences accepted what they viewed literally, and thus great care needed to be taken to avoid any "tricks" that might confuse or disturb them. "Sophisticated" techniques such as panning, flashbacks, quick cuts, and so forth were therefore inappropriate for African audience. If, for example, Africans were shown a "panning" shot of a building, Sellers insisted "they will think the building rushed by."[9]

Sellers established another rule of colonial cinema after screening one of his films titled *Machi Gaba* ("the village that crept forward"). The story contrasted the experiences of two families suffering from infection by hookworm. One family is cured by a colonial doctor; the other goes to a traditional healer and continues to suffer. Sellers was struck by the fact that audiences often laughed at the sight of the miserable family. Rather than attribute this to callousness or some melodramatic quality in the film, he chose to interpret the response as an expression of sympathy, little understood by Europeans, or indeed by the Africans themselves. Sellers thereby deduced a third axiom of colonial cinema: to be effective, films made for Africans required the assistance of "experts" who understood the peculiarities of "native psychology."[10]

Finally, Sellers's experience convinced him that Africans lacked the imagination to visualize the context within which a given scene was taking place. He reasoned that since the camera projects an incomplete picture, although "sophisticated persons" could fill in the missing background, "illiterate people . . . find great difficulty in using their imagination in this way, or making this visual adjustment."[11] His solution was simply to discourage cinema operators from showing films to Africans that included any unfamiliar scenes, situations, or characters.[12]

It took Sellers a few years to develop his formula for making films, yet even while he was conducting his tests, other observers were interpreting his results quite differently. These alternate readings are worth examining because they suggest the tenuous foundation of his conclusions. A British journalist, L. M. Ross, writing in the journal *United Empire* in February 1940 describes a film screening he witnessed in Nigeria. Though he does not identify the film by name, he was almost certainly watching *Machi Gaba*. Ross described the audience's response to a scene depicting a family suffering from hookworm:

> The object of this scene was to impress upon the people the tragedy that results from dirt and disease. To our surprise they were neither saddened nor depressed. On the contrary they found it highly amusing! The sight of an old man, wielding his pick so feebly that he merely scratched the surface of his farm, was the object of unsympathetic laughter and ribald remarks. The sight of a creature so deformed that he no longer had the use of his legs, but had to push his body along in a recumbent position, did not bring home to them the awful realization that illness might reduce them to a similar state. On the contrary, they roared their delighted appreciation![13]

Ross did not attribute these responses to the audience's "primitive psychology"; rather, he proposed two possible alternative explanations:

> The answer to this question lies partly in the native conception of life, which differs from ours because of their social background. . . . The Hausa people are Mahommedans and the Mahommedan is a fatalist. He does not view sickness and death with our eyes. He considers them as inevitable and natural events. Allah wills it. There is no more to be said. To impress upon them the fact that Allah wills it because they are a careless people might be a diffi-cult proposition. But the will of Allah is not usually a matter of mirth.[14]

Ross ultimately discounted this Orientalist interpretation in favor of a more practical explanation.

> Now, this crowd laughed because, in their simple logic, they re-jected the authenticity of the picture. Where had anyone ever seen a village so utterly miserable, so utterly destitute? If you showed an ordinary village with some rich men and some poor, some good some bad, some clean some dirty. Then, I think, the spectators would have been properly impressed. After all, one of the first principles of the drama (and propaganda, to be effective, must be dramatic) is that, to arouse the sympathy and understanding of the audience, the principal character must be admirable.[15]

Sellers's film, Ross argued, was simply implausible, and there-fore the audience failed to identify with the plight of the char-acters. This was to become a common critique of colonial cinema.[16]

Another colonial official drew very different conclusions about the audience fixated on the chicken. John Wilson, an in-formation officer with the Gold Coast government, appears to be describing the screening of a Sellers film in an interview he gave in 1961.[17]

> This man—this sanitary inspector—made a moving picture in

very slow time, very slow technique of what would be required of the ordinary household in a primitive African village in getting rid of standing water—draining pools, picking up all empty tins and putting them away, and so forth. We showed this film to an audience and asked them what they had seen, and they said they had seen a chicken, a fowl[,] and we didn't know there was a fowl in it. So we very carefully scanned the frames, one by one[,] for this fowl and, sure enough, for about a second, a fowl went over the corner of the frame.

Like Ross, Wilson found an explanation in Sellers's technique rather than in the psychology of the audience. "Perhaps it was the sudden movement of the chicken. Everything else was done in slow technique, people going forward slowly picking up the tin demonstrating and all the rest of it and the bird was apparently the one bit of reality for them a fowl that sort of flew away in terror."[18] (Louis Nell, a filmmaker with fifty-four years of experience of producing films in Africa, told me that any audience would be likely to notice movement on a screen when the actors were speaking without moving.)[19]

Sellers's research seemed to provide empirical evidence to support the assumption, long held in imperial circles, that African audiences had needs and capabilities that were different from their European counterparts.[20] Sellers reinforced this supposition by disseminating several anecdotes from his experience that became standard tropes of African credulity. These stories appeared repeatedly in public discussions of colonial media. They served to underscore the simplicity of African audiences and the importance of strictly controlling the screen images they saw.

The most famous and most often recounted was Sellers's tale of the giant mosquito. It first appeared in the 1927 report of the Colonial Film Committee, where it is probably the source of Sir Hesketh Bell's comment that "illustrations of the life history of the mosquito or of the devastating effects of the hookworm, which might be understood by more or less civilized coloured people, who have some notions about microbes and microscopes, would be quite bewildering to unsophisticated natives who have not the faintest idea of modern science and have only a rudimentary sense of proportion."[21] The mosquito tale surfaces again in L. A. Notcutt and G. C. Latham's 1937 book *The African and the Cinema*, where the authors frame it as a caution for future filmmakers: "it is well to remember as a warning the story of the Natives who were shown on the screen a very much enlarged picture of a mosquito. No wonder, they subsequently remarked, that white folk are frightened of the mosquito if they have them that size in their country."[22] After the war, when the magazine *Colonial Development* reported on the work of the Colonial Film Unit in Africa, it managed to squeeze two of Sellers's stories into the article's first paragraph.

> On one occasion, during the showing of a serious instructional film in Nigeria, the audience was unaccountably rocked with laughter. It was afterwards discovered that the behaviour of a white hen that had strolled into the picture had distracted attention from the main purpose of the film. A film on malaria being shown to a bush audience made little impact because at one point a greatly enlarged picture of a mosquito filled the screen so that its structure could be explained. The audience declared that there was no reason to fear the tiny mosquitoes they knew, which were quite different from the huge and terrifying creature they saw on the screen.[23]

George Pearson, who became the Colonial Office's chief filmmaker in 1939, related the story in an article published in 1949: "The reaction among the natives was ruinous to the film purpose, for they said there would be no need for them to worry about the little mosquitoes they knew; those in the film were enormous and terrible things quite different from anything in their country!" Pearson then explained the obvious lesson: "What had been overlooked was the complete ignorance of [magnification in] the primitive mind."[24] Pearson could not resist retelling the story a decade later in his autobiography,[25] and it lives on in Southern Africa today: the historian Tim Burke found it circulating among white professionals in the advertising industry in Zimbabwe in 1991.[26]

The mosquito anecdote was merely the most popular of several in similar vein that found their way into colonial folklore. Most of these tales focus on the literalness with which Africans accepted screen images. One example was the case of the mobile film crew who showed a wildlife film one evening only, allegedly, to find villagers searching for the lion's spoor the next morning.[27] Another story was told of audiences becoming confused and alarmed when an actor whose character had died in one film reappeared in another.[28] Yet another story appears in several versions, all describing audiences fleeing from one or another terrifying screen image—a snake, a pointed gun, an airplane. Perhaps the most famous example of this "panicking audience" phenomenon was attributed to Tanganyika, where the showing of the British propaganda film *London Can Take It* during World War II purportedly sent audiences streaming out of a theater in terror.[29] Another common story had a member of the audience assuming that a local actor shown on screen suffering some tragedy or affliction (death, for example, or contracting syphilis or smallpox) had met with this misfortune in real life.

Sellers's story of the audience who laughed inappropriately continued to circulate widely as well. It appeared, retold by another author, in revised form in a 1950 article titled "Laughter": "Africans in a certain audience laughed outright at a tragic scene of a badly maimed leper who appeared in one of the sequences in a film. When questioned afterwards as to why they

had laughed they were quite perturbed; they seemed quite un-
aware that they had laughed, and emphasized that they were
very sorry indeed for the poor man they had seen in the
film."[30] The author supplied an interpretation that Sellers
would have appreciated: "laughter such as this might be . . .
the subconscious expression of a feeling of superiority roused
at the sight of inferiority in the person of the leper on the
screen."

Such tropes of African credulity had their parallels in colonies
outside the British sphere.[31] In the Belgian Congo, during the
1940s the administration conducted a series of experiments into
film cognition among Africans. These experiments, poorly
conceptualized and executed, reached conclusions that were
amazingly similar to those of Sellers and his supporters. From
these stories several tales of African credulity emerged. One
popular story involved the screening of a cartoon (presumably a Disney short about Donald Duck joining the army).
At the end of the film, a soldier supposedly asked, *"Y-a-t-il
vraiment des Blancs de cette espèce et sont-ils nombreux?"* ("What
kind of creature is this, and do the Whites have many of
them?")[32]

One's first impression is that these stories are apocryphal,
particularly since the specifics of the incidents are rarely
given. Even if genuinely recorded, such accounts are of course
certainly open to alternative interpretations. Megan Vaughan,
in discussing the reaction of the audience to the mosquito on
the screen, has pointed out that Sellers and his successors
never considered that such comments might have been meant
ironically.[33] My own experience in Zimbabwe suggests the
likelihood of this possibility. Two former mobile cinema operators of the Rhodesian Information Service separately recounted to me their experiences showing rural people films
explaining the life cycle of a new strain of maize. The use of

time-lapse photography inspired members of their audiences—
two separate audiences—to ask, "Why doesn't our goverment
give us this maize which grows so fast?" Both informants related this story as evidence of the credulity of their audiences.
However, when I told a third retired cinema operator this
story, he merely laughed, saying, "Didn't they realize the people
were only joking?"[34]

Given the likelihood that such stories happened at best infrequently, what purpose was served by their frequent repeti-
tion by colonial "experts"? The historian finds an interesting
parallel to these tales of audience credulity in the earliest era
of the cinema. Reportage about the first motion-picture audiences frequently recounted the behavior of "panicking audiences" that ran in terror from images projected on the screen.
The most popular of these stories involved the image of an on-
coming train, which was frequently cited as the source of audience panic. Recent scholarship examining the "panicking
audience" phenomenon has drawn into question its very existence. As in the case of the giant mosquitoes, there is some
question as to whether any audience ever ran fleeing from a
locomotive in a theater. Film historian Steven Bottomore has
suggested that, while there were probably a handful of such
incidents, they were embellished and overreported.[35] Tom
Gunning has argued that these anxious audiences were in all
likelihood thrilled by the spectacle of the cinema, without actually believing that they were in jeopardy from the images.
Gunning points out that early cinema shows were meant to be
not narratives but short visual effects, not unlike a magic act.
Thus it should not surprise us that such audiences would have
a thrilled reaction that could easily be construed as fear,
rooted in credulity.[36]

Why, then, did such stories circulate? Both Gunning and
Bottomore use the work of psychologist Christian Metz to ex-

plain this situation in a way that casts light on the African versions of these stories. Metz argued that such tales circulate as a way of allowing "modern" audiences to assert their mastery over the medium. As Metz said, "To believe that people of the past or from more primitive societies may have run in fear at train films, proves how much more sophisticated we are today."[37] Such tropes of credulity also serve to outline and reaffirm group identity and coherence. Bottomore argues that these stories were originally spread by "sophisticated" urbanites and were told about yokels from the countryside. As the film scholar Nicholas Hilley explains it, these stories serve largely to define who is inside and who is outside the group, "revealing boundaries and reinforcing coherence."[38] In line with such an interpretation, the dissemination of these stories in Southern Rhodesia reflects an effort on the part of the colonizer to differentiate themselves from their African subjects.

However, it is not unlikely that there was some confusion for audiences when they were first introduced to this novel medium. In his study *Early Cinema in Russia and Its Cultural Reception*, Yuri Tsivian remarks on the position of what he calls the "innocent viewer . . . a viewer with untrained cognitive habits."[39] Such viewers, with little context for understanding their initial introduction to the cinema, undoubtedly experienced some learning curve before they became adjusted to the peculiar kinds of images that constitute motion pictures. Other writers have suggested that some of these perceived "misperceptions" fit logically within the worldview of African audiences. Thus the perception of images on the screen as "spirits" is consistent with the belief systems of many non-Western communities.[40] Brian Larkin observes that in Northern Nigeria cinema was dismissed by some Muslim leaders as supernatural; he also points out that the Hausa word for cinema is derived from the word for magic.[41]

That said, we are left with the fact that such stories took on a life of their own in their telling and retelling. To modern audiences, the image of the early spectators fleeing the train is unsophisticated, but we recognize that the audience was made up of people much like ourselves, living in an era before they had learned to understand the medium. The lesson therefore is essentially "look how far we have come." Colonial observers, however, circulated these stories for precisely the opposite reason, as proof of the intellectual limitations of Africans.

The first attempt to test Sellers's rules of African cinema was undertaken by BEKE. In preparation for making their own films, the experimenters wanted to see how Africans with no prior exposure to the cinema would respond to the medium. In Notcutt's words, they sought to "elucidate the principles which govern the use of the motion picture as an instrument of education and as an aid for tribal society in the two fold struggle to preserve old traditions and to adapt to the modern world."[42] According to their sponsor, Notcutt and Latham arrived in Africa with no predetermined notions of what shape these principles would take.[43] They had, however, read Huxley's report closely and knew enough of Sellers's work to quote approvingly his tale of the giant mosquito.[44]

In their *The African and the Cinema*, Notcutt and Latham presented a set of rules for making films for illiterate Africans that in the main supported Sellers's approach. First, African audiences required a slower pace than Western audiences: "The speed with which films were displayed to western people is entirely too fast for tribal Africans."[45] Second, African audiences accepted films literally, and thus filmmakers should avoid depicting antisocial behavior. This meant, in particular, that Africans should not be shown criminal activity in movies because "if anything wrong is shown as happening in a film without disapproval being clearly expressed, the Native is apt to think that we approve of it."[46] Despite these condescending views, Notcutt and Latham concluded that "the African is not essentially different from other races";[47] and they noted that "the moving picture is understood by unsophisticated natives to a degree which astonishes people who have experienced their comparative inability to recognise still pictures."[48]

After BEKE ceased operations in 1937, the Colonial Office lost interest in the theoretical question of film's influence over Africans. However, their interest revived two years later with the advent of World War II. In September 1939, Britain's Ministry of Information was charged with the task of mobilizing support for the war throughout the empire and working with the Colonial Office to develop appropriate propaganda. Initially, colonial authorities felt some trepidation regarding the possible influence of film propaganda on Africans. As the governor of Northern Rhodesia informed the secretary of state for the colonies, Malcolm McDonald, films "would be novel to many villagers. If we overdo propaganda and introduce such novelties there is a danger of unsettling the Natives."[49] However, the Ministry of Information determined that film was among its best tools for reaching African audiences, and in late 1939 William Sellers was seconded from the Nigerian government to organize the Colonial Film Unit (CFU). Sellers would serve as the head of the unit until the late 1950s, thereby indelibly stamping his views on African film audiences onto the organization.

Though the unit was colonial in name, the Ministry of Information believed that it was in sub-Saharan Africa that its productions would prove most effective. As one official put it, "Indians have notoriously a keen nose for propaganda, which they reject as soon as they sniff it," while "the native peoples of the colonies are more gullible."[50] Sellers appointed George Pearson, an experienced silent-film director, as his chief filmmaker, and together they began making films.

Because the unit could not film in Africa during the war,

and because its main brief was the production of propaganda films, Sellers was not able to employ many of the techniques and rules of African film production that he had developed in Nigeria. However, the CFU films still adhered to a "specialized type of filmmaking which they considered suitable for primitive people; the films should be slow in pace, avoid trick photography, leave nothing to be inferred, and pay special attention to continuity."[51]

By 1945, the Sellers style had established a kind of orthodoxy among colonial filmmakers throughout the empire, and in the postwar era, when the French and Belgian administrations turned to film as a tool of education and propaganda, they, too, adopted it. The French took films to rural peoples throughout their North African and sub-Saharan empire, and the Belgians took them to an estimated 8.5 million Africans in Congo. Initially these governments purchased CFU films for their libraries; however, shortly after the end of the war, both governments began making their own films.[52] These French and Belgian directors relied upon the CFU cinema style. As a leading Belgian filmmaker declared:

> The African is not yet ready for the cinema as we know it; he is bewildered by its conventions, fails to grasp psychological subtleties and is unable to follow a rapid succession of different scenes. Consequently, if we wish the cinema to have a real influence on the African public, we must adapt its technique to the primitive mind. We must take a step backwards and abandon all the recognized cinematographic conventions, all originality, all personality, and revert to the primitive simplicity of the early cinema.[53]

However, just as other colonial groups were adopting the orthodoxy, it began to be openly questioned for the first time from within the British filmmaking community. One of the first Europeans to question Sellers was Julian Huxley. As seen in chapter 1, Huxley's experiments in East Africa had led him to question the assumption that African audiences were in any way unique. In a public debate during the war, Huxley challenged many of Sellers's conclusions.[54] At approximately the same time, a critic within the Colonial Office began expressing reservations regarding the subject matter of the Sellers's films: "The Colonial peoples want sympathy, not films on soil erosion, humanity, not lectures on how to kill bed bugs. Can we not discard this pose of instructional superiority and get down to learning from the people as well as teaching them?"[55] In the colonies, other critics appeared as well. For example, during the war a British officer in charge of a mobile recruiting troupe in East Africa complained that many of the CFU films were either dull or incomprehensible to his audiences.[56] An information officer who showed them in East Africa criticized CFU films for "the employment of untrained African actors and a rather patronizing told-to-the-children English commentator."[57]

In the postwar era, the British government was increasingly pressured to make some material contributions to the welfare of its African populations. For planners at the Colonial Office, film seemed to offer a "modern" and effective tool for furthering their developmental agenda. With such issues in mind, in 1948 the British Film Institute sponsored a conference on "The Film in Colonial Development." The meeting proved to be the high noon of the Sellers school, with many of the speakers presenting the old CFU prejudices as established "fact." One of the speakers at the conference was Alan Izod, who had worked with the Colonial Film Unit during the war and would go on to become an important figure in Southern Rhodesia. In his address, Izod told an audience categorically, "The cartoon is definitely beyond the comprehension of the primitive African."[58] Other speakers noted the "meager mental outlook of African audiences," the proclivity of Africans to laugh at the wrong times, the imitative nature of African audiences (particularly where scenes of crimes are concerned), and the importance of "quantity not quality" in colonial film production.[59]

However, the conference also saw new doubts expressed about the Sellers style. An African student named A. R. Baëta, from the Gold Coast, presented an address that challenged many of the views aired at the conference. "I wish . . . to point out that some of the remarks made . . . [regarding the] effect of films on primitive Africans are very far from the truth. . . . A speaker said that it was wrong to show people in the Northern Territories of the Gold Coast films showing docks and ships. Another suggested that the primitive African will think it magic if he were shown huge electric trains speeding on the countryside."[60] On the contrary, she argued, such films performed a service by broadening the horizons of isolated peoples with no other context for understanding the world beyond their village. Ms. Baëtta concluded with a criticism of colonial cinema that was growing in popularity: "The European trying to think in terms of the primitive African fails, and what he gets is anything but the way the primitive African thinks."[61]

Among other dissenting voices heard at the conference, the most famous was that of the keynote speaker, John Grierson, the founder of the British documentary film movement. Grierson's work during the 1930s had greatly influenced the work of Notcutt and Latham. However, in his speech he brought into question the foundations of the colonial cinema rules they had espoused, stating, "I am going to say directly that there is now no considerable body of knowledge in this field. Some experiments have been made, but in pretty piecemeal fashion."[62]

The next challenge to the Sellers technique appeared in the pages of the Colonial Office journal *Colonial Cinema*. In June 1950, an employee of the newly established Gold Coast Film Unit, J. Oduntun, wrote: "What a lot of nonsense has been written about the illiterate African and films. How little solid sense, how much debatable theor[y], and how much high-falutin nonsense! . . . To achieve some results with film-making in Africa we have got to abandon the current stereotyped methods and adopt new techniques and a new approach."[63] Odunton also criticized the failure of colonial filmmakers to instruct their audiences in the techniques of cinema. "The assumption was that the uneducated African does not understand films, and for that reason films must be made on a definite pattern and should follow certain rules. These rules were subsequently sanctified and given the name of 'Specialised Technique.'" Odunton warned that such techniques were patronizing and would fail to influence audiences.[64] He finished by promising that his Gold Coast unit would learn from the mistakes of his predecessors: "We are determined not to make our films dull."[65]

Simultaneously, as the Sellers orthodoxy faced criticism from outside of the filmmaking community, it began to unravel from within. A handful of CFU directors were beginning to consider the accusations leveled at them. While George Pearson dismissed Odunton's assertions,[66] Norman Spurr, a filmmaker working in Kenya, acknowledged the validity of the criticism.[67] Spurr had been one of the first CFU employees to air his doubts about the unit's work in public. In a March 1949 article in *Colonial Cinema*, he acknowledged the difficulty he had encountered in his attempts to gauge African comprehension of the unit's films:

> It soon became evident that the system of finding out what an audience thought of the films was completely inadequate: there was

far too much opinion, too little fact, and sometimes we were deliberately misled. Questionnaires were not possible, because the audiences were illiterate and the ordinary question by word of mouth was little better "for," argued the Africans, "we like these films shows, and they will continue as long as we say they are good"—a most understandable sentiment but not much use to us.[68]

By 1949, the rift between Sellers and his critics was widening. As A. M. Champion, an information officer in Kenya, stated, "Due to the lack of adequate information about the audience reaction of backward peoples, controversy rages about their capabilities of appreciations [*sic*] and understanding the films."[69] It was in the interests of solving this debate that in 1951 the Colonial Office decided to finance and supervise a systematic study of the question.[70] The Colonial Office, which on the one hand was becoming increasingly confident about the future of film as a tool of education in Africa, was also becoming sensitive to the critiques directed at Sellers and his followers.

The Colonial Office supplied a grant of £18,150 to fund the experiment. Their interest was not merely academic: the British treasury was being asked to invest large sums in films for development after the war and it was imperative that the Colonial Office produce some evidence of their efficacy. "As a medium of education and entertainment, the cinema in African society is known to be effective, but the modes of its effectiveness are still largely unknown . . . systematic investigation into audience reactions should enable reliable techniques (for making films) to be developed much more rapidly than under present conditions."[71] The Colonial Office hoped the experiment could settle several thorny questions about African film perception once and for all. The areas to be considered read like a catalog of the rules of colonial cinema:

Among the problems urgently demanding attention are the following . . . "Vision" many primitive people don't have two dimensional art . . . "Mental reactions" particularly use of cartoons . . .
"Psychological reactions" . . . "The habitual associations of ideas
of African peoples are very different from those of Europeans and
the study of audience reactions can provide . . . information about
the kinds of associations that arouse the different emotions. In
particular, research into the causes of laughter is necessary."[72]

The Colonial Office sent the British anthropologist P.
Morton-Williams and several assistants to Nigeria to monitor the reactions of various communities to motion pictures.
They screened a variety of colonial and European films over a
culturally diverse region of the colony. They interviewed audiences after each screening and noted comments made during performances. Morton-Williams published his findings in
*The Cinema in Rural Nigeria*.[73] His report refuted much of the
prevailing orthodoxy of colonial cinema and provided a stun-
ning rejoinder to the Sellers school. Regarding the fundamental question of the ability of illiterate audiences to properly
"see" the images on the screen, Morton-Williams felt his findings were conclusive: "It seems quite evident that the physio-
logical aspect of the problem can be ignored; that all audiences
can see what is projected on to the screen, after a very short
period."[74] Nor did African audiences have difficulty understanding sophisticated techniques: "The means by which the
transition from shot to shot is accomplished do not seem important for the audience's understanding. Mixes, fades, cuts
are all acceptable, provided that shot succeeds shot in the
order dictated by the logic of the events in the action. Within
this condition, audiences were not baffled by rapid changes of
scene that took them over long distances or that compressed
time."[75] To underscore this point, Morton-Williams experi-
mented with a malaria film similar to that shown by Sellers a

quarter of a century earlier: "It was found that this demonstration using photography at very high magnification—a mosquito filling most of the screen—was acceptable; it also used an animated diagram to explain how a mosquito injected poison and germs into the blood, and some at least of the spectators were able to understand."[76] More evidence was also forthcoming: a concurrent experiment in Tanganyika concluded, "It seems to us that certain things did not need to be investigated. . . . For example, whether audiences understood close-ups easily or just how they looked at moving images. Good continuity should do much to control wandering eyes, and with close-ups there was nothing that time would not cure, as it did in Europe"[77] Moreover, officials at the Colonial Office were not the first Europeans to conclude that Africans were a quick study when it came to learning the conventions of the cinema. Jean Rouch, the French ethnographic filmmaker and one of many Europeans with long experience showing films to Africans, believed that audiences quickly understood the "language" of the cinema.[78] However, it was Morton-Williams's report that enjoyed the official support of the Colonial Office, and it was circulated throughout the empire.

The Morton-Williams report signaled the end for the Sellers school throughout most of British Africa. Though he continued to defend his principles until he retired in the late 1950s, Sellers's techniques rapidly lost their popularity after 1953. Indeed, by 1958 Sellers himself was acknowledging that the CFU suffered from the fact that "European filmmakers did not have sufficient understanding of the customs and culture of the people for whom they had made the films."[79]

In the following years, the CFU's focus shifted from the production of films to training the staff of the various colonial governments to produce their own films. New units such as the Gold Coast Film Unit and the Federal Film Unit in Nigeria began the Africanization of their production crews, a process that quickly phased out the devotees of the Sellers rules. As the Colonial Office prepared its colonies for independence during the late 1950s, Africans took over production completely, and the "rules" of colonial cinema were soon in desuetude.

The Sellers approach was abandoned in British West Africa because it rested on the assumption that Africans and Europeans possessed differing cognitive abilities, a view that was incompatible with the move toward democratization and independence in the region. However, while the rules of colonial cinema were being abandoned in British West Africa, they were finding new life in the Federation of Central Africa, a federal union that integrated the British colonies of Southern Rhodesia, Northern Rhodesia, and Nyasaland. There an ambitious project was launched in 1948 to utilize film as a tool for the adult education of Africans. From its inception, the colonial officials (the federation was a self-governing British colony) responsible for founding the new film-production unit, CAFU, insisted that special rules had to be employed in the unit's productions.

# Chapter 3

## The Central African Film Unit

### Films for Africans, 1948–1963

> Colonial Films ingenuously reflect the image of the colonizer.
>
> —Luc de Heusch, quoted in UNESCO film survey, 1962

The Southern Rhodesian government's enthusiasm for film production was checked, but not discouraged, by World War II. After the war, the government revived its plans to provide specially made films to their African subjects. The result was the Central African Film Unit (CAFU), which was created in 1948 to produce and distribute motion pictures to audiences throughout Southern Rhodesia, Northern Rhodesia, and neighboring Nyasaland.

This chapter analyzes the films made by CAFU. Few scholars have examined the hundreds of productions made by this organization between 1948 and 1963, yet these films constitute an invaluable resource for the study of the colonial era. Housed today at the National Archives in Harare, Zimbabwe, the films of this state-sponsored production company can be divided into two categories: films made for audiences of European ancestry; and films intended for "natives." The collection of films for whites consists of newsreels, travelogues, and documentaries about the history, economy, and society of the Central African Federation (modern Zambia, Zimbabwe, and

Malawi). Featuring a 35-mm format, English-language sound-
tracks, and relatively high production values, these films
project an image of the federation as a vigorous outpost of
Western civilization.[1] They were intended to popularize the
lives of white Rhodesians and encourage immigration to the
now-self-governing colony.[2] The films made for rural Africans, which constituted the majority of the unit's productions,
are 16-mm silent movies, most of them fictional stories intended to educate and influence their audiences. The subject
matter of the films was wide-ranging; some popularized new
methods of agriculture or animal husbandry or encouraged
the adoption of Western medical or hygienic practices; some
were cautionary tales intended to instil law-abiding behavior
in those who saw the films or to keep rural people from mi-
grating to the city; others were based on stories extolling the
benefits bestowed on Africans by the settler state.

Scholars interested in the colonial history of Zambia, Zimbabwe, and Malawi will find in this collection a valuable resource. The creators of these films aspired to recreate African
life so convincingly that audiences would identify with the
productions and, in effect, see themselves on the screen. These
films thus allow us to gaze on the colonized through the eyes
of the colonizers—to see Africans and their societies as the
filmmakers saw them and as the filmmakers desired them to
be. Consequently, these films reveal a great deal about the
colonial state that produced them.

The limited scholarship about CAFU has misconstrued its
goals, functions, influence, and political sympathies. These fail-
ings are attributable to a narrow selection of sources. While
scholars have relied on a viewing of a limited number of CAFU
films and interviews with one or two members of the film
unit, none have examined the extensive documents relating to
colonial film production held at the National Archives in

Harare. These include private letters, memos, scripts, and official correspondence relating to the CAFU. By evaluating these records, and with the benefit of several interviews with members of the film-production group, this chapter constructs a more complete picture of the unit's activities. In so doing, it reaches several conclusions that are at odds with recent historiography. It demonstrates that the unit was the brainchild of a group of Southern and Northern Rhodesian officials who had begun investigating the potential of film as a tool for education and propaganda before World War II. As such, the unit served as an instrument of policy for the colonial governments of Central Africa. Despite recent characterizations of its personnel and film productions as "liberal," the unit was chiefly composed of individuals sympathetic to the paternalism of white society in Southern Africa, particularly that in Southern Rhodesia.

It also demonstrates that the unit's filmmaking techniques were derived from the film-literacy theories inherited from William Sellers and the Colonial Film Unit. The CAFU filmmakers embraced the Sellers technique, and their approach changed little during the fifteen years the unit was in operation. Finally, dissenting from the view of one historian of the unit, this chapter establishes that the CAFU's importance as a vehicle of education and propaganda grew in the last years of the Central African Federation and demonstrates that the CAFU's personnel went on to form the nucleus of the film-production unit of the Rhodesian Information Service, carrying their cinematic ethos into the Rhodesian Front era.

As outlined in chapter 1, during the 1930s several departments of the Southern Rhodesian government responsible for "native affairs" became increasingly interested in the potential of teaching rural Africans through motion pictures. World War II temporarily halted their efforts to organize a

Rhodesian Film Institute (RFI), which would have had as its goal the production of educational films for Africans. The war, by inspiring Britain to introduce new tools of propaganda throughout its African empire, ultimately provided a fillip to the production of films for Africans.[3] The CFU was just one part of an effort that also included the introduction of radio and the expansion of the vernacular press.

At the war's beginning, officials in Southern Rhodesia expressed little interest in experimenting with new propaganda techniques. Concerns over enemy "subversion" were weighed against the potential of propaganda to inadvertently confuse or alarm the colony's subjects. In the war's first year, with little movement in Europe, authorities proved hesitant to "unsettle" Africans by exposing them to new forms of media. But with the German invasion of France in the spring of 1940, officials in the colony became concerned that Britain's dilemma might undermine the morale of colonial Africans. On 15 June 1940 the Southern Rhodesian prime minister, Sir Godfrey Huggins, wrote to the leading settler papers in the colony expressing his fear that "the Natives are unable to distinguish between official news and German bulletins, and as the latter are as often as not untrue it would be of great assistance if you would refrain from publishing them."[4] A German attack on the motherland seemed to be imminent, and the Southern Rhodesian government believed that it had to act to reassure Africans about the status of the empire. An Information Office report stated: "With the Battle of Britain at its height and the opportunity that the present phase of the war gives for false reports likely to shake the native morale, some . . . means of keeping the native population correctly informed and reassured seems essential."[5] Given the dire circumstances of the moment, keeping the population "correctly informed" was apparently not enough: "While 'straight' news talks for natives are considered unwise, it is felt that 'propaganda-news' talks, giving background and explanations, would be beneficial."[6]

Southern Rhodesia was one of the last colonies in the region to push modern media on their subjects. While radio was already a fixture of Northern Rhodesian life by 1940, southern Rhodesia had not yet introduced broadcasting to its African population. This was in part because of the settler prejudice that radio might become an instrument of instability or subversion. As the territory's chief native commissioner put it, "broadcasts were dangerous because of the possibility of distorting information picked up by the ear."[7] Others feared that the radio was too complicated for Africans. As an official in Northern Rhodesia explained, "the native's brain works too slowly for him to grasp wireless news."[8] However, the exigencies of the war ultimately overcame such prejudices. The danger of disturbing colonial audiences was weighed against the perceived likelihood that an uninformed public might become vulnerable to rumor. At the Southern Rhodesian Information Office, W. D. Gale was particularly impressed by a 1940 memo from a hospital administrator who warned that "the natives are very amenable to mass suggestion and if not controlled, to mass hysteria."[9]

In contrast to concerns about broadcasting, colonial administrators offered little opposition to the dissemination of films. Colonial governments in Northern Rhodesia, Nyasaland, Kenya, Tanganyika, and Uganda all showed CFU productions from mobile cinema trucks to African audiences. In 1944, a Kenyan information officer drew up a report on the feasibility of joining these units into one unit for Central and East Africa.[10] This was the genesis of the postwar Central African Film Unit. After the war, the creation of a joint film unit became one of the first orders of business for the Central

African Council, an organization established to coordinate activities between the Central African territories of Northern Rhodesia, Southern Rhodesia, and Nyasaland. The council consulted with the information officer for Northern Rhodesia, Harry Franklin, and Gale, his counterpart in Southern Rhodesia. Gale, organizer of the prewar Rhodesian Film Institute and a leading advocate of the "films for Africans" scheme before the war (see chapter 1), had lobbied the council to create a film production unit in early 1946.[11]

The Northern Rhodesian government was also enthusiastic. Indeed, the colony had hoped to participate in Gale's film institute for Africans in 1939, and during the war the governor had sent Gale two importuning notes inquiring into the future of a film library for Africans.[12] The governor's pleas stemmed from his desire to provide African miners on the Copperbelt with a steady diet of acceptable films. When the Central African Council began considering the prospects for a film unit, Harry Franklin, representing the Northern Rhodesia government, pushed for the use of 35-mm film since that was what the projectors at most mine-compound theaters were equipped for. But Gale preferred the cheaper 16-mm format, successfully arguing that the film unit's main purpose would be "to produce films *for Africans.* Africans are not discriminating and will accept inferior standard films."[13]

In 1946 the Central African Council agreed to form a unit to produce films for Africans in the Rhodesias and Nyasaland. Officials viewed it as a significant step in the postwar plans for the region: "It is a project of some importance in the development of the three countries as its aim is *inter alia* to produce films demonstrating the benefits resulting from the employment of improved methods of agriculture and animal husbandry and the activities of the unit will be primarily directed to the African as part of a campaign to improve his productivity and standard of living."[14] Southern Rhodesia contributed 50 percent of the unit's operating costs, and Northern Rhodesia and Nyasaland received a grant from the Colonial Development and Welfare Fund to make up the balance of the expense.[15]

From its inception, it was apparent that a Rhodesian film unit would rely on the colonial-cinema approach for its productions. In early 1946, when Gale related his views on film production to the Central African Council, he reflected both the abstract theories of Sellers and the popular prejudices of white Rhodesia: "I would stress the value of the film as a means of developing the African; his natural medium of receptivity is the eye, what he sees he will absorb, but—and this is important—the film must be made in surroundings that are reasonably familiar to him (in country similar to that in which he lives), the customs depicted must be similar to his own, the story must be simply told and straightforwardly photographed."[16] A similar warning was received from E. D. Alvord, the chief of native agriculture in the Southern Rhodesian Native Affairs Department: "Films made with the object of conveying certain ideas and impressions to members of a European Audience, do not unfortunately convey the same ideas and impressions to Native audiences. At best, the educational or propaganda films made for Europeans may be of little value when shown to Natives. At worst, they may convey altogether erroneous impressions and therefore be harmful from the point of view of education and propaganda."[17] Alvord went on to insist that such films must be in color (an assertion soon to be refuted by Morton-Williams) and that, in general, "these films, to be of any real value, will have to be made by persons having an intimate knowledge of the native, his customs and psychology and the way of life in the Reserves."[18]

Gale's and Alvord's views on the subject were commonplace in the region. The settler newspaper the *Rhodesia Herald* greeted news of the new government film unit with a front-page editorial stressing the unique problems African audiences posed to European filmmakers:

> A film designed for European consumption is not necessarily suitable for Africans. It is, indeed, often quite unsuitable. The action of a European film is too quick (with shots lasting from five to eight seconds); such devices to indicate the passage of time as fades, mixes, etc., are confusing; and the steady progression of fact upon fact is beyond the African's grasp.
>
> Films for Africans require a very different technique to those for Europeans—simple photography, long shots to allow plenty of time for assimilation, a plain, straightforward approach to the subject with repetition of the main point, some slapstick humour, and so on. . . . The eye is their main organ of receptivity; seeing is even more than believing—it is understanding, provided the material is properly presented.[19]

The newspaper published a similar editorial three years later:

> A special responsibility . . . rests on the producers of films for natives, because the screen is no land of make believe for them. It has been found that they believe implicitly what their eyes see, and there must be no shuffling of what to them are facts. For example, the actor who plays the villain is forever linked in the minds of the audience with villainy; he cannot later be cast as a hero. Such is their belief in the screen.[20]

The general enthusiasm for employing film as a tool of education in the three territories contrasted with the Central African Council's protracted debate regarding the creation of a broadcasting service in the region. This difference can be attributed to the fact that film offered to territorial governments a form of propaganda that they believed they could easily control. The screenings took place for the most part in public venues—at urban welfare centers, in missions, at mining compounds, or from mobile cinemas traveling in rural areas. Radio listening, conversely, was done in private, usually in homes, and thus permitted a significant degree of autonomy on the part of the audience. With the introduction of inexpensive "saucepan special" radios in the 1940s and the proliferation of regional broadcasts originating outside of the colony, officials in Southern Rhodesia became increasingly fearful of the medium's influence on Africans.[21] As Gale told the Central African Council, "It was known that many employers of African Labour were dubious of the wisdom of relaying broadcasts to Africans in Southern Rhodesia from Lusaka, as they feared—rightly or wrongly—that such broadcasts might not be in line with Southern Rhodesia Government native policy."[22] Suspicion of the radio, and a strong faith in the power of motion pictures over Africans, would make the cinema the most reliable medium of communication between the Southern Rhodesian state and its people.

The Central African Council advertised for a man to lead their new film unit in 1947.[23] Their shortlist was a Who's Who of colonial filmmakers, including feature-film director Geoffrey Barkas and CFU veteran Norman Spurr.[24] The council chose Alan Izod as the administrative head of the unit—a position to be titled "producer." Izod was a British filmmaker who had made films for the Royal Navy and the Colonial Film Unit during the war. Upon his appointment, Izod hired two men to actually make the movies, Stephen Peet and Louis Nell (each was given the title of director-cameraman), and a scriptwriter, Denys Brown, and proceeded from London to his new headquarters in Salisbury. These four men formed the initial core of a film-production unit that grew to more than one hundred employees during the next decade. While Peet left after six years, both Nell and Brown remained with the unit until its demise in 1963. Both served as unit producer after Izod was promoted to a senior position with the Federal Information Department in 1962.[25]

The selection of Izod as the administrative head ensured that the unit would employ the colonial-cinema technique pioneered by the Sellers school. Izod's views on technique were a matter of public record. He had, for example, declared in 1948 that cartoons were incomprehensible to African audiences.[26] In general, Izod shared the views of Sellers—which also were similar to those of his new superiors—regarding African cognitive abilities. In an early report he declared, "The greatest problem the Unit has to face is that its audiences are not yet capable of assimilating information put over in a film of a straightforward educational or documentary type."[27] Izod had found that the experts in the colony shared a pessimistic view of the sophistication of African audiences. Harry Franklin, the head of the Northern Rhodesian Department of Information and a supporter of the film unit, in 1950 gave the following appraisal of their potential: "The appearance of a lion on the screen has more than once caused a stampede and the audience has had to be brought back and reassured of the beast's two-dimensional quality. Cartoons are not understood, nor are diagrams, maps, or any kind of trick filming. The ideal film for the villager should be of slow tempo, on a subject with which he is familiar."[28]

The colonial officials charged with making films for Africans in Southern Africa were unimpressed with Morton-Williams' research in Nigeria. Izod considered the experiment a waste of money, complaining, "By all means let's have research, but let's try to make sure that the research is seeking information that is really necessary and will help us in future."[29] Franklin agreed: "Audience research is much better done locally. We know our own Bantu, and the Department has spent nearly ten years watching their reactions to the various types of film. I would trust the verdict of an experienced D.C. [district commissioner] on the effect of a film on an African audience far more than I would the opinion of a 'sociologist with anthropological experience.'"[30]

Izod's initial team was a diverse group. Nell was a pioneer of colonial filmmaking, having gotten his start in Northern Rhodesia during the war. Some of his early films were among the most popular to be circulated by the Colonial Film Unit. Brown was an Oxford-educated writer with no screenwriting experience. Peet was an idealistic, slightly bohemian person who cultivated friendships among educated Africans and generally ruffled the feathers of the colonial establishment.[31]

The rest of the positions in the unit were staffed by Africans and "Coloureds" hired within the territories. Some of these employees were with CAFU for many years, and several contributed to the production of the films, usually without receiving any onscreen credit.[32] As the historian Rosaleen Smyth has observed, while the CFU had "devoted all of its energies to the training of African film-makers" in CAFU "the role of the African . . . was that of actor, interpreter, and cinema van operator."[33] Why no African was trained to become a director-cameraman during the unit's fifteen years of operation remains a sensitive issue to the surviving members. Izod and Nell insist that Africans were not willing to remain with the unit long enough to become properly trained in camera work because of the poor government pay scale.[34] In 1997, veteran director-cameraman Anker Atkinson expressed the view that Africans were never permitted to operate the cameras for the CAFU because they lacked the aesthetic sense to make visually interesting films.[35]

Virtually all of the articles written about CAFU have been based on interviews with Stephen Peet, perhaps because he alone of all the original members still resides in the United Kingdom.[36] Peet, a Quaker, cared little for the conventions of Southern Rhodesian society. He socialized with the African musician Alick Nkhata, whose subsequent involvement in the nationalist movement inspired the Native Affairs Department in Southern Rhodesia to ban a CAFU film of him performing.[37] His specialty was "uplift" films—movies with a self-help theme; he made several between 1948 and 1954. He was responsible for perhaps the best known of the CAFU films, *The Wives of Nendi*, which was based on the true story of the founding of a women's club by the wife of the Southern Rhodesian leader Chief Mangwende.

It is because of Peet's influence that David Kerr has characterized the CAFU as being composed of "liberal filmmakers."[38] Interviews with Peet and documents relating to his career certainly indicate that he was a more progressive and thoughtful colonial civil servant than most. His sensibilities are well illustrated in a letter he wrote in 1954 to Izod about a script for a film meant to introduce the federation to overseas audiences: "By starting with miles of endless bush into which come the early settlers it may give the impression that the country was uninhabited until the white man came. And everyone knows it wasn't. Thus shouldn't the early scenic scenes have deliberately some huts at least in the foreground, or somewhere about?" Peet also asked, later in the same letter, "Is all lack of mention of Asians and Euroafricans in the commentary and visuals deliberate, or an oversight? I suggest they should be remembered at any rate whilst shooting."[39] He frequently shared ideas with Izod that reflected such liberal sensibilities. One of his early proposals was for "a 'Misunderstanding' Film." As Peet described the idea to Izod:

> This is a rather vague idea as yet. But something on these lines:
> • European employer, African employee.

- They meet only during working hours.
- But the film shows, (and therefore the audience are let into the secrets of) their private lives.
- Each has, at different times during the story, private (family) difficulties.
- The reaction of the employee to his private troubles may be silent misery. But this is interpreted by the employer as dumb insolence.
- Conversely the reaction of the employer to his own troubles may be violent temper. And this will be misunderstood by the employee.
- Circumstances can then cause the employer and employee to find out the real cause of each other's unexpected and misunderstood behaviour.
- The misunderstandings are now not only patched up but the employer and employee find ways in which they are able to help each other, and to continue to work on a more solid foundation of understanding.[40]

Kerr relies on his interview with Peet to sustain his assertion that "the experimental and educational nature of CAFU's policy made it a target of some racist criticism from Southern Rhodesia"; also to say that "there was a feeling among many Southern Rhodesians that the filmmakers in CAFU (like the broadcasters in Central Broadcasting Services in Lusaka) were flirting dangerously with participatory 'do-goodism' which could give the Africans 'too many ideas.'"[41] There is little evidence that colonial officials were displeased with Peet's work. In general, irrespective of his personal politics, Peet's films were very popular with officials at the Southern Rhodesian Native Affairs Department, and they assisted in the planning and filming of many of his productions. For example, Peet's *The Wives of Nendi* was based on an outline provided by E. D. Alvord, Southern Rhodesia's chief officer for native agriculture.[42] The department's only recorded criticism of his oeuvre seems to have been directed at the ponderous length of his early films.[43]

In general, Peet's work embraced the same themes as those of his colleagues, and all championed the colonial hierarchy. He appears to have been an enthusiastic member of the CAFU team throughout his tenure with the unit, and there is no evidence to support Kerr's assertion that Peet was forced out for ideological reasons. Peet certainly does not mention this in a 1988 interview he conducted with Izod. By and large, Peet's colleagues tolerated, but did not share, his liberalism and idealism. Izod's correspondence suggests that he was anxious from the beginning of his term to take his lead from his superiors. He was a supporter of the Central African Federation and served the Rhodesian Front regime for several years during the 1960s.

Most of the other filmmakers who later worked for the unit were drawn from Southern Africa and appear to have shared many of the prejudices common to the white community that produced them. For example, Atkinson, the longest-serving member of the unit, was a Southern Rhodesian farm boy. He was hired when, as a teenager, he responded to an advertisement he had seen in the *Rhodesian Herald*. Atkinson began making films as an assistant for Nell, and he worked in Rhodesia through the federal and Rhodesian Front periods.[44] Another member of the early team was Henry Beriff, a Southern Rhodesian who was bitterly remembered as a racist by one of his African CAFU colleagues; Beriff once informed this man, his elder, that he was "allright for a kaffir."[45] Other early members of the unit such as Brian Usher and Geoffry Mangin were also drawn from the white community in Southern Rhodesia. Mangin, a supporter of the Rhodesian Front, left CAFU to set up his own newsreel production company in the early 1960s. When the foreign media began covering African riots in Southern Rhodesia in 1962, Mangin offered to assist the regime by secretly providing European and U.S. television networks with footage favorable to the government. His pitch was based on his promise that the members his staff were "true Rhodesians" whose coverage of the events might discourage foreign correspondents from coming to the country.[46] Mangin was one of several CAFU filmmakers who went on to work with the Rhodesian Front regime. Others were Roger Fairly, Dick Raynor, and Louis Nell.

In any event, the personal politics of the staff mattered little, for all worked under the supervision of Izod, who was content to take his instructions from the Southern Rhodesian authorities. He wrote in 1948:

> The Film Unit can only make story films successfully if it has the fullest assistance from those who have long experience and full understanding of the African mentality. The members of the Unit have been recruited for their technical ability; most of them are quite new to African conditions, and it will be a long time before they are able out of their own experience to prepare stories which are an accurate interpretation of African life; yet unless the Unit's films have this quality they cannot hope to succeed in being convincing.[47]

The departments of the colonial governments in the region were delighted to guide the new unit. Most of the early scripts were prepared with the assistance of staff members of the Southern Rhodesian Native Affairs Department and the Northern Rhodesian Information Department. Izod invariably deferred to them,[48] and he underscored his reliance on these officials in a speech he delivered at the 1949 premiere of the unit's first films: "One of our greatest debts of gratitude throughout the whole of the first year has been to the Secretary for Native Affairs, Mr. Powys-Jones. It is quite natural, and indeed essential, that we should not move a single step without the advice and guidance of the Native Affairs and other departmental officers who really know the African and what he wants and needs."[49]

The CAFU films conformed to a formula that reflected both the prevailing theory of colonial cinema and the developmental agenda of the Southern Rhodesian government. All CAFU films for Africans were set in African rural or urban locations; they all took place in the present, and all presented potentially "realistic" situations. None of the films included any element of fantasy. This was because one presumption Izod adopted from Sellers and the CFU was the belief that European filmmakers could recreate a compelling, "realistic" African world on film, and that African audiences would identify with it and respond to it.

Izod stated this ambition in a 1950 radio address: "We believed that we could interest audiences, and so 'sell' our lesson, if we could get the people who were seeing the films to associate themselves with the people whose struggles, difficulties, and achievements we were showing in our films."[50] Izod thought that the unit was able to establish this kind of identification with the audiences: "I think in all we felt that the films were accepted so completely as fact that this placed a very considerable onus on us not to betray the sort of trust that was being put in us by the audiences . . . we always had great regard to the truth in what we were doing and what we were saying, because we were dealing with people who were believing us."[51] Peet also believed that they had succeeded in reaching their audiences. "We've found that the falling on a banana skin type of gag is not considered funny by our audiences because they identify themselves too much with the actor. His discomfort is theirs too."[52]

The film team's colleagues in the Southern Rhodesian Native Affairs Department shared their faith in the audiences' identification with the films. In the first report of the department's new Information Services branch, J. F. Bowles, the chief information officer, wrote of the CAFU productions: "These films have been immensely popular and effective wherever they have been shown. . . . The reason of course is not only that the characters of the films are Africans but the whole background and environment are known and understood by African audiences, so that they can derive entertainment and instruction from the films without having to adjust themselves to a strange environment of fantasy outside the orbit of their experience."[53] He attributed this success to the guidance of the information office, which "co-operates closely with the Film Unit in planning them."[54]

The CAFU directors followed a basic procedure in making their films. An examination of this process provides insight into their aspirations and preconceptions. The production of a film began with the selection of one of six specific genres that had been handed down to Izod by the Central African Council. These were:

1. The illustration of a general principle, such as the benefit of a certain standard of agriculture or hygiene. In all the principle of self-help will be stressed.
2. The short film, intended to illustrate the benefit of one particular phase of agriculture, hygiene, etc. Such films might well be made in series.
3. Films to illustrate the value of governmental services.
4. "Profile" films, showing the achievements of individual Africans in various fields on behalf of themselves, of their people, and of their Country.
5. African traditional stories, used to put over such morals as Honesty is the Best Policy.
6. Crime doesn't pay.[55]

With a few notable exceptions, the unit did not deviate from these guidelines.

Once the genre was selected, the scriptwriter would consult with colonial authorities in drawing up an appropriate outline or "treatment" that would integrate the desired lesson into an appropriate setting and provide a plot involving "traditional" African environments and characters. In some cases, the films would be made in what Izod called "an African idiom." This meant weaving the message into the fabric of an African folk genre. In an effort to find stories that would resonate with African audiences, Izod and his staff tried to adapt African folk tales. Toward this end Izod ran a contest in the *African Weekly*, an African newspaper, promising that the best contribution would be filmed.[56] Although he claimed the responses gave him insight into the "several main pre-occupations in Africans' minds," he complained to Peet that "in the first 500 I have found nothing even remotely resembling a film story."[57] The story he eventually selected was the basis for one of the most inventive and entertaining of the CAFU films, *The Box*, directed by Louis Nell.[58]

*The Box* is a crime-doesn't-pay film that was intended to impress upon Africans the power of colonial law-enforcement. It begins by showing two men carrying a large, coffin-shaped box approaching a truck shop in a rural area. The two stop and ask the owner for permission to store their container in his shop overnight. The owner consents. During the night an accomplice climbs out of the box and robs the store. This scenario is repeated at three different shops until an African storeowner figures out the ruse and calls the police. Several African constables lie in wait for the criminal to emerge from his hiding place and apprehend him after a prolonged struggle—the latter played for comic effect. The film ends with the crooks dressed in striped prison garb working on a chain gang.

*The Box* made only minor revisions to the original story, but in general the unit found it difficult to convert traditional stories into films: such tales could not easily be turned into the kind of "uplift" stories that made for good colonial cinema. This is apparent from a series of unused plot treatments suggested by African employees of CAFU. For example, Peet's assistant Gaston Nakumwa contributed "The Story of Enoch and His Wife and A Witch Doctor," which he based on a Malawian folk tale. In this story, Enoch, desirous of a better harvest, consults a traditional healer ("witch doctor," in the treatment) for assistance. The healer demands the sacrifice of Enoch's daughter as payment and plans to decapitate her and plant her head in his garden. Though the film was never made, Peet rewrote Nakumwa's ending to show the healer in court being warned to change his ways and Enoch being taught "proper native cultivation" by his neighbors.

Nakumwa also drafted a treatment for another film, *Ten-Ten and his Wife*, in which Ten-Ten abandons his home and family in the rural areas and ends up living a miserable existence with a prostitute in the city. Given its failure to provide the requisite "uplift," it is hardly surprising that the story was never filmed. Another story, contributed by "The Reverend Gazi," presented a lurid tale of adultery, attempted murder, and kidnapping in an urban township. There are many such stories in the CAFU files that were never used, most of which depict rural people in tragic situations, sometimes escaping their troubles, sometimes not. In their gritty quality, these movie scenarios resemble the popular culture of rural people the world over. They also tell of the less-appealing side of modernization, replete with its dislocations, alienation, and perils. Though such tales probably reflected quite closely the traditions and life experiences of African audiences, they clearly did not embody the "African idiom" that Izod had in mind.

Once the outline of the story was finished, the director traveled to the location and negotiated with local leaders (invariably with the assistance of the local district commissioner) to secure actors and actresses for the film. Once he had filmed the scenes, he sent the negatives to Salisbury to be edited. Because of the long distances involved in making films throughout the federation, director-cameramen would often stay out in the field for months. Operating in remote corners of the colony, they had a great degree of latitude to interpret Denys Brown's outlines. For the most part, however, they left major decisions regarding filmmaking to Izod and Brown, who kept up an extensive correspondence with the filmmakers in the field.[59] Much of this correspondence about filmmaking can be found in the CAFU files, which contain voluminous notes made in the early days of filmmaking when the unit members were new to the country and still felt obliged to articulate their aims and preconceptions. These notes, as much as the films themselves, provide insight into the ways in which the CAFU directors viewed their mission.

Based on an examination of the unit's production notes—as well as viewings of the completed productions—it is possible to draw some general conclusions about these films. The majority fall into the "agricultural instructional" genre. These were intended to encourage Africans to adapt new technologies or techniques or to teach them how to grow new cash crops. An early example of a film in this genre was *Zimbani*, which was commissioned by the government of Nyasaland in 1949 to encourage Africans to grow tobacco for export. Peet developed a film script that contrasted a successful farmer with an unsuccessful one.[60] This was one of the first of many CAFU films to utilize the "Mr. Wise and Mr. Foolish" formula, a format that had been pioneered by Sellers in Nigeria and that provided the framework for most films produced by BEKE and the Colonial Film Unit.[61] It offered a simple, stark contrast between the hero, who is rewarded for embracing the

modernizing project of colonialism, and the villain, whose intransigent traditionalism inevitably brings suffering and hard-
ship to himself and his family. This model made colonial films
into simple morality plays, dividing the colonized world into
modernizers and traditionalists, winners and losers.

In *Zimbani*, the "Mr. Wise" character is called George, and
George, according to the film's treatment, is the "personifica-
tion of the good, hard-working steady villager . . . At all times
when he is in the picture, he should stand out, as far as the
story allows, as an active and positive character."[62] Peet had
ambitious plans for the actor who would portray George: "He
must be human, with a sense of humor. He must be able to ride
a bicycle and play a guitar. He dresses throughout the film
sufficiently well to emphasise his standing in the village, which
is high."[63] George's wife rarely appears on the screen, but his
daughter is an important character, requiring very specific at-
tributes from the actress who plays her. In the film treatment
we read:

> Age and appearance important here. She must last three years,
> looking attractive (by African standards) and be nubile at the end
> of the film. I think that if she were nubile at the beginning an
> African audience would expect her to get married long before
> three years were up, and rather look down on her, and therefore
> on the George family as a whole, if she didn't. So somehow, in
> dress and so on, she must only come to a proper marriageable age
> at the time of Andrew's return from gaol. Send for the make-up
> man! But she must be attractive, whatever happens.[64]

Peet's "Mr. Foolish" is a character named Andrew—

> the typical villain of the piece, but not the out-and-out typical
> Western villain. There should be a definite feeling of "There but
> for the grace of God go I." He personifies the side of the African
> that doesn't fit in with modern life, and which, I think, the ad-
> ministration is trying to—for want of a better word—reform. He

is idle, shiftless, and suspicious and jealous of anything and any-body differing from the old ways. He has also a nasty streak in his character, and it is this that takes him beyond the passive laissez-faire attitude to active opposition to George, first in words, then in deeds. He likes his sundowner more than somewhat, and is always dirty and scruffily dressed.[65]

Andrew's long-suffering wife is Mrs. Andrew, "an anti-thesis to her husband, and an African parallel to the European peas-ant wife who works like a horse and is the backbone of the family."[66]

This long passage in the notes contains many stereotypes that these filmmakers believed their audience would relate to. George, "Mr. Wise," the "steady, hard working villager" is a thoroughly modern, Westernized farmer already reaping the benefits of Western innovations in transport and leisure. His wife is a nonentity, but his daughter, by dint of her being "at-tractive (by African standards)" is permitted a larger role as the love interest of Andrew's son James. Andrew is "the typi-cal villain of the piece, but not the out-and-out typical West-ern villain." Rather, "He is idle, shiftless, and suspicious and jealous of anything and anybody differing from the old ways," as well as being a tippler. He is not evil, but rather "unre-formed." He represents the tragic future for the African man who fails to heed the colonial gospel of modernization and progress.

Beyond such blatant stereotyping, the production notes reveal several subtle messages and assumptions that perme-ated the CAFU films. They reflect the unit's rather Victorian view of the ideal African family. Despite the widespread prac-tice of polygamy in the region, films like *Zimbani* presented their heroes as monogamous. In films where men were de-picted as having more than one spouse (as in the venereal-disease story *The Two Wives*), the relationship was usually a source of trouble to all concerned. CAFU films were also generally temperance-minded: Mr. Foolish characters invariably preferred inebriation to hard work. Moreover, *Zimbani* is typical in its promotion of a crude capitalism in which Western-manufactured consumer goods such as radios, steel plows, and cloth (as well as George's guitar and bicycle) are the rewards of thrift and diligence. Such films also presented scientific, agricultural, and medical technologies as central to the modernization of African life. In this connection, the CAFU films were relentlessly critical of traditional medical practices: they depicted "witch doctors" as both comic and sinister.[67] They also disparaged traditional subsistence farming in favor of export-oriented agriculture. However, in the case of *Zimbani*, Peet was to some extent troubled by the potential dislocation that might accompany such a transition. He wanted the film to encourage Africans toward "adopting and adhering to better cultivation methods"; however, he also recognized the potential danger—that this "may encourage the Bantu to grow tobacco only, to the detriment of food production."[68]

Another typical example of this type of instructional film was *The Two Farmers*, made in 1948. The film begins with a scene of a farming family leading their oxcart into town to sell their produce. The family looks relatively poor, and the script describes the father, Panganai, as appearing "very worried . . . he wanted to get better crops so that he could buy all the things he needed for his house and land." After selling his crops in a state cooperative, Panganai inspects a beautiful shiny cart parked outside the office. He slowly counts his money, but realizes he does not have enough to purchase the cart.

Panganai then meets another farmer, Washoma, and the two venture off together to listen to a white agricultural demonstrator explain how to cultivate maize. The crowd watches in impressed silence, many of them craning their necks to see the demonstration and hear the lecture. Panganai sits rapt with interest. Washoma looks disdainfully at the assembly and then leaves. The scene changes to show an African agricultural demonstrator teaching Panganai to survey his fields and plant his crops in rows. The camera then shows Washoma sitting in his village drinking beer. As the script describes the scene: "Washoma, who didn't believe in work except when it *had* to be done, was enjoying himself drinking beer with his cronies. He had drunk so much when Machiri [the African agricultural officer] came round to his village that he quite forgot his manners, and was very rude to Machiri when he tried to get him to protect his land from erosion." Later Panganai is seen harvesting a bumper crop, while Washoma is admonished by the African demonstrator for the poor quality of his maize. The finale shows Panganai driving his new cart to town assisted by the workers he can now afford, while Washoma looks on sullenly.[69]

*Zimbani* and *The Two Farmers* are typical of the agricultural instruction films. They contain none of the moral complexities evident in the film scenarios proposed by Africans. In their place are the simple dichotomies of modern and traditional, cooperative and intransigent, wise and foolish.

Another common CAFU motif was crime-doesn't-pay. Films produced in this genre emphasized the power of the colonial state and the role of traditional authorities in maintaining order. One of the first was *John Meets Trouble*, made in 1948. Denys Brown prepared the script inspired by a story contributed by C. Sapsed, an employee of the federal broadcasting station in Lusaka, Northern Rhodesia. *John Meets Trouble*—originally titled *The Temptation of the People*—is the story of two African men who loot tinned food from an abandoned truck, only to be quickly apprehended by the authorities. The film begins with a scene of an African truck driver loading his vehicle. Soon after he begins his journey he becomes ill. His truck careens off of the road, almost hits an African cyclist, and finally stops.[70] The driver then staggers out of the truck and walks several paces into the bush before collapsing. Two Africans walking along the road come upon the truck and after some deliberation begin to loot its contents. The driver eventually wakens, makes his way to a village, and there alerts an African policeman. Several constables are dispatched on bicycles in time to catch the thieves who, having fallen out, are apprehended in the process of fighting over their loot. The film ends as the police lead the criminals off in handcuffs, light-heartedly poking them with truncheons.[71]

*John Meets Trouble* is a cautionary tale intended to impress upon rural people the power of colonial law-enforcement. Like many CAFU films, it features only African characters. The entire process of criminal investigation and apprehension is conducted by African officers of the British South African Police (BSAP) with the assistance of the chief of the thief's village. In keeping with the colonial-cinema approach, the action is simple, the film is brief, the number of characters is limited, and the camera techniques are rudimentary. The film presents a vision of African society in which men are either agents of the colonial state, such as the police and chiefs, or menial employees of a colonial business, such as the truck driver, or criminals. The aptitude of African men outside of the colonial system to lapse into criminality is demonstrated through the inclusion of a character who stumbles onto the two thieves dividing up their spoils and immediately insists on being included in their enterprise. One message of the film is thus that African men unaffiliated with colonial institutions are potential criminals. Another is that wrongdoers will be punished, and that the colonial state's powers of retribution are absolute.

Another genre of CAFU film trumpeted the value of community development and "self help." The wish to send this message encouraged the production of one of the earliest CAFU films, *Mujenji Builds a Bridge*. The story for the film was contributed by the Southern Rhodesian chief secretary for native affairs as an inspirational example of "self-help" intended to encourage community participation throughout the region.[72] The film relates the tale of a village that requested assistance from the Southern Rhodesian government to build a bridge across a river. The native commissioner agreed to provide the technical expertise if the local people would supply the labor. From this brief synopsis, Peet produced *Mujenji Builds a Bridge*.

The film documents the construction of the bridge under the watchful eye of a stern government foreman. The sophisticated tasks involved in building the bridge are all supervised by white engineers. The climax comes when the team prepares to dynamite a rock quarry in a dry riverbed. A white official arrives in a large, gleaming American truck and proceeds to lay the charge. The African laborers scurry in terror and wonder, with several surveying the action from a distance while hanging in trees. The shots of the fascinated workers are cross-cut with similar scenes of baboons running away. The film, screened at a special preview in 1949, received favorable comments from many Europeans in the audience. One spectator, a future information officer with the Rhodesian Front, complained of the film's length, but thought the "good points were—baboons, blasting, & in fact most scenes where action was intense."[73]

The CAFU also made several films that Izod called "African traditional stories, used to put over such morals as 'Honesty is the Best Policy.'" A typical offering was *The Thief*, produced by Peet in 1949. The idea was provided by an

African assistant, Lawrence Gumunyu, from a traditional story, though Peet changed the ending to impart an appropriate lesson.

*The Thief* opens with a chief holding court in his village. Peet describes the scene in his treatment: "Many years ago there was a Chief called Mandebvu. People used to travel many miles to hear him taking cases under his indaba tree for Chief Mandebvu was a great and powerful Chief, feared by one and all from far and near. On the advice of his witch-doctors, he wore a false beard, which was strong medicine and enabled him to judge cases very cleverly—or so people believed."[74] The chief is hearing the case of a suspected thief. In a flashback (an unusually "sophisticated" technique for a CAFU film), a witness recounts the details of a crime. We see the thief leaving a shoe along a path ahead of a man herding goats. The herder ignores the first shoe only to come across another shoe—the pair of the first—further up the path. When he returns to collect the first shoe, the thief steals the unattended goats. The action then returns to the chief's deliberations. After tugging on his false beard, he renders judgment against the accused. The film ends on a comic note with the goats eating the thief's shoes.

Peet prefaced his treatment of the film by explaining, "The story of this film is adapted from a humorous African legend and is not intended to be taken seriously."[75] However, this simple comedy serves a similar purpose to the more obvious *John Meets Trouble*. Both films depict African men committing crimes and traditional authorities quickly punishing them.[76]

The extent of Peet's changes to the ending of the storyline for *The Thief* are unclear. But the original story quite likely celebrated the guile of the thief rather than the sleuthing abilities of the chief. If so, the tale would conform closely to a regional folk tradition that championed the exploits of a trickster character, usually a rabbit, who was known for his cunning. In Shona folk tales, the rabbit's wits bring him success in some stories, failure in others. Peet's revision of the original story to include a crime-doesn't-pay message suggests that there was no place for such ambivalence in the world being created by CAFU.

CAFU also made several films extolling the benefits that the colonial state had bestowed upon Africans. One of the first of this genre was *Lusaka Calling*, which was produced in 1949 to advertise the Central African Council's African radio service. *Lusaka Calling* is a fictional story that follows a white broadcast engineer as he travels to an African village to record traditional music. After listening to the villagers' performance and creating a stir by playing their music back to them, the engineer invites the local chief to accompany him to Lusaka to see the broadcast station. The remainder of the film follows the chief as he receives a tour of the station and ultimately purchases a radio. The finale finds the chief back home listening to his people's performance on his own receiver.

*Lusaka Calling* was intended to encourage Africans to purchase the "saucepan special," a simple radio receiver the Northern Rhodesian government marketed to Africans in the 1950s. Like many other CAFU films, it imparts its message through a story intended to contrast a technologically sophisticated, modern colonial world with life in a "simple" traditional society. Thus the Africans in the village display shock, amusement, and alarm when they first hear their music and voices on the recording. During his tour of the studio, the chief gawks at all technological demonstrations and is chastised for speaking when the broadcaster is on the air. At the end of the film, the villagers sit and listen to their radio, apparently relieved of the burden of having to make the music themselves.[77] The extent to which this represents an "improvement" is questionable. In general, the film emphasizes the technical prowess of Europeans, whose mastery of science leaves traditional authorities dumbfounded.

There is an interesting postscript to the story of *Lusaka Calling*. In an article outlining the history of colonial filmmaking in Africa, the French ethnographic filmmaker Jean Rouch stated that the showing of the film had led to a riot in Northern Rhodesia when local suppliers ran out of radios. I did not find any evidence corroborating this story in the colonial files, and the historian Rosaleen Smyth makes no mention of the incident in her exhaustive study of the information services in Northern Rhodesia;[78] it therefore seems likely that this is yet another embellished tale reflecting European faith in the power of the cinema.[79]

Though films showing rural Africans the perils of urban life were not part of the Central African Council's original list of genres, CAFU was asked by the Southern Rhodesian Native Affairs Department to make several such films. The drift to urban areas was a long-standing concern for whites in Southern Rhodesia, and colonial officials had first suggested making films to help stem the tide during the 1930s (see chap. 1). After the war, the pace of migration quickened, and the late 1940s and 1950s were characterized by rapid urbanization. Typical of the "urban drift" films was *Benzi Goes to Town* (in ChiShona, *benzi* means idiot), directed by Atkinson in 1958. The plot was written by the chief information officer of the Southern Rhodesian government. As he described it, "The theme is 'A fool and his money is soon parted' [and was] aimed indirectly at shewing the folly of being hoodwinked by individuals with the 'get rich quick' outlook, including the growing number of Africans who start some sort of Association, collecting funds from illiterate people for same. It also has the moral 'Your parents simple standards are often better than those which seem to promise more material advantages.'"

The film begins with Benzi, a young farmer from rural Mashonaland in Southern Rhodesia, watching several men pass through his village on their way to the big city. After a scene in which Benzi is shown half-heartedly doing manual labor on his parents' farm, he asks his father if he can leave to find work in the city. His father reluctantly agrees, and Benzi departs carrying his meager possessions at the end of a stick slung over his shoulder. Along the way he meets a man who offers to tell his fortune. Benzi agrees, and the man puts several questions to a mask lying on the road next to him. Smoke blows out of the lips of the mask after each question. At the instruction of the fortune-teller, Benzi reluctantly inserts money through the lips of the mask, which emits more smoke. The man interprets the smoke, and Benzi departs satisfied. Once he has gone, the camera reveals that the mask lay on top of a hole in which a second man has been hiding. The latter climbs out of the hole and the two laugh as they divide up the dupe's money.

Benzi then comes upon a native reserve, described in the film treatment as consisting of "serried rows of kraals and industrious people hoeing their newly allocated plots with an occasional demonstrator in evidence." There he stops to listen to two Africans dressed in Western suits addressing the crowd. The narrator's script reads, "A man was making a speech to the crowd, saying that he and his friends were fighting for the young people of the country, to free them from the rule of the old people, from the old customs, to give them liberty to go where they wanted and make their fortune." An elderly chief warns Benzi not to listen or give the speakers money, but the two men notice Benzi and begin pressuring him to contribute. Despite the chief's warnings, Benzi contributes. The treatment describes what follows: "The Chief spoke to Benzi and told him that he was a great fool for giving money to these people. They were fighting no fight, they were doing nothing but lining their own pockets, and Benzi was an idiot to have given them anything. Benzi began to realise that perhaps his father had some knowledge after all." By the time Benzi arrives in the city, he is almost broke. In town a young African man, also in a suit, spots him and promises that for a small fee he can find Benzi a job. He absconds with the last of Benzi's money and leaves him waiting in an empty office. When Benzi realizes he has been had, he finds an African policeman. Together they find all of the sharpers who have cheated Benzi sitting together in a beer garden. The officer arrests the criminals and the film ends with Benzi back at his father's farm, ignoring the stream of men who continue to pass through his village on their way to the city.

The scenes involving African politicians in *Benzi Goes to Town* make it unique among "urban perils" films. It was made in 1958, at a time when African nationalism was developing in Southern Rhodesia and the Southern Rhodesian Native Affairs Department was trying to represent African politicians as urban, rapacious spivs intent on cheating or dominating simple, hard-working rural people. The politicians are represented as merely one of a variety of confidence men who await Africans who venture out of rural areas. The world of *Benzi Goes to Town* is one that CAFU had made familiar to audiences by 1958. Rural people are seen as simple, naive, and honest. Urban Africans conversely are identified by their adoption of "fancy" Western clothing and are invariably dishonest and clever, though never smart enough to outwit BSAP officers. African politicians and traditional healers (in *Benzi Goes to Town*, the latter represented by the man with the smoking mask) are shown to have no interest in the fate of Africans beyond swindling them.

By focusing on such urban perils, CAFU hoped to stem the tide of migration to the cities. To achieve this and their other goals, they had to reach the largest segment of their audience, women. If films like *Zimbani* or *Benzi Comes to Town* relied on crude characterizations of rural men, this may have been well received by the unit's target audience, the rural women who made up the majority of the adults who saw their films. In targeting women, the CAFU was responding to a commonly held sentiment in colonial circles that, in the words of one Southern Rhodesian district commissioner, "we shall never raise the standard of living of the African people and improve their culture until we raise the women up from their ignorance and backward ways."[80] This belief carried great weight in the calculations of the colonial states in Central Africa. In a letter to Izod in early 1954, the chief information officer of the Southern Rhodesian Native Affairs Department discussed the opportunities for influencing women audiences. "It appears," he wrote, "that Africans, women in particular, are remarkably susceptible to pathos, and perhaps it should be played on more. The effect of tragedy and of not having always the happy ending might be worth investigation; might it not have a much greater emotional impact and thus indirectly impress the lessons of a film more forcibly on the audience?" He finished his letter with a restatement of his "belief that we must always have the women in the forefront of our minds in planning films, and that they are probably the most educable element of the audiences."[81]

Despite the focus on female audiences, the only CAFU productions that regularly featured female protagonists were the "profile" films intended to popularize stories of Africans who had successfully adopted some aspect of colonial life.[82] Many of these showcased the role women played in the adoption and dissemination of Western practices. For example, Peet's *Wives of Nendi* was intended to inspire the formation of women's clubs in rural areas.[83] Another example is the docudrama *Rachel Hlazo*, a fictionalized account of a real government-trained nurse whose family, according to the film's narration, "do not believe in witchdoctors or spirits; they learned long ago that the white man's medicines were much stronger and safer than those which the old witch doctors used to use, such as the tail of a baboon or the bones of a hyena."[84] Such films promised that women who adopted Western methods of hygiene and nutrition would improve the health and social position of their families.

But CAFU was not solely interested in transforming African women into homemakers. Some films encouraged women to adopt a second role as wage laborers. In 1950, the Northern Rhodesian secretary for native affairs asked Izod "whether it would be possible to put out propaganda to persuade African women to work, and particularly to go into domestic service." The secretary asked Christie Lawrence, the head of the Lusaka Department of Information, to work with Izod on the project. Lawrence proposed a scenario of an African disk jockey working in Northern Rhodesia, "the glamour of whose life might appeal to Africans." Lawrence recognized that such examples might not inspire women to enter domestic service and asked Izod, "Can you show that an African woman is happier or better off if she is working than if she is idle?"[85] Izod, not one to question his superiors, dubbed the idea "a worthy subject" and suggested the unit produce a series of such films.[86] His only question was the kind of work they should depict. "Do you," he asked, "want to show them working for Europeans in houses and farms, or do you want to show them working rather harder than usual in their gardens at home, or again do you want to show them as independent farmers?" Lawrence was more blunt:

The aim of the propaganda that I have been asked to put out, is to persuade African women into jobs that are now being filled by African men—housework, cooking, etc. The idea is to provide some outlet for employment for wages for the "compound" woman, who does little but sit all day at her front door. I agree that our woman announcer is a rather exotic exception, but after all, there are a few "housegirls," cooks, and so on, and we want to encourage more.

Lawrence considered African opinion on this subject "obdurate" and believed "something indirect would be more suitable than a documentary."[87]

Thus CAFU addressed African women in a contradictory fashion. On the one hand, the unit saw them as their primary audience and therefore expected them to be the bearers of the messages contained in the state's films. On the other hand, women were marginal in most films. In the CAFU universe, it was the African man who came into contact with the colonial state—the African man who usually had to choose whether to be wise or foolish. CAFU proved itself perfectly capable, however, of brushing aside this acquiescence to Western stereotyping of gender roles when their superiors in government needed more domestic help.

Virtually all of CAFU's films were made with extraordinarily simple camera angles and plots and included only a few characters. The unit, and Izod in particular, assumed that African audiences had special needs and limitations.[88] As Izod explained in a 1988 interview: "Technically, I remember that from the beginning we had deliberately decided against the use of complex techniques. We had decided right from the beginning that simplicity of approach was really the way that we should tackle this."[89] This self-consciously simple approach conformed to the Central African Council's mandate to make 16-mm silent films accompanied by a script that could be translated into the region's many vernaculars. In a 1952 memo, however, Izod defended the technique that experience and expediency had handed him. In it he attributed the unit's simple style of filmmaking to technical limitations.

> We haven't yet heard enough about the showing of our films to be able to form any very definite opinions about their suitability for our audiences, or to make any striking changes, ahead or astern, in our technique. In any case technique is controlled to a large extent by the fact that we are working entirely in 16 m. m. Kodachrome, and so opticals are limited to those which we can do in the camera—mainly fades and an occasional mix.[90]

After four years of film production in Central Africa, however, Izod began to express some reservations regarding the conventional wisdom of colonial film production:

> it would be fatally easy to underestimate our audiences. So far I have seen no indication that they cannot follow any sort of straight-forward technique just as easily as an unsophisticated European audience. After all, if a technique obtrudes on the audience it's usually a sign that it's out of place, or badly handled. Be that as it may, we are going ahead with ordinary story films, and using every technique we can lay our hands on—not with the idea of being sensational, or of astonishing the "boys," but with the hopes of making better and smoother films. We do realize that there are some techniques which may cause a little astonishment and puzzlement at first; but we also realize that the sooner we get these into regular use, the easier it will be for us to make good films.[91]

Izod's conviction that obtrusive technique was a sign of poor craftsmanship reflected the prevailing wisdom of the day: classical cinematic language (or the Hollywood Style) sought to create the illusion of transparency. Any technique that reminded the spectator that a camera filtered his or her perceptions was to be avoided.

Izod concluded this letter with a scathing assessment of the theories of the Colonial Film Unit. "As you know, I hold that the greatest condemnation of the Sellars' [*sic*] creed is the fact that after making and showing films in West Africa for many years (is it 15?) the C.F.U. still finds it necessary to use only the simplest techniques. What the hell does it matter whether an audience is able to distinguish and appreciate the techniques themselves, providing that the end result is good."[92] How does one explain Izod's apparent ambiguity on the question of colonial filmmaking? First, it is worth noting that despite his invective against the Sellers approach, Izod failed to distance himself from its tenets in practice. He refused to allow CAFU to produce documentary films because he assumed that their messages would prove incomprehensible to African audiences. Instead he continued to produce short fictional films that aspired to recreate African experiences in a "realistic" way. He employed the increasingly threadbare "Mr. Wise and Mr. Foolish" format despite its tendency toward characterization. He also seems to have believed that his unit could learn little about filmmaking from its audience and remained disinterested in their responses to the films. Izod's condemnation of Sellers and his unit may be rooted in a conflict between the two when they worked together during the war, which is hinted at in a 1952 memo.[93] However, despite his ridicule of this system of filmmaking, Izod made no effort to discourage his directors from following it long after it was being reevaluated in other colonies.

Another possible explanation for Izod's growing ambivalence toward the Sellers creed may lie in the increasing complexity of the messages he was being asked to put across to his audiences. While the early films were meant to convey simple themes and situations, the unit increasingly found itself trying to explain sophisticated concepts such as programs for land alienation and the workings of the Central African Federation.

As Izod informed Peet in 1954, "The time has definitely come for us to find a faster technique, i.e., a method of cramping more into any given footage."[94]

Finally, if Izod's views on African film literacy were becoming less rigid, he clearly understood that his superiors in the federal and territorial governments, and Rhodesian society in general, subscribed to Sellers's view. For example, a *Rhodesian Herald* article contained in Izod's CAFU files describes an experiment undertaken by the films officer of Southern Rhodesia, Frank Goodliffe (a colleague of Izod's who shared office space and equipment with CAFU) that aspired "to ascertain whether the African mind is receptive to the conventions and techniques of modern film production especially as applied to propaganda."[95] The experiment showed a locally made film about bilharzia to a class of African schoolchildren and asked them to answer questions about what they had seen. It was pronounced a failure when only 64 percent of the children successfully answered the questions put to them. This conclusion came as no surprise to W. D. Gale, whom the paper quoted to the effect that "The Department, after years of experience, is well aware that a film for European consumption is not necessarily suitable for Africans, who need a simpler technique."[96] Gale, like most of white Rhodesian society, would discourage CAFU from straying too far from the Sellers model. Regardless of Izod's personal reservations about the colonial-cinema style, the views of his superiors and public opinion in the colony discouraged any reassessment of his unit's approach.

In 1953, the British government approved the federation of the three Central African territories of Southern Rhodesia, Northern Rhodesia, and Nyasaland, and responsibility for CAFU was transferred from the Central African Council to the newly created Federal Information Department. This change had important consequences for the unit. The priorities of their new masters were, at least initially, the production of 35-mm films to popularize the federation at home and abroad. As Izod informed the chief information officer of the Southern Rhodesian Information Service in 1957, "since this Unit became part of the Federal government it has had to work almost exclusively on films for European audiences and particularly for overseas audiences."[97] Izod assured the officer, who had inquired about the production schedule of 16-mm films for Africans, "It is our earnest hope that we shall be able to return to some African film production before long, though it is unlikely in future to reach the volume which we achieved in the past."[98]

The pace of filmmaking for Africans slowed to a trickle between 1953 and 1957, and Peet resigned and returned to England. This refocus of the unit's mission has led some historians to view the federal period as insignificant insofar as films for Africans were concerned. However, while film propaganda became a low priority for federal authorities between 1954 and 1957, the government of Southern Rhodesia retained its enthusiasm for teaching rural Africans with films. CAFU's films-for-Africans program eventually received a new lease on life after 1957 when the growing dissatisfaction with the federation among Africans throughout the region forced the federal government to redouble its propaganda efforts.

In August 1957, CAFU's production of films for Africans revived after the Federal Information Department was severely criticized in the federal parliament for losing touch with the state's African population.[99] As one member of the parliament complained, "I have heard a great deal of criticism about the Federal Government's apparent inability—sometimes I have heard it described as unconcern—to trying [*sic*] to put across to the mass of African people those points which occur from time to time due to the activities of the Federal Government which are of considerable benefit to the African people." In September, under pressure from MPs, the cabinet of the federal government instructed CAFU to begin producing a newsreel for the federation's Africans. This was a clear departure from the "story-films" of the past. Izod initially expressed his concern that this format "would become absolutely stereotyped, and would offer no scope for imagination."[100]

Despite Izod's misgivings, CAFU prepared an edition of the *Rhodesia and Nyasaland News* every month from 1957 until the end of federation in 1963. Its purpose was to encourage the people of the region to support the federation by showing the benefits that the government bestowed on its subjects. As will be seen in chapter 4, reports of the officers showing these films indicate that the newsreels did more to undermine than to further the federal cause among Africans. An analysis of the films themselves suggests why. Standard fare for the newsreel consisted of scenes of white dignitaries addressing gatherings of Africans, chiefs being invested by government officials, and federal and military and police parades. There were "African advancement" stories that focused on the professional accomplishments of "assimilated" Africans and also stories intended to highlight racial cooperation in the federation. Many of these seem unintentionally inflammatory, such as a segment showing a multiracial track-and-field competition in which whites win every event; another is a profile of two white adolescent girls in Bulawayo who were teaching their adult farmhands to read. As a white priest in Southern Rhodesia complained to a mobile cinema officer, the newsreels had "not enough Africans and Europeans mixing together. . . . He thought it would do a lot of good if we showed Africans and Europeans, drinking, dancing, and swimming, etc., with a camera[;] that should not be hard to do, and everybody would be pleased."[101] However, there was little likelihood that this kind of social mixing would find its way into *Rhodesia and Nyasaland News.*

The films unwittingly documented realities that were not always perceived by the filmmakers. As Izod reported to the federal minister of home affairs, the difficulty in producing documentaries highlighting successful Africans in the federation lay in the fact that "it is difficult to find suitable stories."[102] Outside of the federal health and postal services, Izod pointed out, there was little tangible evidence of African advancement. This difference between the dream and reality was a recurring problem, as the following anecdote illustrates. In a government memo, a white agent of the Federal Information Office recounted that he had

> brought to Nkata Bay for distribution purposes, a number of the Health photo posters. While at Mzimba, he also placed one in the Post Office with the consent of the African postmaster. This individual was dressed in very tattered clothes and had a large bandage around one foot. He read the photo poster very carefully and then turned and realised I was watching him. He immediately said "But we do not have these things here" presumably referring to the X-ray and other facilities depicted in the poster. I pointed out the pictures were taken at Zomba and Blantyre and were meant to show how Africans were given careers by the Federal Government.
>
> His reply took my breath away. He said he had injured himself on Wednesday and had called the ambulance, which did not come until very late in the afternoon. I asked him how he was injured. Someone had trod on his foot during tug of war practice for the Queen's Birthday Celebrations.[103]

Within the circle of his fellows, the information officer dismissed the objections of the postmaster with ridicule, as if the relevant point was the African's misunderstanding, rather than the government's misrepresentation. However, the anecdote highlights the challenges facing filmmakers intent on popularizing the economic development and social equality of the colonial state.

Despite the limited supply of stories, *Rhodesia and Nyasaland News* never resorted to presenting "news" per se. This was in part because CAFU's attempts to cover newsworthy events were censored by the federal authorities. Even before the newsreel program got under way, Izod realized that it was likely to be heavily censored: "As this is a government Unit it could be possible for the situation to arise where unbiased film reportage might be viewed with some dismay by the governments, and we should of course have to take notice of any instructions which might be issued."[104] For their part, the CAFU cameramen accepted such control cheerfully.[105] Most appear to have been ardent supporters of federation who believed, like their colleague Henry Beriff, that "objective" reporting only permitted "the overseas Press [to] turn 20 or 30 paid demonstrators into newspaper headlines and thoroughly misrepresent us to the British public."[106] The unit's newsreel for whites, *Rhodesia Spotlight*, was also censored in Rhodesia, a harbinger of future media control in that colony.[107]

By 1958, several departments of the federal government were calling for an increased commitment to the films-for-Africans program. A report issued by the Federal Department of Education argued for a reinvestment in film propaganda:

> Every pound spent on the production and distribution of documentary and instructional films is worth many times a pound spent on any other method of mass communication. The Press, Broadcasting and Television are all ephemeral; their impact is transitory and their value lies largely in the sphere of entertainment. Documentary films alone combine the visual impact with

such qualities as durability of material, flexibility of use, infinite repeatability, and availability for use where they are needed, when they are needed. Money spent on documentary films is money invested.

The report went on to lament the state of CAFU's films-for-Africans' catalog: "Government films are not reaching the wide audiences they should reach, particularly African audiences in both rural and urban areas. . . . The recent production of films for African consumption has been negligible. Productions made by the CAFU some three or more years ago, especially for Africans, are now over familiar and are no longer greatly welcomed."

The report concluded with a request for a new fleet of forty federal mobile film units to take the new productions to the people of the federation.[108]

In the last years of the federation, the unit became an integral part of the Federal Information Department's campaign to "put over Federation and to allay fears" among Africans. In 1959, CAFU received instructions to cancel all plans for future productions "but to keep the lines clear, so that the unit can concentrate on the production of a series of films to put the federation over to audiences overseas, and to put federation over to Africans in our three territories."[109] It was with great satisfaction that the head of the Federal Information Department, Vernon Brelsford, could report in 1959, "The 1959/60 Estimates provide for a considerably increased output of films by the Central African Film Unit of which a substantial part is designed for African consumption in the Federation as one of the best means of propagating the Federal idea."[110] Though the Federal Information Department ultimately failed to convince their audiences to support federation, many observers in the government and in parliament believed that the CAFU propaganda had proven tremendously influential in rural areas.[111] Impressed with the film program's progress throughout the federation, the Southern Rhodesia Information Services Department purchased a new fleet of mobile cinema vans in 1962.

Despite the best efforts of the Federal Information Department and the Central African Film Unit, in 1963 the peoples of Northern Rhodesia and Nyasaland voted to dissolve the Federation of Rhodesia and Nyasaland. Northern Rhodesia and Nyasaland became the independent nations of Zambia and Malawi in 1964. In the wake of the federation's breakup, the white regime of Southern Rhodesia renamed their colony Rhodesia. In distributing the assets of federation among the three nations, Rhodesia ended up with the Central Film Laboratories, one of the most sophisticated film labs on the continent, and the equipment of the defunct Central African Film Unit. However, the new Rhodesian Front regime balked at the costs of continuing to produce films for Africans without supporting funds from the other territories, and the Central African Film Unit closed in 1963. The privatization of the unit's assets resulted in a scandal that implicated several prominent members of the settler government. Most of the employees of the unit chose to remain in Rhodesia, and many found work in the colony's fledgling commercial motion-picture industry. When the Rhodesian Front regained its enthusiasm for filmmaking in the late 1960s, it was able to take advantage of this large pool of trained colonial filmmakers within the colony.

How are we to assess the work of the Central African Film Unit? For African audiences, the obvious contrast was the commercial cinema, which, as will be seen in chapter 6, consistently eclipsed the popularity of the government productions. However, it is logical to compare their work to similar films-for-Africans programs from elsewhere on the continent.

As we have seen, production of the CAFU films was guided by the same principles utilized by their predecessors, BEKE and the Colonial Film Unit. Like its predecessors, CAFU produced short, didactic films that used a fictional narrative to tell simple stories. They employed the most basic cinematic techniques and used only amateur African actors. The filmmakers themselves had little experience in the commercial cinema industry, and many of them learned their craft on the job.[112] Given the conditions under which they worked, CAFU was able to produce films of a relatively high technical caliber. The result, nevertheless, was the production of films that looked decidedly amateurish if compared with even the lowest-grade Hollywood productions. In technique and content, they reflected a very limited confidence in the abilities of their audiences to comprehend sophisticated concepts or images.

Given the prevailing colonial prejudices and the conditions of production in Africa, could CAFU have done otherwise? An interesting comparison can be made with the work of the film units at work in the Belgian Congo. There a government film unit, largely patterned after the British CFU, began making films for Africans after World War II.[113] At about the same time, Roman Catholic missionaries in the Congo began worrying about the pernicious influence of commercial cinema on Christian converts. They established the Congolese Center for Catholic Action Cinema and began producing their own films for African audiences. In principle, these clergymen-turned-cineastes shared many of the assumptions about African audiences that were current in British Africa. For example, Pere van den Heuvel, one of the architects of the filmmaking program, believed that the secret to making films for Africans "consists in using the technique of film for children."[114] This meant that "the projection time, as for children's films, must not be long. . . . The scenes will follow each other in a chronological manner; no flashbacks or flash-forwards. Dream sequences will be banished. The ideal is a film in which the action takes place in one day."[115] However, despite their condescending views, the Catholic fathers appear to have produced genuinely popular films. They did so by transgressing several of the basic rules of colonial cinema.

Among their popular productions were a series of cartoons involving the adventures of an antelope, called *Les Palabres de Mboloko*. This was in a genre that was considered beyond Africans by Izod and his team. But their greatest success was the *Matamata and Pilipili* series—short comedies about the misadventures of two friends. In making the films, Father Albert van Haelst, the director of the series, was not afraid to use technical "tricks," such as the simplistic stop-action removal of actors to make it look like they have disappeared. The series was in black and white, which in the eyes of the CAFU should have rendered the films unrealistic to Africans. But most importantly, they allowed two professional (and sorely used) actors to develop characters from film to film, whereas CAFU directors paid little attention to the recruitment and training of actors and actresses, believing that all Africans were "natural actors" and were therefore interchangeable. They were also dissuaded from using the same actors repeatedly because of the stereotype that audiences would become confused if the same actor reappeared in a new part.

Thus the makers of *Matamata and Pilipili* were able to imbue their films with a level of professionalism that the CAFU films could never achieve. While the films were didactic, they were made as comedies first and foremost. Though there has been no exhaustive study of audience response, interviews conducted during the 1990s suggest that the films were extremely popular in the Congo.[116] If so, this is undoubtedly due in large part to the fact that the filmmakers were guided by conventional rules of the early cinema, rather than contrived preconceived notions of African peculiarity.[117]

CAFU was the most prolific colonial filmmaking unit ever created. In fifteen years, it produced hundreds of films, most of which were intended for Africans living in rural communities. It provided a training ground for dozens of producers, directors, and technicians who later worked in the Southern African commercial cinema industry and in film services for the Rhodesian and later the Zimbabwean government. CAFU's work had so impressed the Southern Rhodesian Native Affairs Department that, as we will see in chapter 6, film became an important component of the Rhodesian Front's propaganda machine during the 1960s and 1970s. The members of CAFU, the governments that employed them, and in general the white population of the federation believed that the unit had perfected a powerful technique for influencing Africans.

# Chapter 4

# Monitoring African Film Audiences in the Central African Federation, 1948–1963

Millions of viewers saw the films of the Central African Film Unit throughout Africa and overseas between 1948 and 1963. The largest audiences were in the Central African Federation, where in Southern Rhodesia alone every year nearly half a million Africans watched their films. During the late 1940s and 1950s, cinema became a vital channel of communication between ruler and ruled in the region. By 1963, film had become one of the state's most important tools of adult education and its most reliable weapon for combating the forces of "subversion" in the region.

Producing and distributing films for Africans was a costly undertaking, but officials in Central Africa believed the influence of the films justified their expense. Government agents at every level of film production testified to the cinema's hold over Africans. Virtually every person involved in film distribution—mobile cinema operators who screened films in remote areas, social welfare officers who showed them in urban halls, farmers who organized shows on their plantations, missionaries who screened films for their congregations, and a host of other colonial impresarios—testified to the power of the cinema over Africans.

However, the evidence available suggests that this faith in the power of the cinema was misplaced. Audiences often ignored the messages of these films or ascribed their own meanings and interpretations to them. Their oppositional interpretations at times constituted what Manthia Diawara has referred to as "resistant spectatorship."[1] In some cases, the evidence from these alternate readings is rather dramatic. African audiences on occasion objected vigorously and vocally to the representations of themselves and their culture and to the promotion of unpopular state policies. Their reactions, however, were frequently subtle and often characterized by discreet acts such as ironic comment, laughing at "inappropriate" moments or simply refusing to attend government shows. Such behavior was interpreted by colonial observers not as resistance to the images presented in the films or the ideas they promoted, but rather as misunderstandings, which were believed to be the inevitable result of exposing Africans to a complicated medium.

These forms of resistant and alternative readings are not surprising in light of the methods and goals of the colonial filmmakers. What is extraordinary is the fact that colonial observers failed to appreciate the ambiguous, and often hostile, reactions of Africans to state cinema. Rather than revising or reducing the use of film propaganda, the Southern Rhodesian and federal governments significantly expanded the program between 1948 and 1963, despite audiences' growing resistance. The intransigence of these officials reflected their inability to abandon their preconceptions about Africans that underpinned the film program. CAFU taught lessons of development and modernity that were second nature to whites in the colony, using film, a media that was widely assumed to exert a profound influence on Africans. That these lessons, presented on film, could be questioned or rejected by Africans was virtually inconceivable to most colonial officials. Thus the mounting evidence that Africans were often unmoved by films, or even hostile to their images, failed to shake the confidence of filmmakers and distributors. Rather than abandon the project, and their preconceptions, colonial officials found it easier to ignore evidence of resistance, or ascribe it to the intellectual deficiencies of their audience.

This profound disconnection between the official vision of the state and the realities of its perception at rural cinema performances illuminates a larger communication gap between ruler and ruled in the region. It was not that the state had no interest in the responses of African audiences. Both the federal government and the Southern Rhodesian Native Affairs Department required mobile cinema officers to report regularly on audience reactions; indeed, their reports represent one of the most aggressive attempts to systematically investigate African opinion by a settler regime. However, these documents appear to have been read selectively and used largely to reinforce colonial preconceptions. In retrospect, they present a clear pattern of resistance to state propaganda that grew until Rhodesia was liberated from colonial rule.

Before examining the response of African audiences to CAFU films, it is important to understand the goals of the organizations that showed them and the context within which the films were viewed. When CAFU began its work in 1948, there was no infrastructure in place to distribute their films. The Central African Council (CAC), the organization that sponsored the unit, intended for the films sometimes to be shown in "static" theaters, such as African schools, missions, social-welfare halls, and mining compounds; however, it was expected that the films would be shown most frequently from mobile cinema trucks operated by the three territorial governments. This was the technique pioneered by BEKE and also adopted by various commercial organizations—for example, the Tea Marketing Board and Lever Brothers Soap. There had been some experimentation with mobile cinemas during the war in both Southern Rhodesia and Nyasaland, and by 1948 Northern Rhodesia had a fleet of mobile cinemas and specially rigged boats to show films along the Zambesi River.[2] CAFU anticipated that mobile performances would be their most important outlet and produced their films with this venue in mind.

From the beginning, CAC decided that the films would be silent and shown with narration in local vernaculars. Though they later added sound tracks with music and sound effects, with a few notable exceptions CAFU used live commentators for the entirety of its fifteen-year career. The live-commentator system, which had been pioneered by the Colonial Film Unit during the war, was viewed by administrators in Southern Rhodesia as an inevitable expedient because of the polyglot nature of their audiences. As became apparent from the outset, however, it was fraught with problems that invariably intruded between the intended messages of the films and their reception by audiences. One weakness was that the scripts were written in English and then translated into the vernaculars by poorly paid African employees of the unit. Narrators often found the translations confusing. On one occasion, Alan Izod, the CAFU producer, asked the Southern Rhodesian Native Affairs Department to proofread a translation (it was the script for *Mulenga Goes to Town*), noting that the film "will not be much good unless it is accompanied by a commentary spoken by an African in the appropriate vernacular."[3] The department's reply was not encouraging: "The mistranslations are too many and too serious to be altered on your script . . . you will have to let it go as it is."[4] The chief native commissioner (CNC) did not feel that this should prevent the film's distribution: "After all," he wrote, "you are relying on the pictures to tell their story."[5]

Unfortunately, the films rarely told their intended story simply through images, although a few CAFU directors were able to produce films that required little or no commentary. Louis Nell, for example, made several films that can be understood with virtually no narration. Nell's ability to tell a story in pictures stemmed in part from his being one of the only members of the unit who had not learned filmmaking in Britain or on the job in Southern Africa. He had grown up attending cinema shows at the mines on the Northern Rhodesian Copperbelt. Many of these were silent, or when they were "talkies" they were in English, and the sound track was usually drowned out by a noisy crowd. Nell's films for CAFU were made with such an audience in mind. His *The Five Messengers*, which won a prize at the Edinburgh Film Festival, is one of the few CAFU films that required no narration. This film tells the simple story of five members of the Northern Rhodesian police force. Each is shown performing some task of police work, such as apprehending a criminal, aiding an accident victim, or hunting a dangerous wild animal. The climax of the film is a bicycle chase between a fleeing suspect and one of the African officers—an homage to the horse chases popular in Hollywood westerns. The brief film contains little dialogue and is made of a series of scenes of almost constant action. However, such films were exceptional, and most of the unit's films required a scripted narration to make them intelligible.

More serious than bad translations were films shown with no script at all, which was a common problem. While in Nyasaland, CAFU director Stephen Peet found that the commentators working in the region had no scripts and thus had no idea what the films were supposed to be about. Peet reported a showing at the Chikore Mission: the narrator, having no notion of the film's intended plot, therefore "had a rather difficult time trying to invent a story to accompany the film as it went along."[6] In these cases it can be safely assumed that the original "meaning" of the films was lost, and one can only guess at the messages contained in the invented commentary that replaced them. As Peet complained, "Misuse of our films like that must tend to make the audiences groan when they see the 'CAFU' and its appearing at the start of yet another incomprehensible film."[7]

Situations like that at the Chikore Mission were a concern to the government departments responsible for showing the films. An official at the Southern Rhodesia Native Affairs Department wrote in 1952, "There are at present few good films for Africans other than those of the Central African Film Unit[,] which are largely dependent for their effectiveness on a commentary and on the commentator. Is it wise," he asked, "to let them be out over extensive Native Areas with a commentary by an inexperienced commentator with little or no understanding of the lessons taught by the film? He might even twist it the wrong way."[8] Such comments reflect the authorities' anxiety with the ambiguous role of the African narrators.

It was from CFU that CAFU adopted the technique of having Africans provide a live commentary in a local dialect. Scholar David Kerr, in an article on CAFU history, has called the reliance on these middlemen "a very important innovation . . . because it created a context whereby the 'gate-keepers' of the new media were not only the colonial film makers but local urbanised Africans who could offer their own reinterpretation of the films."[9] In the case of the state-run mobile cinema units, these "gate-keepers" were for the most part educated Africans or "Coloureds" employed by the territorial or federal information offices. These men occupied an uncomfortable position between their audiences and the regime that employed them. They were often supervised by whites who had at best a poor understanding of the vernacular in which the films were narrated. They also found themselves frequently presenting films that were in part objectionable to their audiences. Moreover, the films often portrayed complex scenes and themes that may have been difficult to put across to rural peoples. CAFU staff had anticipated such problems, and they expressed their concerns to the Central African Council: "From what members of the Unit have seen of the present system whereby commentaries are delivered 'live' in the vernacular, it seems obvious that under the best circumstances, such as good training and frequent supervision, this method can be extremely effective. On the other hand it is equally clear that it can be a miserable failure."[10]

Throughout the unit's history, the role of these narrators vexed white administrators in both the territorial and federal governments. A mobile cinema officer with the Southern Rhodesian Native Affairs Department expressed this apprehension in a report filed in June 1952: "The commentator John Moyo is doing well as a commentator but needs constant supervision. He is not the type who would ever be trusted on his own. As an interpreter I have to pull him up as he wants to say what he thinks should . . . be said." However, the officer did not suggest his replacement, saying, "He is a great improvement on the first one I had."[11] A much later report by an officer in the federation's Department of Information reflects the growing fear that African narrators were misrepresenting films to their audiences. In appraising the abilities of a white officer supervising a cinema van in Nyasaland, a department official noted, "I suspect that his lack of understanding of the African language will seriously limit his usefulness to us. For a start, how can he be certain that his own team is reliable and loyal unless he knows of what they are saying behind his back? How can be sure that they are not distorting the commentaries to the advantage of the nationalists?"[12]

Similar frustrations were being voiced in the Southern Rhodesian legislative assembly. When the minister responsible for the Southern Rhodesia Information Service proposed hiring additional African staff for the cinema units, an MP asked, "Is he quite certain in his own mind that by employing Native Information Officers he is in fact putting over, through them, the information that he intends to put over? There is a danger at the moment, to my way of thinking, of putting people into the field and putting out information which may not be the sort of information that you want the Africans to follow."[13] Clearly, colonial officials recognized that this precarious link between producer and audience made the films vulnerable to misinterpretation. However, this realization only encouraged policymakers to attribute most misunderstandings or acts of resistance to the inept or inflammatory role of the African narrator, rather than to the content of the films themselves.

In CAFU's first few years, the unit's films were not widely distributed. Then beginning in 1951 two developments expanded the audience considerably. The first was the creation of the Southern Rhodesian Information Service (SRIS). The service was an agency of the colony's Native Affairs Department and was established, in 1951, to keep the rural African population informed about departmental schemes and policies. The creation of the SRIS was an attempt by the Southern Rhodesian government to establish a link with the rural people and reflected the government's acknowledgment that Africans

in the colony were increasingly coming into contact with the
outside world. As the CNC for Southern Rhodesia explained:

> The establishment of the Branch constitutes a recognition of the
> growing interest of Africans in matters outside their immediate
> environment and of an awakening political consciousness which
> is extending that interest to national affairs and even, though
> perhaps yet superficially, to international affairs. There is an in-
> creasing tendency amongst Africans to think about these things,
> but if such thought is to be rational it is essential that it should be
> founded on facts and given a wider than parochial horizon to pro-
> vide an appropriate setting.[14]

He went on to observe that films were a crucial part of such a
program.

The commissioner was careful to point out that the service
was not merely a propaganda department: "It cannot be too
strongly emphasised too that the Branch is not a propaganda
agency in the worst and generally accepted sense of the term;
it will put out 'propaganda' in the best sense of the term to
promote, for example, the adoption of improved methods of
agriculture or standards of hygiene, but it is not a political
agency to propagate the merits of Government policy on the
lines well-known in totalitarian states." However, he apparently objected to such methods for practical rather than ideological reasons:

> For the average attitude of the conservative African to anything
> new is one of innate suspicion based on ignorance of the facts. If
> that suspicion can be removed and the facts explained there is no
> reason to suppose that the thought of Africans on any new mat-
> ter, in so far as they are capable of comprehending it, will be any
> less rational than that of any other section of the community.
> The fund of wisdom and good sense amongst many of the older
> people, even though they are illiterate and uneducated, is an in-
> dication of this.

The new information service saw film as an important means toward furthering these ends. As seen in chapter 1, the government of Southern Rhodesia had been eager to use film as a teaching tool since the 1930s, and this enthusiasm continued in the postwar years. In 1947, while the Central African Council was mulling over the creation of CAFU, the Southern Rhodesian government founded the Public Relations Department Film Unit to make films for white and African audiences in the colony. With the advent of CAFU in 1948, this unit directed most of its attention to films for white audiences, but among its earliest planned productions were several for rural Africans. The unit did produce at least one film for this audience, *We Were Primitive*, completed in 1948. The plot of the film as described in the Rhodesia House catalog in London

> shows the impact of European knowledge on a primitive people. [It is a] story told by an African Demonstrator who is conveying the knowledge he has gained at a Government agricultural school to his people on a Native Reserve. The previous primitive misuses of the soil and the unhygienic way of living are seen to be giving way to better farming and to a higher standard of health. Produced by the Departments of Public Relations and Native Agriculture, this film is entirely factual and is an interesting survey of the result of imparting knowledge to the African, through the African.[15]

In its subject matter and approach to its audience, *We Were Primitive* foreshadowed the films for African development that the Native Affairs Department would help CAFU to produce after 1948. Unlike CAFU films, it has a sound track in English, because it was originally intended for British and Commonwealth audiences. It contains many images that would not have made it into CAFU productions, such as scenes of people dressed in "traditional" clothing, and dramatizations of precolonial slave raiding in African communities.

The SRIS had three main media—cinema, radio, and the "native" press, which it subsidized—at its disposal. As seen above, the Southern Rhodesian authorities were particularly suspicious of radio. When the Central African Council tried to organize a regional broadcasting service for Africans in 1946, Southern Rhodesia's native-affairs secretary voiced his reservations: "I think it will be some considerable time before the radio will serve as a potent arm in the mass education of Southern Rhodesia . . . the visual form provided by the 'movies,' with a running commentary in the vernacular, together with the printed word, provide the most suitable methods."[16] His objection to broadcasting lay in the potential of Africans to misunderstand the medium: "Wireless propaganda easily becomes suspect, as was amply demonstrated when it was used for this purpose during the War. We did not use the method ourselves, but the Union Authorities did to some extent, sometimes with results somewhat different to those anticipated."[17]

The African press, the other preferred media of the SRIS, was served by several African papers sponsored by the Native Affairs Department. White officials believed that written propaganda could not be easily misunderstood or subverted. As the head of the SRIS wrote in 1960, "The printed word is the most durable method of distributing information which, when produced in local languages, cannot so easily lend itself to distortion, misrepresentation, and the subsequent poisoning of minds."[18] However, the value of newspaper information, even when written in Shona and Sindebele, was limited by the high adult illiteracy rate in the colony (in 1961 the colony's adult illiteracy rate was estimated to be 70 percent, and would certainly have been much higher in rural communities). Thus because of the perceived dangers posed by broadcasting and the limitations of print information, cinema became by default the most valued and trusted tool of the new department.

When the Federation of Rhodesia and Nyasaland was created in 1951, it established its own information department to inform rural peoples about their government and the peoples of the federation. The new department provided its own fleet of mobile cinema units to show CAFU films throughout the region. The federal vans originally left distribution in Southern Rhodesia to the SRIS, focusing in the first years of federation on Northern Rhodesia and Nyasaland. By the end of the 1950s, however, several hundred thousand Africans in Southern Rhodesia were seeing CAFU films annually on both federal and territorial circuits.

Once CAFU had completed its first batch of films, it began testing them on hand-picked audiences in Southern Rhodesia. The first test was held for local white officials and literate Africans in the Matopos region in September 1949. The program included *Zimbani,* a story about African tobacco cultivation, Stephen Peet's "self-help" film *Mujenji Builds a Bridge,* and *Mulenga Goes to Town,* an "urban peril" slapstick comedy. After the show, an African employee of CAFU, Gideon Naminesu, distributed questionnaires to the audience. The written comments of Africans at the show contain a good deal of specific, though muted, criticism of the films. Many of them commented positively about the goals of CAFU, and several were clearly pleased to see their government making films starring Africans. However, others appeared anxious to keep in the good graces of the local white authorities (this was especially important since the questionnaires were not anonymous). Still, their responses contain a significant amount of guarded criticism of both the techniques and the content of the films.

One common complaint was the simplistic technique of the filmmakers. *Mujenji Builds a Bridge,* in particular, was criticized for its dull and plodding technique, with one viewer complaining that the methodical scenes of building the bridge took too long and that as a result "it makes people tired."[19] Another common criticism was that the films presented the inequalities of the colonial state too baldly. One respondent deplored the fact that the bridge builders received no remuneration: "It is unfair & does not encourage people to do such a job without a bit of pay to help their families at home as it is known today life is hard. I know these people did it in that way but I doubt if it can be done in other places." Another, although first saying of the film *Zimbani*, "the show . . . was a good one," added, "one disappointment to me was that his African carriers were overloaded very much. Man is not an animal but a human being and should deserve some respect, though it was a good lesson to people who do not go to school to receive education and get better jobs." The film aggravated this same viewer by depicting the state's control over local agricultural producers: "I did not like the government controlled price which made the hard worker Simon sell his cows at such a low price for such big cows."[20]

If some critics found aspects of the films too true to life, others complained about their unrealistic and unflattering portrayal of Africans. Several complained of the clownish behavior of the title character in *Mulenga Comes to Town*. They found Mulenga's behavior implausible and criticized in particular a scene in which he sits down in a city street and begins making a cooking fire, oblivious to the danger posed by the passing traffic. One man found this "very unsatisfactory in that all what happens there is not practicable eg no fool can ever make fire in the centre of the road."[21] This respondent was one of several viewers who felt that the film offered an unnecessarily provocative depiction of the African colonial police. In a more general criticism, one viewer complained "one thing which worries me is this it seems as if there is too much of being down looked upon. looking at the films it seems as if we are the only dirty lazy & foolish race and yet not considering that we are a race that is downpressed more especial on the point of money."[22] Such criticisms were more direct than most. Perhaps typical of the comments was the ambivalent response of one man who wrote, "I hope and trust next time we should have more interesting and helping films on our side."[23]

The white members of the audience had a dramatically different view of the program. To be sure, many of them complained about the facile techniques and several said that they themselves were bored by the style of the films. However, they assumed that the plodding pace and simple techniques were appropriate for African audiences. As one white observer commented, the films "seemed to go down well with the Africans, but albeit long drawn out in some places, although these were doubtless introduced to attract the African mind." Another respondent echoed this view, stating that he found *Mujenji Builds a Bridge* "a bit too long and drawn out," while concluding that this made it "allright for the native audience."

In general, the white respondents found the films too complicated for African audiences. One viewer's brief comment, which seemed to reflect a concern with the ability of Africans to distinguish between "real" and "make-believe" at the movies, stated, "I think the basic *mistake* was to combine *fact* & fiction."[24] Another respondent found "films generally too long & too much emphasis placed on the incidental adventures of the natives. This perhaps appealed to the native mind but reduces the instructional value of the film. I suggest simple emphasis on the correct way of doing things and leaving the wrong way out entirely as the native has a genius for misunderstanding instructions."

Despite such reservations, the films were much appreciated by the white members of the audience. In a revealing critique, a white land-development officer stated, "Having lived in close contact with Africans for the past 25 years and understanding their ways and customs perfectly, I think that these pictures were splendid. The acting could not have been more natural and those responsible for their direction have my complete admiration."[25] Though these initial screenings were intended to aid CAFU in planning future films, the staff expressed little interest in the criticisms of the Africans in the audience. Gideon Naminesu told his superior, Izod, "At the conference we had an advanced type of African so I do not think their views would be the same as the backward sections of the reserves."[26] Izod for his part shrugged off the criticisms of these "advanced type" of Africans. When Harry Franklin, an information officer with the Northern Rhodesian government, suggested he make revisions to *Mulenga Comes to Town* in light of African opinion, he politely declined.[27]

Shortly after the inaugural showing, CAFU and the Native Affairs Department hosted an official premiere in Salisbury. White officials and educated Africans were invited to view the films and to offer written comments. Again the show elicited contrasting responses from the two communities. White opinion was highly complementary, with Sir Godfrey Huggins, prime minister of the federation, personally commending the unit on its work. However, Lawrence Vambe, an African reporter for the newspaper *African Weekly*, offered a much more critical view of the performance. Although he published a glowing review of the films in his newspaper, he sent a letter to Izod that sketched out several criticisms of the productions. He objected to the cumbersome techniques ("not enough excitement," "too long tends to bore") as well as the general representation of African life on film ("In parts unrealistic . . . unAfrican . . . dirt rather exaggerated"). However, Vambe apparently believed that "primitive Africans" were likely to imitate screen action, and warned that the crime-doesn't-pay film *John Meets Trouble* "should not be shown to primitive Africans" because it "encourages superstition" and would likely "encourage Africans to do mischief."[28]

Izod could shrug off the criticism of what he called "the more advanced type" of Africans because they were not his intended audience. It was the reactions of rural people that counted. These were solicited and recorded by employees of the territorial and federal governments and shared with Izod on a regular basis. These reports represent one of the few opportunities presented to rural Africans to communicate with the colonial state. Though the cinema operators were interested mostly with determining the level of audience comprehension, the nature of the films meant that African comments on them inevitably included oblique or direct criticism of state policies. Thus they represent a rare and fascinating articulation of African views of their colonial predicament. However, interviewer and interviewees shared an interest in muting or deflecting critical responses, and such reports must be read critically. Audiences were often hesitant to offer any opinions at all. Many mobile cinema operators found African communities fearful of the units and suspicious of the officer's motives. As one mobile cinema operator reported of his potential audience, "They were reluctant to come some fearing it to be conscription." He found that "on the whole they are very suspicious of any European who comes around."[29] Those Africans who watched the films and shared their opinions with cinema operators were frequently guarded in their comments. One white official, commenting on this phenomenon, remarked on "the African's sense of propriety in saying things which he hopes will please the European. This makes investigation by the method of direct inquiry very difficult for the African's sense of politeness will never allow him to say that which is discreditable to your efforts on his behalf."[30] An African cinema operator was more candid: "Africans will never speak their minds out in presence of officials and police."[31] This reticence was not always rooted in fear. Many Africans did not want to be seen criticizing the films because the shows were very popular in many areas, and some respondents feared that too much adverse criticism would lead to their discontinuation.[32]

If the audiences had reasons to be reserved in their opinions, mobile cinema operators had their own interest in doctoring responses. In most cases, African information officers had a great deal of latitude in interpreting audience reactions because they were usually supervised by white officers who were not fluent in local languages. Many African cinema officers conducted their shows unsupervised by white officials and thus could take liberties with their narration. They were also in a position to show films that were the most popular and least controversial. Since they knew what the officials in the information departments and CAFU wanted to hear, it is not surprising that these men embellished their accounts of audience reactions. At least one CAFU filmmaker suspected the African cinema officers of "playing to the gallery" in their reports of the film shows.[33]

Before delving into the question of audience responses to the film shows, it is worth considering the context in which they were screened. In the early days of CAFU, many members of their audiences had never seen motion pictures before. For such viewers, the shows would have been a novel experience. By the early 1960s, the proliferation of cinema shows presented by government and private interests had worn away the novelty of the medium. Still, many rural Africans would have viewed the cinema, at least initially, as a tool introduced into their lives by the colonial state. Seen in this context, the early criticism of these programs appears all the more remarkable.

Given such considerations, there is a significant amount of evidence in reports from mobile cinema vans that suggests that audiences were often unresponsive or hostile to the film shows. In the early days of the mobile cinema, such sentiments were expressed in very vague or diffuse comments; however, as Africans became more accustomed to the shows, as the films began traveling with their intended commentaries, and as the messages became increasingly partisan and political, audience criticisms became more vocal and more hostile.

Many of the examples of audiences misinterpreting films are reminiscent of the stories told by Sellers and other early filmmakers (chapter 2). For example, in one instance a mobile cinema operator remarked of the film *The Wives of Nendi,* "In the scene where the women are having a heated discussion at the well, a man on a bicycle, who has no relation to any of the actions of the story, passes far in the background. Nevertheless, they never fail to notice him and usually make audible comments about him. Thus that which was meant to be merely incidental background becomes for the moment foreground."[34] This report reminded Izod and his colleagues of the danger of providing unnecessary distractions for audiences, and Izod was pleased to report several years later that this incident had inspired his unit to take pains to simplify their films even further.[35] In another episode reminiscent of Sellers's early experiences, mobile cinema officers were unnerved when scenes of children with malnutrition in a film entitled *Food for Life* were regularly greeted with laughter.[36]

Evidence of resistance, rather than mere misperception, appears in a 1952 mobile cinema officer's report. After showing CAFU films to more than four thousand people, he found the

newest CAFU production, *The Wise Father*, "very disappoint-
ing and unconvincing."[37] Audience reaction, he explained, had
impressed upon him "the necessity for accuracy in depicting
social customs and taboo which seems to regulate kraal life to
a large extent in most reserves." He cited the example of
people "objecting strongly" to the scenes in the film during
which an African family shared a meal. "No self-respecting
African father ever has his meals with his children."[38] Such reports were not uncommon and were to some extent expected.
It was an accepted tenet of colonial cinema that Africans invariably found representations of Africans from other cultures
amusing or offensive.[39] Thus, rather than considering that
such images were, like the unrealistic, foolish behavior of Mulenga, unbelievable to Africans, white observers assumed that
Africans lacked the imagination to respond to scenes that
were in any way foreign to their own experience.

A 1954 mobile cinema report provides more evidence of the
kind of diverse and subtle criticisms present at these showings. The officer had shown *The Three Wives*, a film about the
dangers of venereal disease. The film—which is also an
oblique critique of polygamy—shows an African father who
resists receiving treatment for his disease from a colonial doctor; he finally relents after one of his infected children suc-
cumbs to the disease. In his report, the cinema operator
observed that audiences were upset by the depiction of a
child's funeral. "When the film reached the stage where it
shows the people bearing the coffin from the house to the
[graveyard], each time the audience becomes sad and start
murmuring "we do not want to see this."[40] The officer however was quick to downplay the significance of this response:
"The film is so very impressive that people who are not of
weak character like it very much more especially fathers and
mothers." Despite these obvious objections, he claimed that

the film had exerted a strong influence on the audience and pointed out that one child at the show was immediately diagnosed with symptoms of venereal disease and sent to a local clinic.[41]

At the same show, the cinema operator also found that the film *The Box* bothered some in the audience. "They did not like it for they fear it is teaching people especially young people how to start [stealing]." Others objected to the film *Mangwiro and Mudzimu* because it portrayed a traditional healer as a charlatan. The African cinema operator conceded, "Old, old people do not like it for the reason that white people want to discourage us to carry on our old customs." Thus three separate films in a single show, early in CAFU's history, inspired criticisms from the audience. In each case, the cinema operator downplayed the significance of such comments and testified to the efficacy of the film to influence audiences.

These early reports indicate that rural Africans soon tired of the educational films produced by CAFU. Cinema officers frequently complained that audiences were unwilling to make the effort to attend. When they did come, the crowds often demanded that they be shown commercial films. In one such instance an officer reported:

> A very big and undisciplined crowd of about 400 who had attended a *muchato* [beer-drink] during the day all very excited all wanting to come in at once. . . . They refused to be controlled and threats were of no avail. A great shouting and screaming went up especially from the women when the first picture came on. As this atmosphere was not very conducive to the more instructional type of film we kept to the entertainment side after the first picture. As the novelty wore off they soon became restless and uninterested and at the showing of the fifth some shouted that they had seen enough and made their exit.[42]

Colonial observers read this kind of response as evidence of the limited ability of the audiences to comprehend educational films: "The Natives only wanted the comic type of film; the little mental exertion needed to follow the simplest educational film required a mental [exertion] the local Native was not prepared to make. If sensational and comic films were not shown repeatedly the Natives lost interest and wandered off and back to the beer pots and their own dancing and merry-making."[43]

Here two colonial prejudices came into conflict: on the one hand, the belief that Africans were undiscriminating audiences and therefore willing to sit through anything, and on the other the conviction that Africans did not have the intellect or patience to comprehend even simple plots and images. The latter prejudice supported the popular conception that Africans should be permitted to view only films that were made especially for them. Thus in the eyes of most colonial officials, CAFU films were the only safe films for African audiences.

This posed a problem because the unit could not make films quickly enough to satisfy the mobile cinema circuits. Colonial observers deftly theorized their way out of this dilemma by deciding that Africans needed to see each film repeatedly in order to understand it. Thus a white provincial agricultural officer with the Southern Rhodesian Native Affairs Department wrote in 1950, "I believe that each film should be shown twice in the same evening for an unsophisticated African audience in order to obtain the full educational value."[44] A colleague in Northern Rhodesia thought this was an absolute necessity: "It often happens that we can show the same films to the same audience several times without them really getting on top of the information presented."[45] A similar view was expressed by CAFU scriptwriter Denys Brown four years later: "We all know that Africans do not as a rule object to seeing films more than once."[46]

The most extreme example of this attitude was expressed when an official of the Native Affairs Department tried to dismiss audience objections to films about the Native Land Husbandry Act. This act had been passed in 1951 to alleviate some of the environmental pressures caused by growing populations on the African reserves. The provisions of the act permitted African families to retain no more than five head of cattle and eight acres of land. The district commissioner—not the chief, the traditional authority—allocated land, and families were forced to sell off cattle in excess of five at artificially low prices. According to a leading monograph on the nationalist struggle in Zimbabwe, the act was "a futile attempt to arrest a situation they had themselves created . . . generat[ing] more bitterness against the settler government than any previous legislation."[47] One of these films, *New Acres*, was one of the first to elicit vociferous opposition from audiences. Though it was eventually pulled from circulation, the Native Affairs Department ran it long after it had clearly begun infuriating audiences.[48] As the SRIS's chief information officer reported in 1961, "In some areas agricultural films are not popular due to the campaign against the Land Husbandry Act. . . . These films are shown continuously, however, and their message is slowly sinking in."

There exists, not surprisingly, a great deal of evidence that suggests Africans quickly tired of seeing repeats. Cinema officers' reports are replete with complaints from viewers expressing irritation at being subjected to the same films repeatedly. For example, the following conversation was recorded by a mobile cinema officer in 1958:

"We saw this picture about three weeks ago, why do they show us the same pictures?" asked one person. "My friend, by showing us this picture they want us to learn, particularly our wives, how to look after our children carefully," explained his friend. "Yes that is true. But I still do not see any point in showing us the same picture many times. I think they are running short of films." said the first person again. "No, they cannot run short of pictures, they are making more and more every time. They simply repeat showing them to us because such pictures are important," argued the second man.[49]

A similar report echoed this view: "Agricultural films continue to receive a very varied reception. They are still popular in the areas in which they were made but elsewhere, when the actors are not known personally and where the films have been shown frequently, they are apt to be greeted with groans and the audience reaction of 'Not this one again, please!' is sometimes reported."[50]

Audience resistance grew steadily throughout the 1950s. An important turning point came when CAFU began producing a newsreel for Africans. The newsreels about life in the federation that CAFU had begun making for white audiences in 1953 had also often been shown to Africans. The newsreels CAFU began making in 1957, specifically designed for African audiences, were intended to broaden the horizons of Africans and to give them a better understanding of the community of peoples that made up the British Commonwealth and the Central African Federation. They were initiated mainly to mobilize support among rural Africans for the federal government. However, the mobile cinema officers' reports suggest that in fact these films sowed dissatisfaction with the colonial status quo. That these films should cause disaffection is not surprising. As seen above, newsreels tended to focus on the power of the colonial state and were filled with scenes of white politicians or soldiers. For colonized peoples used to the privations of war and the press gang, such images would almost inevitably concern audiences. As one viewer commented after seeing film of the British army, "We were shown the soldiers in England simply because they wanted us to march in the same way in order that if the soldiers of England are conquered by the Russians we Africans would also go and help."[51]

This became an increasingly common concern. When an American anthropologist, Hortense Powdermaker, conducted a study of film and radio audiences in Northern Rhodesia in the 1950s, she found a lot of this kind of anxiety in response to government newsreels. In one instance, scenes of UN troops arriving in Formosa were greeted with the panicked comment, "War is on. They will kill us all." Another newsreel showing flood victims in Europe was also interpreted as posing a threat to Africans: "Those people do not have an easy time at home. Perhaps that is the main reason why they have made this Federation of theirs, so that those who have no homes in England or anywhere in Britain, may come and live here, where we do not have floods."[52]

But federal newsreels did not always alienate African audiences. Indeed, their depiction of African businessmen, politicians, and athletes made them one of the most popular elements of government film shows. It was through these newsreels that many Africans in the federation learned that there were African representatives in the federal parliament. As one cinema operator reported, "People like to see African MPs in Federal films"; audiences held such events to have been "undreamt of . . . before Federation."[53] Another operator working in Southern Rhodesia wrote, "Some say these films are good in that they have 'no colour bar'—by this they mean that they show all races mixed together like scenes of opening functions by the Governors and Officials."[54]

Such films also offered opportunities to voice criticisms of the federal government's leadership and policies. Scenes of the federal prime minister came to be greeted with derision throughout the federation, while on at least one occasion a white federal Information officer in Nyasaland was able to quell a potential riot by showing films of the nationalist leader Hastings Banda.[55] In many cases, the response to the federal newsreels was simple skepticism or bemusement. A cinema officer recorded the following conversation: "'Can you tell me why they show us these pictures?' asked one man. 'They want you to see the progress that is taking place in your country because of the Federation,' answered another. 'What progress you mean, we want money,' said the second man, then laughter."[56]

The introduction of African newsreels was one of several developments that encouraged rural audiences to articulate their resistance to CAFU films in the later 1950s. Another was the replacement of white operators by black and "coloured" cinema operators, who, working alone, were more likely to hear frank opinions about the films. In the early days of the mobile cinema, rural peoples were often suspicious of white officers, and by the early 1960s in many regions this had grown into hostility. One Southern Rhodesian audience warned an operator in 1962, "If you were a European Operator we would not have allowed you to come here."[57] A similar incident was reported the following year: "While we were getting ready for the show people started gathering little by little. One boy that I would call a kid said to his friends, 'Lets hit these people' and others said, 'Oh no. These are Africans, sons of the soil. If they were Europeans yes we would hit them.'"[58]

Resistance to the films was growing also in response to the increasingly sensitive subjects dealt with in the films. It was not just the newsreels that were becoming more partisan and political. After 1957, the Federal Information Department asked CAFU to attempt to popularize the benefits of citizenship in the Central African Federation. As the future of the federation became more precarious, the federal government introduced ever more heavy-handed propaganda in support of its continued existence. Perhaps the most controversial example of this effort was a CAFU film entitled *Free from Fear.* The idea for the film probably originated in a memo from the director of the Federal Information Department, K. D. Leaver, in 1959. Leaver wrote to the CAFU producer, "To combat the insidious development of Congress movements in the three Territories of the federation it is suggested the time is most opportune for the production of a historical film for African consumption on the growth and development of Central Africa."[59] Leaver suggested the production of a long film that would dramatize the extirpation of the slave trade in the region as well as "the ending of the internecine wars between Amandabele and Shona" in Southern Rhodesia, the "advent of law and order," and the "development and new openings for Africans" in the modern period.[60]

The result was *Free from Fear.* A documentary, produced in 1960, it was intended to publicize the legacy of white rule in Nyasaland since the end of the nineteenth century. It begins with reenactments of slave raids undertaken in the 1890s and a dramatization of the British government's suppression of the trade. These scenes are followed by film of contemporary urban life in Nyasaland, with a voice-over, in English, explaining the many benefits that the colonial government had bestowed on modern Nyasas. The federal government is credited with supplying many services, including education and medicine, as well as with maintaining peace in the colony. The last part of the film, an attack on the pretensions of Hastings Banda's Malawi Party, features grisly footage of victims of disease and violence in the newly independent Congolese Republic.

There were many aspects of *Free from Fear* that made it

unpopular with African audiences. First, the film's early scenes presented an unflattering depiction of the "primitive" nature of nineteenth century African life. It is perhaps the only CAFU film to show Africans wearing "traditional" dress. Most CAFU productions featured actors and actresses wearing Western-manufactured cotton clothing. In *Free from Fear*, however, the films showed African women bare-breasted, and men in loincloths. Second, it was filled with morbid scenes of murdered Africans that were much more explicit than anything previously presented to rural audiences. If the staged funeral of *The Three Wives* upset audiences in 1954, the scenes of corpses in *Free from Fear* proved far more unsettling and offensive.

Rural audiences voiced objections to *Free from Fear* at its initial screening. Cinema operators who worked in Southern Rhodesia during the early 1960s remembered it as a particularly difficult film. An African cinema officer's report from the Essexvale region of Southern Rhodesia complained that because of the film "we have been accused as stooges in places like Luveve and the main Police Camp in Bulawayo"; at showings in the Goromonzi area, *Free from Fear* was labeled "false propaganda to thwart Africans."[61] Many colonial observers refused to accept this hostile reception at face value. In their opinion, the problems with propaganda like *Free from Fear* stemmed not from the subject matter but from the technique employed in making such films. As one white cinema officer explained, "The film *Free from Fear* which you sent me in the last batch of films is in my opinion not fit for general viewing. . . . The commentary is very difficult for an African audience to follow, and I feel that people would have the wrong impression from this film . . . this film should be reserved for selected viewing."[62] Here again is the assumption that the African audience was incapable of comprehending the medium. Audience dissent was attributed to a "wrong impression" rather than to the actual content of the film.

Another production that proved particularly problematic was the agricultural film *Uncle Mupari,* which was intended to teach Africans how to grow tea as a cash crop. Reports quoted audiences calling the film "rotten" and accusing it of "opening old wounds." However, government observers continued to attribute such responses to the complicated nature of the film. A typical report explained "Uncle Mupari is not understood by the people. Only one teacher could follow it."[63]

By the end of the 1950s, resistance in Nyasaland and Northern Rhodesia had become much more active. As Vernon Brelsford, head of the Federal Information Department, reported in 1958, "The Nyasaland Chief Information Officer informed me that mobile vans had been stopped on several occasions by road blockages from which the vans had to turn back. There had been incidents of men standing in front of the projector with their hands raised to block the light. One tough African in charge of a mobile unit on one occasion tackled two of the thugs, bundled them into the van and took them to a nearby Police Station."[64]

More overt resistance developed over the next four years. By 1962, a typical mobile cinema report from Nyasaland reported, "This show was a failure. Village people were kept away. . . . We do not want Sir Roy's[65] pictures here nor F[ederation] R[hodesia] N[yasaland], After one and half hours showing we closed down as crowd looked dangerous."[66] A similar report was filed two months later: "A good number of leaflets were torn up. One could hear them say 'Sir Roy is dead,' 'Federation is finished.'"[67] By April 1963, the criterion for a successful film show in Nyasaland had become one unmarred by violence. "This show was well received. A few of the audience kept shouting 'We don't want Federation or Federal films here.' When asked if we should come back again the answer was 'NO.'"[68]

The resistance in Nyasaland was mirrored in Northern Rhodesia. By 1961, the territorial government in Northern Rhodesia had taken steps to end federal film shows.[69] In Southern Rhodesia, however, active resistance to the films came later than in the northern territories. When it did develop, it was in large part inspired by news of disturbances to the north. But it was also the result of events within the colony: specifically, the banning of African political parties in Southern Rhodesia and the attempt to implement the Native Land Husbandry Act.

The story of CAFU's involvement in the campaign to promote the Native Land Husbandry Act illustrates the increasingly difficult task confronting the filmmakers. In 1950, before the act was passed into law, the Native Affairs Department had asked CAFU to produce a film that would explain some of its more controversial provisions, such as the creation of fixed-tenure landholdings and the destocking of cattle. The department provided CAFU screenwriter Denys Brown with a brief story that they hoped would serve as a basis for the film:

> In 1946 many farms in Emhlabtini and Willsgrove were being 'kaffir-farmed'—i.e., absentee owners allowed Africans to farm the land without control. . . . These Africans were doing quite nicely, thank you—they had good quality land, and when they had exhausted one plot with their unenlightened farming they moved on to another. All that was lacking from their point of view was *security of tenure*. The government faced unrest when the farmers were forced to move to lower lying areas with poorer soil.[70]

The department suggested a format that provided a "comparison of old and new." Brown quickly perceived the problem:

The thing that stands out a mile is that by no stretch of imagination can the people concerned be said to be materially better off because of their move. That doesn't mean that their standard of home life and farming isn't higher—it certainly is. But while to the European eye the improvement is obvious—good farming and homes for bad—to the African it is not so. Put at the most extreme level, they might say "We now have less land, less cattle" (they were destocked for the move) "and more rules, all to get poorer harvests."

Brown despaired at bringing this story to the screen. "I fear this won't make the outstanding movement story I'd hoped for. The main reason is that it's quite impossible to contrast present prosperity with previous penury, or anything like it. In fact the contrast is unfavourable enough to ruin such a story."[71]

Brown's solution was to produce *The Story of Mdhlongwa*, a film based on a true story of a farmer whose land had been taken while he was working in Bulawayo. The story was decidedly more downbeat than he would have wished: "This being a true story, I have left it exactly as it stands." However, Brown wrote the treatment without any important revisions to the original plot because, in his words, "I am advised by African members of the staff that this story, unembroidered, will hold the attention of African audiences." The film is unique in the CAFU collection as a Job-like story of an African farmer forced off his land by a retrogressive government policy. Brown described it as "a portrait of a kindly and home-loving man slowly goaded by adverse circumstances into a final anti-social outbreak: then of his growing appreciation of the good work done by the group-leader and demonstrators and of the respect and esteem they command in the villages: and finally of his own rehabilitation and success, so that at the end his relations with other people are even better than ever before, because he is now doing something for them."[72] There is no record of the film's reception by a Southern Rhodesian audience, possibly because mobile cinema units showed it infrequently.

When CAFU was asked to make more films to explain the Native Land Husbandry Act's provisions, it responded with *New Acres* and *A Stake in the Land*. Unlike with *The Story of Mdhlongwa*, where little is known about the film's reception, there is ample evidence that the two new productions caused significant disaffection among rural peoples.[73] In fact, by the end of 1961 the new CAFU films appeared to be creating more problems than they were solving. The Information Office in Southern Rhodesia reported to Alan Izod in September that older CAFU films and newsreels retained some popularity, but the new "'Free From Fear' . . . and 'New Acres' are films most criticised." The Native Agricultural Department pulled *New Acres* from circulation in 1961;[74] however, this decision was rooted to some extent in the perceived misperceptions of the audience. The department was particularly impressed with a report from the director of native agriculture that warned that African audiences were not interpreting the film correctly: "New Acres is not suitable for showing to rural areas or urban areas these days. Above all people think the group that follows the tractor is actually fighting the driver and chasing him away. . . . What bad criticism we heard from people can not be stated here. . . . People think the driver is being chased away because of disapproval of the Native Land Husbandry Act."[75]

Growing resistance to the native land-husbandry films reflected a larger dissatisfaction with the Native Affairs Department's campaign to transform African agricultural methods. From its inception, agricultural films were a staple of CAFU's productions. The need for these films grew as the reserves in Southern Rhodesia became increasingly overpopulated and the Native Affairs Department became concerned with the developing rural environmental problems. As the crisis intensified, agricultural propaganda became increasingly pointed, and was in turn increasingly resisted. By 1962, the cinema officer's reports reflected the growing outrage of the audiences with the agricultural films that had formed the backbone of most CAFU shows since 1948.[76] By 1961, the agricultural films were serving largely to remind audiences of their rural poverty and the inequality of land distribution in the colony. One mobile cinema operator reported that when "showing of film on Soil Conservation, one man said 'We do not have enough land."[77] Another audience told him, "We do not want to see those demonstrators splitting our land into acres for we know better ways of farming."[78] A more thorough critique was offered by a member of an audience in Gwelo (Gweru), who informed a cinema operator:

> We quite understand improved methods of farming but certain factors hinder us from achieving the practical objectives of these films—
>
> i)  prices of our crops too low to enable us to buy modern farming implements and things like fertilizers.
> ii)  Some of our younger men have neither land rights nor grazing permits to enable them to utilize these skills.
> iii)  Our Cattle are [in because] of limited grazing areas and poor grass, consequently they are unable to transport manure and the like to our fields.
> iv)  Soils are sandy and any attempt to reach minimum yield specified become unsuccessful.

In general, the reports indicate that African farmers found the films dull and condescending. The same operator noted, "Agricultural films are said to be boring. The general reaction to these agricultural films is that we know how to look after our crops, lands and animals." The reactions to agricultural films became increasingly hostile during the early 1960s, and by

November 1963 a cinema operator commented, "People complain why we have to show farming films in police stations."[79]

A Southern Rhodesian government document from July 1963 marked "Confidential" reported widespread African disaffection. An officer of the Southern Rhodesian Information Service recounted the following comments heard at cinema shows throughout the colony: "People warned us not to touch on their wounds by showing them how their land was divided and the best land given to Europeans."[80] A viewer in another town commented, "You cannot teach us farming, we know it, you must show us things from other countries which we don't know."[81] In general, the officer explained, "The remarks I could overhear from people were as follows, 'We do not condemn the achievement in the agricultural films but we would rather like "deceive" [*sic*] the purpose of showing us such films when the government knows the actual fact that the common farmer like ourselves here in the rural areas have no chance of improving our lands just because the lands happen to be poor even for a good farmer.'"[82] Complaints were apparently widespread throughout the colony and were noted by numerous employees of the Southern Rhodesian government. There seems to be little doubt that by the end of 1963 agricultural films were not transforming economic behavior in the rural areas but rather creating resentment against the government.

The hostility toward the agricultural films eventually spilled over to CAFU films in general. By the early 1960s audiences were objecting vigorously to other topics and images. For example, the representations of African politicians on film produced strong criticism. Before the early 1960s, there had been little political content in the unit's films. Certainly all of the films represented the leadership of the federal and territorial governments in a positive light, and a few took oblique swipes at African politicians (in such films as *Benzi Comes to Town*).[83]

Politics, however, was a topic considered by the colonial authorities to be relevant to town life, and since most CAFU films were situated in the rural areas, representations of African politicians were largely confined to newsreels. However, with the rise of organized political movements during the 1950s, African politicians became a part of the CAFU newsreels.

By 1962, film audiences in Southern Rhodesia were becoming increasingly politicized. Cinema operators frequently complained of the influence of the Zimbabwe African People's Union (ZAPU) nationalists on their audiences. An African member of the Federal Information Department's film unit operating in Northern Mashonaland in 1962 reported of his audiences:

> Most of the people in these areas are very hostile against the government. . . . After this tour of the rural areas, I came back with the conclusion that it would be almost impossible now to try to explain the advantages of the Land Husbandry Act. This, I think, should have been done long before the Act was introduced and implemented. If this was done, I do not think it was done fully and clearly. . . . People in remote areas to-day look to ZAPU as their only source of "true" information.[84]

The film screenings inspired nationalist feelings in audiences in unintended ways. In several cases, cinema operators warned that a film series called *Ngoma* that showed traditional dancing was inspiring spontaneous expressions of support for ZAPU. As one operator warned, "Care must now be taken to ensure that no fur hats are shown in future Ngoma films" because "Z.A.P.U. calls were stimulated at several shows."[85] In general, the atmosphere at these film presentations was growing uneasy. One operator reported, "We were, in addition, quite impressed with the way Chisumbanje audience behaved. There were no political demonstrations. As for subterranean movement, that could only be noticed when it comes to the surface. So far things were reported calm and quiet."[86]

One film sequence that elicited a particularly violent reaction was part of the newsreel series *Rhodesia and Nyasaland News*. The segment, entitled "Claim Your Vote," encouraged Africans to participate in the impending federal elections, but when it was shown at several locations in Southern Rhodesia it was greeted with hostility. A colonial official reported to the prime minister's secretary, "Claim Your Vote was again treated with scorn . . . people are reluctant to claim their vote as they do not feel they are getting a fair deal . . . others want to know why all chiefs and headmen automatically get the vote when most of them are completely illiterate and others say they will not claim the vote because they have nothing to vote for."[87]

Similar comments were encountered at other showings: "At a certain school we heard numerous bad remarks and stones thrown at a classroom where we had put up after the show. This was caused by 'Claim Your Vote film RNN 63.' . . . Bad remarks were shouted such as 'this film (Claim Your Vote) does not help us in any way, it only helps the minority to govern strongly therefore we do not want anything to do with it . . . we do not want to be shown this thing because it fails to meet our needs.'"[88] Another officer, working in Northern Mashonaland, reported a conversation with an older man that reflected many of the common complaints that were frequently voiced at these shows: "One man aged about 50 said 'Even if we claim our votes, whom do we vote for? How can you expect us to vote for people we do not know? What we want is the soil and not to claim our votes . . . why does the government not give us what we want . . . soil?"[89]

By the end of 1963, audiences were objecting to aspects of

virtually all of the government's films. Criticisms were no longer raised against specific policies but were beginning to relate to all representations of white culture and rule. In August 1963, a cinema officer observed, "It is clear at this township that the audience does not like any film that shows Europeans, whether they are singing or acting."[90] At another screening it was reported that "during the projection of the following film 'Jack of What Trade' and 'Commonwealth Students,' half of our audience left in protest. They said they were not interested in films showing Europeans."[91]

Films showing European life infuriated Africans for the obvious reason that they inevitably highlighted the differences between the way Europeans behaved at home and in Southern Africa. (For a discussion of the spread of commercial cinema throughout the region, see below, chapter 5.) As one mobile cinema officer commented, "People were very excited to see white people use ploughs. One man said, 'So these people work hard, they hold *magejo* [plow] like us but when they are here they leave all the job to us. At first I thought England as a whole was full of African servants who performed all the manual and dirty work."[92] Another officer observed, "Some people were a little sceptical about [its authenticity] and find it very hard to believe that Europeans do manual labour."[93]

Even films produced to cast white enterprise in Africa in the best light often elicited criticism: "The showing of a film on game conservation inspired one member of the audience to wonder 'Why was all this being done to save the animals only when many people are suffering? That money could have been given to poor people of all races."[94] Another report stated, "On the film 'The Luangwa Game Reserve' one man said 'Why do they keep the wild animals? They should let us kill them for meat." When the CAFU crime drama series *Casebook No. 1* (produced for Rhodesian television) was shown, a skeptical viewer asked, "Why don't those policemen hit that thief in the film? They usually hit hard even for a small offence or no offence, are they trying to make us think S. Rhodesian police don't hit our captives?"[95]

As the CAFU shows became increasingly unpopular, many Africans, recognizing the power of film to represent, or misrepresent, their lives, began refusing to appear in the films. As suspicion of the unit and its motives grew, CAFU found it increasingly difficult to produce films. An early incident from Barotseland in Northern Rhodesia indicates the kind of resistance the unit encountered. When CAFU proposed to the paramount chief of the Barotse people that a film be made about their agricultural practices, he rejected it on the grounds that it would inaccurately represent his community as being reliant on government assistance. The district commissioner for the province explained to Izod, "The film was considered an insult to the Barotse."[96] The Barotse people did not want such images to be screened to other African peoples, but Africans were also concerned about presentation of their images to Europeans. Gideon Naminesu reported to Izod that, when organizing film shoots, he "stressed the point that films were made about Africans and shown to Africans because many Africans think that these films are going to be shown to European audiences and this keeps some of the good actors from taking part as they think it is a degradation in front of Europeans."[97]

This fear that Africans were being represented as "primitive" was common. An African told the district commissioner for Bulawayo in 1953, "Our government is sly. Our Government has sent to England pictures of primitive Natives wearing 'imisubelo' [traditional dress] to indicate to the British Government that we are still very low, and that we have not come to the stage of understanding federation. The Government has not sent to England pictures of Natives dressed in suits, because that alone would indicate that we are capable of understanding what federation means."[98] African fears of such "primitive" representations later forced CAFU filmmakers to downplay their affiliation with the federal government. One CAFU director reported, "In the rural areas, we find, Africans are extremely hostile towards the term 'Federal' and during my search for a location for the rural scenes for P.157 [*Political Progress*] I found that people shied off when they learned that the Unit is part of the Federal Government." The filmmakers therefore "had to introduce [them]selves as 'more neutral' CAFU, [and] erase 'federal' off of their equipment."[99] This problem ultimately drove CAFU filmmakers on occasion to claim to be from the BBC rather than the federal government.[100]

Critics of the representations of Africans by the unit began voicing their views in public. In 1954 an African member of the federal parliament complained that the films

> are not able to depict the modern life of the African. When they want to depict African life, they show the worst that is in it and they do not show that the African is advancing. They only pick out the Africans in the kraals in very poor huts. While showing that background of the African life, at the same time they could depict the present life to show we have at least advanced, although there is backwardness. There is also advance in the buildings and in the appearance and dress of the people and so on. It is only the old type of African that is shown and there is nothing to show the world that we are advancing.[101]

Similar criticisms appeared in the African newspapers. In the *Bantu Mirror*, a 1959 article entitled "Better African Films Being Shown in England" reported: "Mr. Shamuyarira, a member of the African Newspapers in Salisbury . . . had been asked whether it was true that the people in England were only shown those pictures that showed the African wearing skin and living under primitive conditions. Mr. Shamuyarira said the films of Africans dressed in loincloth were on their way out."[102] Despite Shamuyarira's assurances, fears still persisted. In 1962 a mobile cinema officer filming among the Batonka people of northern Southern Rhodesia reported, "I must record the fact that the Batonka are becoming tired of being regarded as something primitive and unique and are resenting being constantly called upon to perform for numerous visiting teams."[103]

Besides the fear of being represented as "primitive," some Africans were also afraid that appearing in a CAFU film would implicate them as supporters of the colonial regime. A CAFU cameraman's attempts to film an African car owners' club in Bulawayo were thwarted when the members boycotted his film. "The reason given for the boycott," he reported, "was that the cameraman was going to take pictures of the car owners and publish them, saying that these people were in favor of federation, evidently. This is not the first time [cameramen] have been boycotted due to Africans being intimidated by members of African Political Parties."[104] Africans in Goromonzi district voiced a similar concern in September 1963: "People at Goromonzi complain about a film shot at their school which has a S[outhern] R[hodesia] theme song. They want the withdrawal of the film. . . . 'When this film is shown we will be identified with it. We will, of course be intimidated and attacked. Many of us live in Salisbury and Bulawayo. We will be labelled [stooges].'"[105]

Colonial officials could more or less ignore the relatively subtle complaints heard in the first decade of the unit's history, but by the final years of the federation the objections were widespread and loudly voiced. Yet the federal government and the territorial governments that made up the federation never wavered in their faith in film's ability to shape African opinion. Indeed, at the moment when resistance to the films was most apparent, the Southern Rhodesian government began drafting a plan to dramatically increase the number of mobile cinema units operated in the colony.

Why did the films-for-Africans programs continue with little apparent regard for audience reactions? The answer lies in the fact that, throughout the unit's history, white observers—including Izod and his colleagues—doggedly continued to believe that the films were exerting a profound and positive influence on their audiences. In an interview conducted in 1988, Izod indicated that he still believed the films held an almost hypnotic power over audiences: "I think in all we felt that the films were accepted so completely as fact that this placed a very considerable onus on us not to betray the sort of trust that was being put in us by the audiences . . . we always had great regard to the truth in what we were doing and what we were saying, because we were dealing with people who were believing us."[106]

Izod's confidence in CAFU was shared by his superiors in the federal government. Harry Franklin, the information officer in Northern Rhodesia, wrote an article in 1952 extolling the success of the unit's productions: "Since it was set up only five years ago the Central African Film Unit has shown that the film is probably the most valuable means of spreading information amongst the backward peoples of Central Africa."[107] Izod also had the full confidence of the federal prime minister, Godfrey Huggins, who was an enthusiastic supporter of the unit's work.[108]

District commissioners throughout the federation had shared the enthusiasm of the men at the top. The head of the Native Affairs Department in Salisbury in 1952 passed along to the CAFU producer the following comments from one DC: "You might like to know what the man in the District feels about it. My own impression is that it is one of the best things to come out of the Native Dept. for a long time. I thought the films shown were excellent particularly the local propaganda films. Not only were they . . . very well produced but the stories were simple and true to life and easy for the kraal native to understand. . . . At present the film is worth all the radio and newspapers put together as far as propaganda for the kraal munt is concerned and after all he represents the bulk of the population and it is the only means we have of reaching him."[109]

Officials of the Southern Rhodesian Native Affairs Department expressed similar views. The assistant native commissioner for the Nkai district reported in 1954, "The Natives show a keen interest in films. For propaganda purposes, this is the most attractive medium. They learn more readily through the medium of the eye and are prepared to pay to see films."[110] The director of native agriculture had expressed a similar view in 1952: "There is an intense desire for knowledge and they will absorb any number of films on craftwork, agriculture, hygiene, community improvement and what is more they will pay to see them. Let us have as many educational films as possible—films made for them—and let us include some in every programme."[111] Three years later, the district commissioner for Melsetter said of the CAFU films: "The value of this form of entertainment cannot be too highly stressed."[112] Similarly glowing reports were filed by district commissioners throughout the region.[113]

One of the few whites to criticize CAFU's work during the 1950s was a South African director named Blake Darymple, who in 1953 submitted a proposal to the federal government to produce several films for Africans. Darymple's company, Films of Africa, produced short comedies as advertising vehicles for such companies as Lever Brothers and the Nyasaland Tea Board. In a letter to the prime minister of the federation, Darymple outlined a scathing critique of the unit's work:

> An instructional film need not be dull, but can be amusing and exciting. It is really a matter of experience and film-craft, and this company is of the opinion that with all the facilities and advantages behind it, the official film unit has failed to make the most of the available material, and is forging ahead without waiting to see the results of the experiments which it must doubtlessly [carry] out. Much of this may well be due to lack of training or experience in the unit itself, but the whole attitude of approach to the African film must be taken seriously and cease to become a plaything. . . . Films for Africans must not be simply something knocked up in a couple of days by an amateur cameraman with no past experience of his trade.[114]

Darymple concluded with an indictment of CAFU's conservatism: "At the moment all the official films are made down to the African; designed to what is considered by Europeans to be suitable for him and no effort is made to raise the standard of the films."

Darymple had a strong incentive to disparage CAFU's work: he was essentially trying to put them out of business. And his own views were hardly more enlightened. In his letter, he repeats such bromides as "the African's outlook is not unlike that of a child" and "the African believes what he sees on the screen." And his own films for Africans used simple techniques, contained comically deceptive advertising promises, and are astonishing in their racist imagery.[115] However, his critique hits on several of the more apparent problems with the unit—such as the amateurish and lifeless quality of its films—that virtually no other whites were willing to recognize.

Nothing came of Darymple's proposal. In a letter to the Federal Internal Services' Department, CAFU supporter Vernon Brelsford dismissed this "gratuitous attack on the Central

African Film Unit" and lashed out at Darymple's slapstick comedies, which he insisted "disrupt the instructional atmosphere of many film shows."[116]

The government's enthusiasm for films continued despite the growing resistance of audiences. In 1958, as opposition to the Native Land Husbandry Act grew, members of Southern Rhodesia's legislative assembly called for greater involvement by the mobile cinemas in the campaign to convince Africans of the necessity for the legislation.[117] In his annual report for 1961, the chief information officer for the Southern Rhodesian Information Service, reporting that half a million Africans had seen CAFU films during the past year, commented, "This is certainly proof of the increased interest shown in the Cinema Units and the increased impact that this form of propaganda is having on the public."[118] When the Southern Rhodesian government began planning its strategy to combat African nationalism in 1961, one of its first acts was to increase the mobile cinema fleet.[119] In the eyes of government officials, this investment was soon paying dividends, and by March 1962 the SRIS newsletter reported that the growing popularity of cinema shows "is certainly proof of the increased interest shown in the cinema units and the increased impact that this form of propaganda is having on the public."[120]

This enthusiasm for CAFU's work was shared by the colonial press in the region. The *Rhodesia Herald* routinely published articles and editorials effusively praising the unit's work. In Northern Rhodesia, the *Northern News* expressed confidence that the unit's films "would make Africans more useful."[121] In South Africa, the film historian Thelma Gutsche wrote enthusiastically about CAFU in the *Cape Times.* Gutsche found a preview of CAFU films "very remarkable." She reported that *The Two Farmers* "exploited the Mr. Right and Mr.

Wrong theme in an entirely different manner, both characters proving neither priggish nor incredible." She had high praise for two other films as well: "'Mujenji Builds a Bridge' was constructed round the principle of 'self-help' and was a straightforward documentary with an epic tinge shot over a long period. 'The Wives of Nendi' proved outstanding. Its effect in consequence is amazingly powerful." She congratulated CAFU for "embodying an adult approach to the problem, not of propaganda but of straightforward documentation of information."[122] The journal *East Africa and Rhodesia* published a similarly laudatory appraisal of the productions.[123] In a review of *Joe Hlahla*, a profile of an African businessman, the journal reported, "There could be no better corrective than this picture to the idea, sedulously circulated by bitter critics of Britain's civilizing mission in Africa, that Africans are not given fair scope in Southern Rhodesia." This film convinced the author that "the cinema has become a potent force in the spread of ideas, and one need in Central Africa and in East Africa likewise, will be the allocation of further funds for the making and distribution of the right kind of films."[124]

The colonial state's faith in the influence of state-sponsored film on Africans changed little during the unit's fifteen-year history. White officials were confident in 1948 that films made especially for African consumption would transform African beliefs and practices. Fifteen years later, they remained unshaken in this conviction despite the mounting evidence suggesting that their films infuriated more people than they inspired. When the federation of the Rhodesias and Nyasaland disbanded in 1963, the settler state of Rhodesia inherited the federal government's film-production and distribution equipment. It also retained a faith in the influence of film over Africans that would have disastrous consequences for the future of the settler regime.

# Chapter 5

# Postwar Censorship in the
Rhodesian Federation, 1948–1963

Southern Rhodesia's ambitious plans for moviemaking were put on hold for the duration of World War II. The war also dampened discussion of film censorship, a topic of much public debate during the 1920s and 1930s. But in the immediate postwar period, public interest in moviemaking and cinema censorship reemerged. The war having brought important social and economic changes to the colony, a new situation shaped the revived discussion. A booming wartime economy had drawn African laborers to the cities of Southern Rhodesia in unprecedented numbers, and from this growing community emerged a tiny class of educated, urban Africans. They congregated in Salisbury and Bulawayo, where movie houses catering to African audiences blossomed, exposing the new audiences to Hollywood serials and features. The postwar changes also included the arrival of thousands of new European immigrants.

The new public discussion about Africans, cinema, and censorship focused on the growing popularity of cinema in the cities and the potential influence Hollywood films would have on Africans. Over more than a decade, this debate played out in the press and in colonial legislatures. It drew the attention of prominent anthropologists working in the Rhodesias and culminated in a series of federal hearings on film censorship in 1960. This debate reveals that white views regarding the "special needs" of African cinema audiences had changed little since the 1920s. Many of the colonial interests that had supported the campaign to tighten film censorship before the war, including missionaries, women's groups, and members of the colonial civil service, found themselves agitating for the same cause after 1945. Their arguments reflected the same prejudices that had sustained censorship legislation decades earlier, indicating that much of white society retained its preconceptions regarding African film literacy. In this new campaign, opinion makers focused their attention on the perceived pernicious influence of American westerns in the region, the imitative tendencies of African audiences, and the link between crime and cinema.

That these attitudes had changed little is hardly surprising. What is remarkable, however, is the degree to which, in the postwar era, these views were seconded by educated Africans, whose opinions, published in the African press and recorded in government hearings, served to reinforce settler demands for race-based censorship. When calls were heard in the late 1950s to make censorship color blind, it was representatives of the elite African communities in Northern and Southern Rhodesia who challenged the initiative. They warned that public safety was jeopardized by the corrosive influence of the commercial cinema on uneducated Africans. In taking this position, these elite Africans were attempting to draw a distinction between themselves and what they called the "unemerged" community. By doing so, they helped to sustain a myth of African credulity that would retain currency in Southern Rhodesia until 1980.

White fears of African movie audiences during the 1920s had led, in 1932, to the passage of stringent censorship legislation in Southern Rhodesia.[1] Shortly after the war's end, the Southern Rhodesian government returned its attention to the subject of censorship. In 1948, the government amended the Entertainments' Control and Censorship Act by delegating the censorship of all "films intended for exhibition to natives"[2] to a board in Bulawayo. This body consisted of nominees of the missionary-run African Social Welfare Society. It placed films in four categories: "for general showing; for showing to adults over the age of 19; for showing to persons over the age of 12 and for showing to Africans."[3] However, the Southern Rhodesian minister for internal affairs feared that the board would find it impossible to censor inappropriate films while still approving enough movies to meet the demands of African consumers. He identified in particular the problem posed to the censors by American westerns. "Cowboy films with scenes of violence and lawlessness may not be considered suitable," he observed, but he conceded that since "there is little else to choose from," westerns would continue to be permitted. "It would be unreasonable to restrict showings to educational films and cartoons." Ultimately, he could only diagnose the problem, observing, "No solution to the difficulty has yet been found and the matter is still under consideration."[4] Because they constituted the largest part of the movie diet available to Africans, cowboy films remained the one film genre that escaped the net of censorship.

The internal-affairs minister singled out American westerns for mention because they were virtually the only kinds of commercial films shown to Africans in Southern Rhodesia. During the 1930s and 1940s, westerns had become the favorite films of audiences throughout Southern Africa. The South African film historian Thelma Gutsche described the popularity of these films in Southern African mining compounds in her history of South African Cinema, published in 1948: "More than twenty years of film exhibitions on the mine circuit failed to cure the 'boys' of their affection for a mythical cowboy called 'Jack' (no matter what his real name) and his always-successful deeds of daring."[5]

However, in the postwar era this enthusiasm for "Jack" began to unnerve many colonial observers. After 1948, the new censorship board took a decidedly dim view of westerns and committed itself to insulating Africans from their influence. The board was run by the Federation of African Welfare Societies, a Bulawayo-based mission organization headed by the Reverend Percy Ibbotson.[6] The February 1948 issue of Ibbotson's *African Welfare Bulletin* foreshadowed their decision to take aggressive action: "Many films shown to Africans in the Colony were unsuitable, and also there was some evidence that the influence was detrimental to African life, particularly in the case of juveniles."[7] The board wielded its new authority enthusiastically, and four years later Ibbotson's paper could report that, thanks to its efforts, many Africans had been kept from seeing undesirable films.[8] However, Ibbotson realized, as had the internal-affairs minister, that tightening censorship would not sit well with consumers: "The difficulty has been the lack of suitable films for showing to Africans. Representations have been made to the authorities concerned regarding the need for a supply of a better type of film and suggestions have been made as to the kind of film favoured by the Censor board."[9] Despite the paucity of "acceptable" films, the board remained committed to protecting Africans from dangerous screen images, announcing in 1952 that they would employ even tougher standards in their future efforts.[10] The *African Weekly* reported:

> The Censor Board has decided to exercise greater strictness in the censoring of films. Unsuitable films will be banned and in future the following scenes will be removed from films: "Women of

easy virtue: prolonged embraces: Scantily dressed women: Scenes where masks are worn: Manhandling of women: Capture and tying up of members of one racial group by those of another race: Deliberate murder at close quarters, such as shooting in the back or strangling. . . . All scenes of obvious crimes readily understood by Africans: All scenes where attacks are made or threats made with the aid of a knife."[11]

Clearly, the main target of the new measures was the cowboy film (drawing-room comedies do not feature the "tying up of members of one racial group by those of another"). The Southern Rhodesian secretary for internal affairs, in his annual report in the same year, supported the board's call for more stringent censorship:

> Existing arrangements for the censorship of films shown to native audiences are not fully effective, due to the fact that the *Entertainment Control and Censorship Act* provides for the censorship of films for public exhibitions only. It is hoped to extend the scope of censorship during the forthcoming year to cover films which are shown privately as well as publicly, and this will have the effect of preventing the showing of unsuitable films to natives on farms and mines and in industries.[12]

The most popular films being shown at these venues were grade-B Hollywood westerns, which were the least expensive commercial films available. Colonial officials in the region were well aware of the appeal of cowboy films for Africans. In 1950, Harry Franklin, information officer for the Northern Rhodesian government, published an article in the Colonial Office's house magazine *Colonial Cinema* examining the phenomenon.[13] Franklin began with a description of young movie crowds in Northern Rhodesia:

> Groups of African boys, dressed in home-made paper "chaps" and cowboy hats, carrying crudely carved wooden pistols, can be seen

running around the native quarters of any industrial town in Northern Rhodesia shouting "Jeke, Jeke, come on Jeke." Jeke is the nearest African approach to the pronunciation of Jack, and it is a tribute to Jack Holt that every cowboy on the screen is, to the African, Jack. Sometimes the boys affect a more sinister appearance, with a black mask over the eyes and a wooden dagger in the belt.

Franklin was not sure of the extent to which these films left an impression on their audiences: "Are these effects, and others which are not so apparent, harmful? That is not an easy question to answer." He went on to state that he doubted the films had a profound or negative impact on their audiences, though he concluded:

> The best evidence of the effect of "Western," or "Gangster" films comes from responsible Africans themselves. The general tenor of complaints made in African Urban Councils and similar bodies is something like this: "We ourselves understand that these films are only plays and that Europeans do not really behave in the way the pictures show. Some of us like them, others do not bother to attend them because they get no benefit from them and their desire is to be educated by films.

Franklin's ambivalence toward westerns was in all likelihood influenced by the fact that his department regularly showed westerns in their mobile cinema vans to encourage Africans to watch educational films. While Franklin viewed westerns as relatively harmless, other members of his office were not so sure. A 1952 issue of the *African Listener*, a magazine published in Northern Rhodesia in conjunction with the Lusaka station's service for Africans, featured an article entitled "Films for Africans: Cowboy Films" that intimated that Africans had the wrong idea about westerns. The article warned, "These films cause a great deal of misunderstanding among many Africans in Central Africa . . . There is plenty of action in Cowboy films, and that is why so many people like them, but do remember when you see one of these films next at a cinema, that you are seeing a picture of the sort of life that some people led in the very remote parts of America 100 years ago."[14] In general, the authorities in Northern and Southern Rhodesia recognized the appeal of the cowboy film, and in contrast to the mission-run board of censors, viewed them as a fairly anodyne entertainment.

The African Welfare Society's plea for films that were appropriate for African audiences was in the process of being answered by CAFU. Because the unit charged admission to its shows, they immediately found themselves competing with westerns for the pennies of African film audiences.

When cameramen for the film unit began traversing the colonies, they queried white officials regarding the cinematic tastes of their target audience. Their informants all reported that Africans enjoyed cowboy films, though they offered an interesting variety of opinions as to why this was the case. One of the first explanations came from J. D. Reinhalt-Jones, an adviser on native affairs to the American Corporation of South Africa. In a 1948 memo he stated:

> Wild West films are the most popular. . . . We have no evidence on the effects of films upon the native mine workers. My own impression is that they invariably side with the hero and the forces of law and order in Wild West films . . . but there is no information as to the ultimate effect. The sharp increase in the use of firearms and knives in criminal assaults on the Reef suggests the possibility of the influence of the cinema. . . . It must be remembered that (1) the mine workers need the release which action films give and that secondary exposure of the kind provided by action films helps to satisfy the "drives and needs."[15]

Reinhalt-Jones's analysis deserves our attention because it raises several key concerns shared by many colonial observers.

First of all, he touches on two paradoxical beliefs regarding westerns: that they may cause crime, and that they discourage antisocial behavior by providing a release valve for African aggression. His response also hints at a fear of what Manthia Diawara calls "resistant spectatorship"[16]—the idea that Africans were subverting the intended order of the films and cheering for the Native American "Indians" against the cowboys.

This does not appear to have been a widespread concern among whites during the colonial period. Indeed, Reinhalt-Jones is himself dismissive of such considerations. However, since the 1960s, belief in such a resistant reading of American westerns has become a part of popular culture. One of the more recent representations of this story appears in the BBC series *Heat of the Sun* (1999), which features scenes of Kenyans watching an old western, and rooting against the cowboys. In South Africa, the writer Bloke Modisane remembered siding with Native Americans against the cowboys in his youth: "I definitely identified with the weak . . . people who were unarmed. Not because they were particularly black, or because I knew anything about Indian versus white culture, but simply because they were unarmed and I saw the same forces against them, the same technologies ranged against them, that seemed to be in play in my own particular situation."[17] Though not implausible, such stories read like inversions of the tropes of African credulity that circulated during the colonial era. They function as a postcolonial antidote to the tales of the giant mosquito and serve as a satisfying testimony to the subversive agency of the colonized.

However, it seems unlikely that such readings were common or widespread, given the narrative power of even the poorest quality Hollywood films. A recent study conducted by an American sociologist underscores this point. In an experiment undertaken on a Native American reservation, sociologist JoEllen Shiveley showed the John Wayne film *The Searchers* to "Indian and Anglo" audiences separately. She found that the Native Americans and the Anglos both sided with John Wayne, despite his character's hatred for the "Indians" in the film. When queried about these views, the Native Americans explained that they had not been provided with enough information about the "Indians" to form any kind of emotional attachment.[18] Also, it is worth noting that it was the character of the cowboy, not the Indian, that was emulated in dress and style in African townships throughout Southern and Central Africa.

If it was not to cheer for the cowboy's victims, why did Africans enjoy the genre? Another Southern Rhodesian official provided Alan Izod with another view:

> The operator of the mobile cinema told me that people like cowboy films best (nothing new about that). . . . The cowboy films certainly cause uproarious amusement at times and the reason is easy to find. For long periods the audience sits completely bemused by pictures without action but with continuous meaningless (to it) dialogue: then violent action occurs, and the audience is released from its embarrassment and its bemusement and reacts almost hysterically. The fact is that the people are so glad to have something they *can* understand that they make a lot of noise when it happens.[19]

Whatever the merits of this analysis, it reflects a popular assumption that westerns were not "understood" in the intended manner.

In 1951, Stephen Peet passed along a similar assessment of the genre's popularity to Izod. While visiting the Northern Rhodesian Copperbelt, Peet met with several representatives of the mines' social welfare unit to discuss African film tastes. The welfare officers complained to Peet about the unsuitability of the films being shown on the mining circuits. The projectionist at the mine gave Peet his impressions of his audience's tastes. Peet summarized their conversation in a letter: "Cowboy films only popular ones, but are not understood. Audience does not follow story, but stops the conversations, etc., to watch screen whenever fights, chases etc. crop up. Films judged by amount of general mayhem in story."[20] He also informed Peet that the mine no longer showed films supplied by the Northern Rhodesian Information Department because "they were so dull that hardly anyone came."[21] Implicitly bemoaning the influence of the more popular action-oriented genres, he went on to tell Peet that "the audiences are so acclimated to background sound & music that they demand it, even though they don't appreciate it. Silent films are a failure for this reason."[22]

However, not all of the CAFU staff felt threatened by westerns. As mentioned above, Louis Nell, who served as a director-cameraman with the unit during the 1940s and 1950s, integrated elements of westerns into his own films. He also had little doubt that the audiences were following the action: "Westerns—always excellent examples of visual story-telling—were easy enough for the audience to follow and always had a rowdy, enthusiastic reaction."[23]

The CAFU staff was faced with the thorny problem that much of their target audience apparently preferred American westerns over CAFU's locally produced films. However, instead of following Nell's example and adjusting the technique, other CAFU filmmakers simply resorted to wishing away the obvious appeal that westerns held for their audiences. Izod and his fellows were aided in this by their African assistants, who frequently assured their superiors that CAFU films were making headway with audiences. For example, in October 1951 the Salisbury-based *African Weekly* quoted Gideon

Naminesu, an employee of CAFU, as saying that when the CAFU productions had been shown together with cowboy films, the audience had enjoyed them equally.[24] Nahminesu also submitted a stream of reports to his superiors at CAFU chronicling the victory of their films over the westerns. Audiences told him, he insisted in an early report, that they "did not like cow-boy films, because they didn't learn anything from them."[25] In the same report, he related approvingly the opinion of a European projectionist who believed that Africans liked "African films" more than cowboy films. His reasoning was based on his observation that CAFU films were watched in dead silence, unlike westerns, "which proved to him that Africans don't understand these other films."[26] Whether Naminesu was attempting to flatter his superiors or put his fellow Africans in a favorable light, his would not be the last African voice to reassure the government of the popularity of its films.

Despite such reports, CAFU was clearly fighting an uphill battle with urban audiences. Their films could not help but look amateurish in comparison to what was available at the commercial theaters. Though they did offer Africans an opportunity to see Africans on the screen, the unflattering depiction of urban dwellers, and educational lessons aimed at rural farmers, seem to have left urban audiences cold. Ultimately, CAFU had to concede that its films could never supplant the western in the hearts of a certain section of their audience. In recognition of this fact, the Southern Rhodesian Information Service quit charging Africans to see the films in the late 1950s. Later, Izod acknowledged that while CAFU films were popular with rural people, "more sophisticated town audiences used to a diet of 'cowboy' films, would have nothing to do with them."[27]

Others keenly interested in the impact of the CAFU films

on Africans were the colony's district commissioners. As seen above, many DCs were enthusiastic supporters of CAFU, and their annual reports, which frequently considered the influence of film in their districts, reflect a guarded hope that CAFU could displace westerns as the preferred fare of African audiences. We know from a report from 1960 by the Northern Rhodesian Native Affairs Department that the government relied on westerns as a draw to gather audiences for state-sponsored productions: "African audiences at present appear to prefer films depicting African life, wild game, comics, and the wild west (blood and thunder) but these shows provide an opportunity to squeeze in educational and propaganda films and the Information Department is fully alive to this."[28] A district commissioner in Southern Rhodesia expressed cautious optimism that CAFU might make headway against the westerns: "The Unit's productions as a whole, comprising as they do, instruction and entertainment, have proved immensely popular even with the Africans who are habituated to the cinema and might be expected to find them tame by comparison with the thrills of the Wild West."[29]

The Southern Rhodesian Department of Native Affairs report for 1951 said of the CAFU productions: "These films have been immensely popular and effective wherever they have been shown, and have in many cases superseded in popularity the ubiquitous "cowboy" films which formed the bulk of the cinema fare available to African audiences." The report went on to explain the appeal: "The reason, of course, is not only that the characters of the films are Africans but that the whole background and environment are known and understood by African audiences."[30]

However, an official in the Southern Rhodesian mining district of Shabani reported in the same year, "Where the Africans have seen the Cowboy type of picture they are less inclined to walk a distance to see a bioscope than those who have never seen a show."[31] Reports from European officials, though generally representing the response to CAFU films as enthusiastic, carry an undertone of anxiety. The district commissioner for Salisbury lamented in 1951:

> The cinema goes on dishing up "Westerns." Although the African cinema fan is greatly attracted by this type of film, they also enjoy films produced by the Central African Film Unit. This is sufficient proof that the better class of pictures would have as many patrons as the other kind, and it is not too late to wean them from the "Cowboy" stuff now, it might be difficult to do so in five years' time; it might even be difficult next year.

Contributing to the anxiety of these officials was the fear that cowboy films were inspiring crime in urban areas. Such concerns were felt widely throughout Southern Africa in the decade following World War II. As rapid urbanization drew rural Africans to the cities of South Africa, Southern Rhodesia, and Northern Rhodesia, ensuing fears of African criminality became linked to the rising popularity of the cinema. A 1950 report, prepared for the South African parliament, reflected these concerns in the Union:

> The location youths, who on account of their education are not subject to any social bonds, lead idle lives. No wonder that most of them drift into gangs with an anti-social tendency . . . films of cowboys, crooks and pickpockets shown to native children in locations and which are decried by native leaders as the children try to imitate what they see, and di[s]regarding the crime does not pay angle, are initiated into crime at an early age.[32]

Again we see the fear of a "resistant reading" of westerns. The report went on to argue, "The mental capacity of the audience is unable to grasp the fact that the hero succeeds in the end, and that crime does not pay. The mental process is circumscribed by the vision of pockets being picked, persons shot and killed by means of firearms and crooks living in luxury on ill-gotten gains."[33]

Highlights of the report were published in the *Bulawayo Chronicle* in 1950 as a cautionary example for the white community in Southern Rhodesia. The African paper the *Bantu Mirror* reported two years later that the cinema continued to encourage crime in South Africa. "The cinema has a disastrous effect on Africans and is one of the big factors contributing to the crime among their race. This is the opinion of Mr. John Coleman, who addressed a meeting of the Durban Parliament." The article quoted Coleman as attributing to films "a decade long 10% per annum increase in crime . . . African audiences in cinemas are gripped in the thrill of pursuit and capture, assault and battery, bullseye marksmen, rough speech and Bacchanalian brawls. These things they witnessed are carried back into everyday life. . . . The cinema in its general conception is disturbing in Mr. Coleman's opinion, and depicts hate, admiration and a host of other emotions." The paper quoted Coleman as saying, "'Zoot-suits' 'tsotsi trousers' and gaily coloured ties are ample evidence of the Africans tendency to imitate and serve only to remind us that the acts of violence and hatred depicted on the screen must also be digested and discussed by African audiences."[34]

Officials in Southern Rhodesia feared similar problems in their own colony. In 1953, the report of the Southern Rhodesian Department of Native Affairs noted that "complaints continue to be heard about the poor type of films available for many of these shows from commercial sources; the majority of the complaints emanate from responsible Africans, who allege that a regular diet of 'westerns' and 'cowboy' films which usually form the main feature of programmes issued by commercial companies has a harmful effect on African youth."[35]

The "responsible Africans" mentioned in the minister's report became increasingly active in the campaign against cowboy movies during the early 1950s. Colonial authorities who favored stricter film censorship increasingly found support for their cause among middle-class Africans. There developed in the colony's urban areas a tiny minority of educated Africans, many of them teachers, journalists, or officials in the lower ranks of the civil service. They communicated through social organizations and in the pages of African newspapers such as the *Bantu Mirror* and the *African Weekly.*

For these self-styled "emerged" Africans, the issue of censorship had several dimensions. One was the fear that constant exposure to the dregs of Hollywood would undermine the values of African youth. This anxiety was articulated frequently in the region's African newspapers. For example, a lengthy editorial in the Salisbury-based *African Weekly* titled "Influence of the Cinema Criticised" declared: "Bioscope has had bad influence on young boys. Many young boys who see films of gangsters are inclined to put what they see on the screen into practice. A case happened at Gatooma some time ago when young boys who were using some of the methods they had seen used by cow boys on the screen were arrested after they had laid waste to many business premises." The editorial concluded with a demand for more stringent censorship: "In this regard it would be to the interests of both the Africans and Europeans if Cow-Boy films were banned from being screened to African audiences."[36] This remained a theme of the editorial and letters pages of the African newspapers in the colony throughout the decade. In general, the subject of the influence of westerns on Africans became a favorite topic of discussion among educated Africans in the cities and was taken up several times by African representatives in the federal parliament.[37]

Many educated Africans also took issue with censorship laws that made no distinction between themselves and what they referred to as the "unemerged"—the vast majority of illiterate Africans. Thus their criticisms of cowboy films were in part inspired by their desire to distinguish their tastes and status from those of their uneducated compatriots. Many African elites adopted the rather contradictory position of demanding the same access to motion pictures enjoyed by whites in the colony, while supporting the censorship of American westerns for "unemerged" audiences.

Some educated Africans took steps to spare their community from the scourge of the westerns by attempting to improve audience taste. In this they received support from white social welfare officers, who were anxious to substitute more edifying programs for the cowboy films. In the late 1950s, elites in Bulawayo began to organize regular screenings of the few films from genres other than that of the western that had escaped the censors' net. They established a new theater in the McDonald Hall, and there, charging higher admission prices, showed a variety of comedies and dramas. It was an alternative to the other main theater in the city, Stanley Square, which continued to show cowboy films. A letter in the *Bantu Mirror* voiced the demand of educated theatergoers for the new venue: "The films that are shown at the Stanley Square . . . have no moral at all, and above that they have little to thrill. It must be remembered that the days are now gone when Africans were interested in the Western type of film. The cowboy with all that goes with it has very little to attract the African of today. That type of film may interest young boys but not grownups."[38] The argument of this correspondent reflected the views of many educated Africans heard on the subject. They insisted that Africans were no longer enamored of westerns and would seize any opportunity to see films of a higher quality.

166 / *Flickering Shadows*

The experiment was not a success, however; audiences proved resistant to "improvement." Few moviegoers turned out to see the more "sophisticated" programs, and many of those who did attend often went in the expectation of seeing a cowboy film. A newspaper describing a showing of the film *That Midnight Kiss*, reported, "There was among them a section still clamouring for the blood racing, action and thrill packed 'Westerns.' This section defied all decorum and shouted without restraint, with some of its members taking the role of unauthorized commentators on a picture they hardly followed."[39] For the most part, African audiences showed their continued affection for the western by voting with their feet; however, some spoke out against these attempts to dictate their tastes. In the *African Weekly*, a letter writer said, "I do not see any harm done by Western films shown to young boys and girls. . . . Cowboy films are the best on the screen because they teach people to be very careful if they go to big cities. Moreover, young boys and girls when they see cowboys being arrested and imprisoned, it teaches them that crime does not pay." Such films were preferable to films made by CAFU, the correspondent stated: "Africans are not interested in seeing local films because they do not want to see their own people dressed in a primitive way."[40]

Another writer criticized the new programs being presented at MacDonald Hall: "The cry is now fairly general from Africans who say that they are deliberately being robbed of their hard-earned money by being given pictures at MacDonald Hall which are very very poor."[41] An editor at the *African Weekly* noted, "The J. M. MacDonald Guild has been featuring a number of films in the MacDonald Hall for the high class Africans and the response has not been good."[42] Another correspondent summarized the frustrations of cowboy-movie fans: "What is your idea of giving us bad and useless pictures.

. . . You must give the public what it wants and not what you think it wants."[43] In a similar vein, a writer to the *African Weekly* complained that the new film shows, "with the exception of a few, were not appreciated by the African cinema going public. Too 'sophisticated' or too dramatic."[44] Yet another correspondent reported that he had complained to an official at the African administration headquarters that "the pictures we get there are very very poor and that we pay too much money for them. He told me that the films are chosen by some Africans there at Macdonald Hall. . . . He told me that Cow Boy pictures are not allowed (This . . . I cannot understand whether it is a law of the choosers of these pictures or of us who pay high money for good pictures)."

The efforts to "improve" cinema programs often turned violent. In a letter to the *African Weekly* quoted above, the letter writer noted that a recent showing had resulted in "a big row because of the poor film shown."[45] Another correspondent confirmed that a recent screening at the hall had ended in a near-riot.[46] This kind of violence was apparently not unusual at Harare cinema shows. A story in the *African Daily News* preceding a 1957 showing of *Abbot and Costello Meet Doctor Jekyll and Mr. Hyde* assured readers that "to maintain order in the hall, African constables from Harare will be in attendance."[47]

Similar efforts to "improve" the quality of film shows also failed in Northern Rhodesia. Testifying before a federal committee on film censorship in 1959, A. J. Harris, a social welfare officer employed by the Northern Rhodesian government, explained: "The outspoken desire of many Africans for good-quality films was not borne out in practice. . . . The cinema was packed with Africans when a 'Western' was showing but there was only a sparse African attendance for a better-type of film."[48]

During the postwar era, the racial censorship laws of the colony became increasingly irritating to educated Africans. In the campaign to have the laws changed, advocates focused on the western movie as a symbol of what was wrong with the current censorship laws. The *African Weekly* reported in October 1959 that

> romantic films, drama, and even War Action Pictures are marked: "Not For Natives and children 4–16." One theater goer who lived in South Africa said "Most of the films that are exclusively for Europeans in this country are shown to Africans in S. Africa." ... African Social and Cultural Club of Salisbury can't see these films [even though they are] cultured, well behaved people. . . . The fact that films which feature both Europeans and Negroes are not shown to the Africans here, shows that the idea of partnership is not catching at all.[49]

One reader of the *African Weekly* found the censorship guideline "Not for showing to Natives or children under 16" "not only puzzling [but] a pinprick to the African. A man of 60 is, in this sense, a child."[50]

Although the African papers would eventually call for race-blind censorship, they moved to this position slowly. Their arguments remained influenced by their fear of the effect of cowboy films on young African men and their desire to differentiate between their educated readership and the illiterate urbanites whose unruly behavior threatened public order. As the editors of the *African Daily News* stated in late 1959, "One wonders whether the law barring Africans to certain films is not out-of-date in respect to many Africans who have been overseas and many places in Africa where they have seen the films in question." Thus the *African Daily News* was not prepared to suggest that all Africans were equally prepared for the removal of censorship: "Admittedly there are many Africans who are not mentally qualified to see many of the films in question, and yet there are many Africans more qualified than quite a good number of European teenagers (who are allowed to see the films and who must rightly feel insulted to be classified together with European children of 12 years of age)." The paper suggested a new qualification for African audiences: "We suggest all those who are over 21 years of age; all those who are married, whether they are 21 or not; all those who are voters, who are holders of Identity Cards; and all those who have distinguished themselves in public service, should be entitled to see any film available." However, the paper appreciated that such a radical revision to the colony's censorship laws might not come quickly. "The African must realise that these things cannot change over-night. Customs and conventional practices die hard, and usually one by one, gradually."[51] The *African Weekly* published an almost simultaneous call for a reassessment of the colony's censorship laws:

> Nobody can question or doubt the necessity for censoring films. The right films seen by the wrong people can cause harm. By the "wrong people" we refer to young people, with little experience of life, who can hardly draw a line between what is wrong and what is right, young people who live in a cloud-cukoo land, and can be mentally perverted by seeing films above their range of understanding. . . . In our humble opinion, there is no reason why all the films, with special exceptions, should not be opened to all exclusive African Clubs and to all the adult Africans who are either educated, married, or 21 years of age. . . . We do not know how much powers the Film Censor Board have got, but we feel that they should recommend more films for Africans than the paltry 20 per cent and better films than the cowboy films which have become the lot of the Africans and are of very little interest, if any, to the majority of them.[52]

The call for an end to racial censorship echoed throughout the urban African community in Southern Rhodesia, and in

October 1959 both the Central African Party and the Salisbury African and Social Club called for a reform of the colony's censorship laws.[53] As public opinion moved against race-based censorship, the *African Weekly* was able to report the following month that the Southern Rhodesian Censorship Board had decided to loosen up its criteria for censoring films.[54]

As the emerged Africans were redefining themselves as "adults" vis-à-vis the European community, the latter found it increasingly difficult to continue treating them like children. The public debate about cowboy films was drawing attention to the censorship policies of Southern Rhodesia, which were beginning to look increasingly obsolete to observers from outside of the colony. During the late 1940s and early 1950s, two anthropologists had become interested in the cinema's influence on Africans in the region. In 1952, B. W. Gussman completed a study of the African population in Bulawayo. In his wide-ranging *African Life in an Urban Area: A Study of the African Population of Bulawayo*, Gussman included a brief description of the role of the cinema in the lives of his subjects.[55] To Gussman, the question of the cinema's effect on Africans amounted to the question of the influence of cowboy movies on Africans, since the program was "almost invariably a Western."[56]

Gussman's assessment of the situation of the African cinema in the colony was similar to that of the secretary of internal affairs and the Reverend Ibbotson's. He wrote:

> All films shown to Africans in Bulawayo are censored by a special Board who have the right to ban a film or to cut it where and how they think fit. This board takes its duties seriously and a high proportion of films offered by the exhibitors are refused altogether. Many of those that are passed are so cut as to destroy their continuity completely. . . . Partly as a result of the Census Board's activities and also because of the lack of any large-scale

film production for African audiences, there is a severe shortage of suitable films. Many films are, therefore, often repeated.

Gussman concluded that cowboy films had no noticeable negative influence on their audiences.

> There is no evidence that the Western films or those shewing Europeans in an undesireable light do the harm to the African audiences that some critics would suggest. If the African wishes to see the European in a bad light he does not have to go to the pictures. Instances are frequent on every hand and such instances, because they are real and in a context that an African can readily understand, can and do affect African morals in their wider sense, very much more than any celluloid fiction can ever achieve. Intensive research elsewhere on the effects that the gangster type stories have upon children has shewn that the actual harm such films do is limited. It is probable that research of the same kind would shew how little Africans are adversely affected by films now considered to be unsuitable for them.[57]

Hortense Powdermaker, an American anthropologist investigating the same question in Northern Rhodesia, reached similar conclusions. In her study of the colony's mining towns, *Copper Town: Changing Africa*, Powdermaker devoted a great deal of attention to the influence of the cinema in African societies. She attended weekly cinema shows held at the mine compounds and made a systematic study of audience responses to the films. She reported that film shows had been a fixture of the mine's welfare program since 1928 and that most programs featured "a cowboy film (old and grade B)."[58] She found that cowboy films were preferred by audiences over the other shorts and features screened at the theaters. This predilection varied little between men and women; she did, however, note a slight preference for cowboy films by educated audience members, compared with the uneducated. Powdermaker also observed that Africans experienced these films quite differently from how they experienced other ones. "During this film men, women, and children rose to their feet in excitement, bending forward and flexing their muscles with each blow the cowboys gave. The shouting could be heard several miles away."[59]

Powdermaker was noting an aspect of the cinema experience in Africa that perplexed many white observers—the often raucous activity of the audience. Such behavior seemed to confirm that films were incomprehensible to African audiences. However, this reading of audience behavior, like much of what Europeans concluded about the cinema in Africa, needs to be understood in a broader context. Historians of the cinema have shown that early audiences initially were much more boisterous and active than their modern counterparts. Early films had no narrative and thus did not require the close attention of those desiring to follow a plot. Even when narrative cinema came into fashion, films still frequently elicited interaction from the audiences, with patrons speaking to the screen. Often these early narrative films would feature a live commentator (similar to that used by CAFU), who would interact with the audience and keep them abreast of the action. Seen in this light, and taking into consideration that the heavily edited westerns they saw probably had lost much of their narrative power all together, the active nature of African cinema audiences appears less remarkable. Colonial authorities, however, chose to interpret this participation as evidence of misperception.

In addition to remarking on the audience's performance, Powdermaker also considered the question of why Africans had become so enthusiastic about the cowboy genre. Unlike many of the opinions cited above, which assumed that the films were poorly understood, or were misunderstood, Powdermaker, argued that audience identification with the cowboy was logical and appropriate:[60] "Through the cowboy films, pent up aggressions were played out in a group; and the African became free and triumphant. The individual's enjoyment was heightened by the sharing of his feeling with a thousand or more others, who were shouting their reactions. There was much greater excitement and overt emotional participation at the movies than at the Sunday afternoon tribal dances."[61] In Powdermaker's view, this identification was particularly strong with cowboy films because of the life-experience of the mining audiences.

> It was not difficult to understand why the Africans strongly identified with the cowboy hero, Jack, or Jake as he was also called. In the past, intertribal wars were part of African life, and success in fighting was one way of gaining prestige. But we do not have to look only to the past. Probably even more important is the manner in which identification with the cowboy hero fits into the present power relationship between European and Africans. It was obvious that Africans resented their low political, economic, and social status in relationship to Europeans and that there was relatively little outlet for the consequent aggressive feelings. The hard-fighting cowboy, moving freely on his horse in wide-open spaces, surmounting all obstacles and always winning, is indeed an attractive hero for a people intensely fearful of losing some of their wide-open spaces to Europeans, who until recently held all the power. The cowboy is white, but not European. Through identification with him, the African can fantasy unconsciously or consciously, being as white as the dominant group and always winning over them. The film likewise gave him an opportunity to learn the popular skill of boxing, which he could then use immediately in intra-African fighting.[62]

Though Powdermaker was against film censorship, she clearly believed that the westerns posed a threat to the colonial order. The public discussion of film censorship was taken up in the federal parliament in 1954, when an African member from Northern Rhodesia first raised the question. He complained to the assembly that his colony's information services continued to show westerns from their mobile cinema vans:

> Cowboy films . . . are a damage to the country. They show fighting and stealing. At the present stage we are not concerned with stealing and fighting, but we are concerned with proper character training. The young people today should not be trained how to fight and steal, but we have to train them how to behave and grow into better citizens of Central Africa. Therefore, the moment you take this Department over please avoid bringing in these cowboy films which are a nuisance and a damage to the country. They only encourage young men how to fight and steal and misbehave. I think the Government must be very careful about these films.[63]

The home-affairs minister commented, "I entirely agree with his views about the possible effects of films of the nature he described."[64] Mike Hove, a former journalist for the *African Weekly* and now a member for Southern Rhodesia, offered:

> Now, the only films the Africans can see are the cowboy pictures. Can the Federal Government not do something to try to encourage a better type of film service . . . very good films have come to this country and the African has not been able to see them. . . . I think if we subsidised a good film like "Cry the Beloved Country" it would be money spent better than money spent by people going to see things which result in a moral erosion of the youths who go to these performances.[65]

However the minister ended the debate by insisting that this was a territorial, not a federal, subject. Hove raised the question again three years later, saying, "The African likes to see pictures. He likes to visit picture-houses very much indeed, but the type of films showing to the Africans has no reference whatsoever to what is happening within his own country and the result is from what is depicted more is known from the Western type of film than of what is happening in the country in which he lives."[66] A white member concurred: "I would like to agree most heartily with the hon. member Mr. Hove when he says the film programmes shown to Africans are trash."[67]

The federal parliament returned to the question of film censorship two years later when members introduced new legislation to censor the new drive-in movies becoming popular in Southern Rhodesia. The bill, which proposed permitting access to theaters on a nonracial basis, drew criticism from several members. One representative argued that he objected "not because I am against having non-racial censorship, but because I think before any decision is taken on that matter there should be adequate ventilation of the matter."[68] Another representative was blunter: "I believe it is unwise at the present stage of our racial affairs in this country to show certain types of exhibitions to the African population, and I make no bones about it."[69] However, a Southern Rhodesia representative urged the parliament to take into account the aspirations of the "emergent" Africans in the region:

> In regard to the African, I am afraid I must look at the problem in the light of that a half per cent, or perhaps one per cent, of the African people have emerged. They want such entertainment. They want stimulating and thoughtful films and matters of this nature, and it is extremely difficult if you are going to band them together with all the less emergent Africans and perhaps prohibit them from attending such films, simply because they are Africans without regard to the standard of advancement they have achieved.

This member's solution was to have new, nonracial censorship in tandem with higher fees for Africans for certain films. She argued that "most of the Africans who are sufficiently emerged will probably be able to afford a greater entrance fee to see such a film than the population to whom damage might be done."[70] She explained that this was already being tried in Bulawayo—with some success, in her opinion: "In the McDonald Hall they charge a greater fee and show a more stimulating film than they do in the Stanley Hall where they tend to show the sort of film which one would show possibly to a ten-year old child, cowboy films and things of that nature. I think possibly on those lines something constructive might be worked out to meet the objections by the non-racial section."

Several dissenting voices were raised in parliament, and not all expressed concern regarding the crime and violence of cowboy films. A Dr. Burrows is quoted as saying (with an interjection from Mrs. Watson, the member whose opinion has just been quoted):

> Let us say quite frankly that we are worried about matters sexual—[Mrs. Watson: And violence]—We must consider the African's attitude to these things. Let me tell the House that sociological studies show that the African outlook on these matters is entirely different to that of the European. I can assure this House that the African has no Freudian guilt. He looks at sexual matters in an entirely open fashion. It would be very little stimulation to him to see these adulterous contacts and things of that sort, because to him that is no crime.[71]

The debate ended with a plea from the federal justice minister to end racial censorship in the federation: "There is no doubt at all that there are many Africans at present who are prevented solely on that racial ground from seeing many films which they would wish to see and which would have no harmful effect on them any more than on any other members of any other race. . . . It is considered now that censorship on a racial basis should in fact be done away with."[72] However, he saw certain dangers in removing all racially based censorship: "On the other hand, it is considered equally imperative that there should be some distinction drawn between those who are considered educated and culturally developed and those who are less educated or uneducated and less culturally developed." He offered what was becoming a familiar recommendation:

> A practical solution would be to deal with it on an economic basis and to channel films for censorship to theatres normally patronized by what one might call the more developed sections of the community, and those places which are usually attended by the less developed sections. Thus, censorship would be directed to the two main groups of cinema audiences, the educated and culturally developed and the uneducated and less culturally developed.

The minister ended by expressing his hope that the bill would "remove most of the objections which now attach to film censorship, whilst it will still provide the protection so necessary to the less advanced section of our community."[73]

The proposed revision led to the creation of a federal committee in 1951 charged with examining the feasibility of creating a common censorship policy for all three territories. As it stood, each of the three maintained separate policies. In Northern Rhodesia, where multiracial cinemas were becoming commonplace, censorship was perceived to be much more lax than that in Southern Rhodesia (multiracial cinemas remained rare in the south). The committee was made up of representatives from the federal government and all three of the territorial governments. Among the federal representatives was Alan Izod, head of the Central African Film Unit. The committee heard testimony from government officials, theater owners, social welfare officers, and a variety of urban and rural Africans. The committee addressed two questions: what did African audiences make of so-called cowboy films? and should censorship in the federation be based on nonracial principles?

The witnesses were nearly unanimous in warning the committee of the influence of cowboy films on "unsophisticated" Africans, but on the question of racially based film censorship they expressed more varied opinions. White officials from the Southern and Northern Rhodesian governments in general supported the case for utilizing race as a criterion in censoring motion pictures. For example, K. D. Leaver, the chief information officer for the Southern Rhodesian Department of Native Affairs, emphasized the danger of showing certain kinds of films to Africans.[74] Leaver, according to the hearing transcript, "instanced an occasion when a film showing people struggling to board a bus caused an uproar in a certain rural audience. His Department, which had exhibited the film, was accused of introducing the South African 'tsotsi' spirit to the area. Likewise, it was out of the question to exhibit films depicting violence (including 'Westerns') in the rural areas." Not all white officials were as adamant about censorship, however. Leaver's superior in the department, R. Howman, told the panel:

> There should be no racial discrimination in the censorship of films. Whilst there was no evidence to prove that Africans were irritated by the present system of censorship, they would undoubtedly become more so as the tide of nationalism grew. Furthermore, Africans were growing tired of continually seeing the "Western" type of film which was served up to them. If censorship was conducted on a non-racial basis, a far greater variety of films would be made available to them.

Questioned as to the effect of films on the African mind, Howman said that there was no yardstick with which to judge African reactions to films. No such study had been made and one could only guess at the effect of a particular film on an African audience. It could be said, however, that no violent incident concerning Africans had been traced directly to the showing of a film depicting violence. Further, an African audience would be unlikely to learn anything from sex films that they did not know already. An official of the Southern Rhodesian Native Education Department had reached a similar conclusion:

> Mr. Murray said that no study had ever been undertaken to determine the effect of films on the African mentality and one could only guess at the effect. A Commission which sat in the United Kingdom some years ago exploded a popular-held theory and concluded that films were in no way responsible for juvenile delinquency. Until a serious study was therefore made, it was impossible to ascertain with any degree of confidence the influence of films on the African population.

Murray went on to say that "all Africans are in favor of nonracial censorship," but a case had to be made for differentiating between "emergent and the uneducated, unsophisticated mass of the population." When pressed for a distinction between the two groups, Murray said that "economics and education are [the] hall-marks of an emergent African."

Few colonial officials shared Murray's views. A Southern Rhodesian police officer gave what to the committee may have been a more worrying account of the influence of films on Africans. Lt. Col. B. J. Price, of the Southern Rhodesia CID, testified that films posed a danger if shown to *any* members of the African community. Of educated Africans, clamoring for an end to racially based censorship, he said: "This type of African could be regarded as a leader amongst his people. To allow him to see all films passed for European exhibition could well be dangerous, especially if he were to discuss some of them with his uneducated 'followers.'" The followers should likewise remain protected from the cinema: "The unsophisticated African undoubtedly thought that films were some sort of magic. Because of this he should only be shown films passed for general release."

Several representatives from white civic organizations

echoed the officer's views. Two women from the Salisbury Business and Professional Women's Club, Mrs. D. P. Cooper and Miss E. Wilkin, told the committee that nonracial censorship was impracticable because "some 'Westerns' tended to excite them too much." Other female witnesses aired similar views. Mrs. Hickman and Mrs. Jarvis of the National Council of Women of Southern Rhodesia testified that censorship should be nonracial but said that they recognized "it might still be necessary to exercise some form of control over the films seen by the unsophisticated mass of the African population." Similarly, Mrs. Greatrex and Mrs. Berry of the Federation of Women's Institutes of Southern Rhodesia, an organization that had been instrumental in drafting censorship legislation during the 1930s, stated:

> Many of the films produced nowadays, especially in Hollywood, were of a very low moral standard and, to an African audience, would show up the European in a very bad light. . . . Even if censorship standards were raised there would still be many films which should not be seen by the unsophisticated, uneducated Africans who attend cinemas in the African townships, municipal locations and mine compounds etc. What would be considered "art" by Europeans would not be appreciated as such by this class of African and would possibly be completely misinterpreted.

Several representatives of the clergy offered qualified opposition to racially based censorship. Father Swift, of the Saint Peter's Mission in Harari, said he believed that cowboy films were not misunderstood by African audiences. He testified: "Western films not harmful, children knew hero was good guy. . . . The children did not attempt to emulate what they saw on the screen and the prevalence of crime and violence in African townships was not attributable to films." However, he still believed that for moral reasons it was "too early" to censor films on a nonracial basis. He was particularly concerned with nudity in films: "Undressing scenes in films . . . were far more dangerous and evoked bad comments from African audiences who were by nature very emotional. African moral standards were very different from European standards and, in African eyes, such scenes were repugnant." The priest, however, was the first of many witnesses to hit on an important problem in drawing a distinction between "sophisticated" and "unsophisticated," between urban and rural, and between "emerged" and "unemerged": "Although Africans in the rural areas generally wanted educational films and those in the towns something entertaining, with the constant movement of Africans from the rural to the urban areas and vice versa there was not a great deal of difference in sophistication between the country and the town." This "drift" between rural and urban areas—which had been perplexing authorities in Southern Rhodesia since the early 1930s and served as the subject of several CAFU films—was erasing the distinctions between these two worlds. The Right Reverend O. F. Green Wilkinson, the Anglican bishop of Northern Rhodesia, told the committee that, despite his general support for nonracial censorship, there was

> a case for exercising discrimination in regard to the films seen by Africans in municipal locations, African townships and mine compounds, etc. Only films passed for general consumption should be shown at cinemas in these areas. Africans who attended such cinemas would easily be encouraged to violence and immorality if all types of films were released for exhibition to them. . . . On the question of the general effect of films on the African population, the Bishop said that films, being visual, had a greater effect than books on the same theme. A very violent or immoral film would be likely to lead an African audience to violence or immorality.

Father K. Flynn, representing the Roman Catholic archbishop of Lusaka, offered a similar view: "The majority of

Africans, with their primitive ideas of morality, needed far greater protection than did Europeans, with their 'civilised' standards." He stated that while it was safe to permit educated Africans to view certain films,

> it was essential to apply separate standards to the rest of the African population. Certain everyday European conventions, such as the kiss, were completely foreign to primitive African society and when depicted on the screen were considered to be grave moral offences. If shown in large numbers to unsophisticated African audiences, films depicting such conventions would have a cumulatively harmful effect, and would lead in time to a general debasement of African moral standards.

—a view that is in stark contrast to the opinion, cited earlier, that Africans had nothing to learn from Europeans about sex.

Among the opponents of continued racial censorship principles were several theater owners. V. D. Mistry, the proprietor of a multiracial theater in Lusaka, told the committee that he had worked at a similar theater in Kenya, where nonracial censorship had caused no problems. "If anything," he said, "the European 'cowboy-type' of viewer was the worst behaved in the audience." P. J. Lashbrook, manager of the Vista Cinema in Broken Hill, Northern Rhodesia, similarly testified that he had worked at a multiracial cinema, in Uganda, and had had no problems in ten years there. However, he also told the committee that "the 'Western' type of film had the most appeal" for Africans and that "cinema had done a great deal of harm to children. Juvenile delinquency was due in a large measure to the cinema. The cinema had a cumulative effect over a period of time and the change in children's behavior over the years (e.g. the present-day lack of respect for parents) could be traced to films."

A. J. Harris, a senior welfare officer from Lusaka, testified, conversely, that his office had never perceived a link between film shows and violence. He said of films: "They were not the cause of any crime or violence. . . . Africans realised that films were 'plays' and, although African reaction to some film scenes was rather different to European reaction, Africans were seemingly no more influenced by films than were Europeans."[75] Harris also gave testimony that was consistent with the results of the failed experiment of the McDonald Hall in Bulawayo, where the screening of "better" films resulted in sparse attendance or outraged customers.

The views of educated Africans were well represented at the hearings. Several journalists from the African press testified that racial censorship was necessary because of the intellectual divide separating the "emerged" from the "unemerged" African communities. Nathan Shamuyarira, a reporter for African Newspapers, Ltd., was recorded as saying that "'Westerns' . . . although they had an immense appeal for the unsophisticated mass of the African population . . . were of no value to their viewers and, in fact, had a very harmful effect on them."[76] E. V. Bwanausi, another reporter for African Newspapers, Ltd., while insisting that she was a supporter of nonracial censorship, actually put forward a strong case for censoring films to all elements of African society:

> Non-racial censorship will make better films available to African audiences, many of whom have written her letters complaining about "Westerns" shown to kids. . . . Violence had followed the showing of films depicting violence and some of the crime which took place in African townships undoubtedly resulted from the showing of these films. The mass of Africans considered that films depicted real life and there was no harm in emulating what they saw on the screen.

However, despite this view, Bwanausi said she was a proponent of race-blind censorship. She "stressed that it was a source of irritation and frustration to the educated, advanced

Africans that they were unable to see all films considered suitable for adult European audiences. There was no reason why this class of African should not see such films and the only way to remove the source of frustration was to make film censorship completely multi-racial."

The managing director of African Newspapers, Ltd., C. A. G. Paver, testified similarly that "besides being irritated by the present racial approach to film censorship, Africans complained of the shocking type of film (e.g., 'Westerns' and films depicting violence) being shown to them. To meet these complaints it would be necessary to conduct film censorship on a non-racial basis, thereby releasing a greater variety of films for African audiences." Like Bwanausi, he went on to warn that films posed a danger: "Mr. Paver said that the gangster and cowboy type of film did untold harm to African audiences. Some of the crime and hooliganism committed in such places as Harari was undoubtedly motivated by such films." However, even with nonracial censorship, there was a need for a certain amount of discrimination on the African side. The uneducated, unsophisticated mass of the African population should not be allowed to see all films available to the educated, responsible type of African, and Paver said he felt that the only method of discrimination that would prove acceptable to Africans would be one based on an admission charge. Paver concluded with a succinct statement of the prevailing view of most "emerged" Africans: "If censorship were put on a nonracial basis, educated, responsible Africans would themselves wish for some form of discrimination to be adopted with regard to their own people."[77]

The committee interviewed many other middle-class Africans, most from within the colonial establishment, who claimed to be against racial censorship in principle, while harboring reservations regarding the cinema's possible influence on their less-educated countrymen. A typical statement was made by J. Savanhu, the federation's parliamentary secretary for race affairs: "Educated Africans should be allowed to see the same films as Europeans, but the unsophisticated African should not be shown any of these films which were of doubtful moral character or depicted crime."[78]

Another government employee, George Saza, identified in the transcripts simply as an "African Civil Servant," argued that "educated Africans should be permitted to see European films. With the present racial discrimination in film censorship, Africans felt that they were credited with having the same mentality as European children." Like many other witnesses, however, he balked at the prospect of abandoning the current censorship guidelines: "The time was not yet ripe for the uneducated, unsophisticated mass of the African population to see all types of films. Certain films would undoubtedly have a bad effect on this section of the population. . . . Censorship should be based on education, not race."[79]

Two teachers at Munali African Secondary School in Northern Rhodesia, Mr. and Mrs. M. Kaunda, offered similar views: "Asked if Africans had no interest in 'better type of film,' Mr. K said 'most Africans had been brought up on "Westerns" and had not had the opportunity of seeing the better type of film. Consequently, being unaccustomed to them, they were unable to follow them.'" The Kaundas said that until Africans were exposed to different films, they could not learn to appreciate them. However, Mr. Kaunda said "it might not be wise to release all types of films to all sections of the African population at this early stage in their development. The emergent African should be allowed to see all films but the unsophisticated element of the population, which still believed that films portrayed 'real' life, should only be shown the better type of film in moderation."

Although a parade of educated Africans testified that despite their objection to racially based censorship they thought the authorities had some responsibility to protect unsophisticated Africans from the potentially dangerous influence of motion pictures, there was a dissenting African voice. It came from a rural community in Northern Rhodesia. Chief Mpanza, asked to describe the influence of motion pictures in his area, offered views that were very much at odds with the testimony of educated urban Africans. Mpanza declared, "Speaking as a chief of 16,000 people in a rural area . . . there would be no harmful result in releasing all films for exhibition to all sections of the African population." The chief reported that the people of his region saw mostly westerns, "and rural Africans were frustrated at the sameness in their film diet." While he believed that "Romance" films might be bad for young girls, he believed that this was not a sound reason to censor them. He also had no fear of films depicting violence; he was confident that they "would not be harmful to the rural Africans."

At the end of the proceedings, the committee announced its conclusions. Despite the views of Chief Mpanza, the final report said that the committee was "particularly impressed by the unanimity of evidence from African witnesses rather than European regarding the need to protect the uneducated, unsophisticated Africans from the impact of films that for them were unsuitable and disturbing."[80] The committee summed up their findings by citing two principles: (1) The need for censorship on a nonracial basis; (2) The need to discover means by which without introducing a racial principle into censorship, something could be done to protect the rural or unsophisticated audience from the effects of unsuitable or harmful films.

The committee's report remained a secret until 1961. By the time it was released, the future of white rule in the region

was clearly in jeopardy, and within two years the three territories would go their separate ways. The debate on censorship
abruptly evaporated when Northern Rhodesia and Nyasaland
achieved independence and Southern Rhodesia came under the
influence of the repressive Rhodesian Front regime.

The federal censorship hearings culminated a decade of
public discussion of African movie tastes. As this debate
raged, African audiences continued to frequent cowboy pictures, resisting all efforts to manipulate their tastes. Tellingly,
the western remains popular in the region today. Urban entrepreneurs still make a living renting old cowboy films and
showing them on 16-mm projectors in remote areas. Neither
colonial officials nor educated Africans have been able to wean
African audiences away from these films. The fact that they
believed they could, however, is remarkable. Their attempts to
transform African cinema habits were rooted in the belief,
held by African and settler elites alike, that the tastes of the
cinemagoing public could be guided from above. It shocked
both educated Africans and colonial officials when this proved
not to be the case.

# Chapter 6

## The Rhodesian Front Era, 1962–1980

The Central African Federation ended in 1963. The handwriting on the wall had been clear since the late 1950s. In the words of one historian, by 1958 Africans had become "pathologically opposed to the whole system" of colonial rule.[1] Resistance to the federation became so intense in Nyasaland that in 1959 the government declared a state of emergency. In 1962, the federal constitution was changed to permit Nyasaland to secede from the union, and Northern Rhodesia was granted the same right the following year. When the people of Nyasaland and Northern Rhodesia were given the opportunity to vote on the future of the federation, they chose overwhelmingly for independence.

With the end of federation, CAFU lost the financial support of the British government. The Rhodesian government chose to disband the unit rather than continue to fund it alone. Some of the members of the unit, including Alan Izod, found work with the Rhodesian Information Services.[2] However, the government of Rhodesia could not absorb all of the dozens of directors, technicians, and writers. Some found employment in the fledgling commercial motion-picture industry in the colony. Many sought work in Zambia (as Northern Rhodesia now came to be known), South Africa, and the United Kingdom. Others remained in Rhodesia and embarked on careers in other industries. The government sold the unit's valuable film laboratory, one of the most sophisticated facilities of its kind in Africa, to Dragon Films, a privately owned local company. The sale embroiled the young government in its first scandal. Critics claimed that the equipment had been sold for well below its market value. The transaction was allowed to go through, however.[3]

The abrupt dissolution of CAFU has led historians to identify significant discontinuities between film policy in the colony during the federal period and that during the subsequent era of Rhodesian Front rule. Two authors who have studied filming under the Rhodesian Front have treated the state's approach to the medium and to its audiences as if it started from scratch in 1963.[4] Certainly, the sudden liquidation of the unit and its production equipment encourages such a conclusion. However, the demise of CAFU did not entail a dramatic end for the colonial film project in Rhodesia. Within a few years of the end of the Central African Federation, a new film unit staffed by many former CAFU members was back in the business of making motion pictures for Africans.[5]

Films for Africans continued in Rhodesia until Zimbabwe achieved independence in 1980. Under the Rhodesian Front, the white settler regime that held power from 1962 to 1980, more Africans saw government films than ever before. There were, it is true, some minor discontinuities with the federal era over this seventeen-year period: since the unit did not have to prepare films for the peoples of Nyasaland and Northern Rhodesia, and since most Africans in Rhodesia spoke either Sindebele or Chishona, the government began producing sound films with narration in both languages as well as in English; and there were brief periods during which film production was halted and reevaluated. Nevertheless, for nearly two decades film was the Rhodesian Front's most important medium for informing and influencing Africans.

The Rhodesian government's assumptions about African audiences altered little after 1963. After the dissolution of the federation and the independence of Malawi (former Nyasaland) and Zambia, the Rhodesian Front faced increasingly aggressive opposition from Africans, and the decade following the end of federation saw a rise of African national consciousness in the colony. To combat the rising nationalism, the government produced films intended to educate Africans about political issues. The productions portrayed aspiring African politicians negatively and extolled the benefits of colonial rule. These productions came to be defined as "propaganda" both by their producers and their audiences. However, colonial officials expressed little concern at their growing reliance on motion-picture "propaganda." They retained their faith in the power of film to shape and guide the aspirations and values of what they took to be a credulous audience. Such a policy would have disastrous consequences for the future of the regime.

With the demise in 1963 of the Federal Information Service, the department that oversaw CAFU, the Rhodesian Information Service (RIS) became the sole government department responsible for communicating with Africans. RIS was a division of the colony's Native Affairs Department, and the new Rhodesian government considered its function a major priority. Many politicians and colonial officials believed that the federal government had failed in large part because it had not provided enough information to the peoples of Nyasaland and Zambia.[6] In the years following the end of federation, members of the colony's legislative assembly emphasized the importance of film to the RIS task on several occasions. As one member told the assembly in early 1964:

> We have here in . . . Southern Rhodesia a very large section of the community that we have got to tell what Government is about, what decisions Government is taking on its behalf and how Government expects it to respond to these decisions. We have got to tell these people these things regularly, but it is particularly difficult to tell them these things through the medium of the written word because of the high degree of illiteracy. . . . I regret greatly the disappearance of the Central African Film Unit [and believe] more emphasis should be given to film units perhaps than to other media in Southern Rhodesia.[7]

Later in the same year, critics in the legislative assembly took RIS to task for failing to counter the propaganda of African nationalist groups. In September 1964, the minister for information, P. K. Van Der Byl, admitted, "We are not getting the message across to our African population in the rural areas. I am well aware of that, and it is a matter of considerable disappointment to me." Van Der Byl attributed this failing in large part to the limitations of the films-for-Africans program: "The only really effective method that we have as a Government is, of course, the dissemination of films. . . . There is no doubt in my mind at all that as a conception and as an idea it is absolutely first class and has, in the past, played a considerable role and will in the future play an even greater role in the affairs of dissemination information to our rural population." Under Van Der Byl, the Rhodesian Front government would remain committed to using film to shape African opinion.

Van Der Byl recognized that the mobile cinemas had not been welcomed in many communities for several years. However, he did not blame the films the unit showed. Like many colonial officials before him, Van Der Byl assumed that audience hostility to

192 / *Flickering Shadows*

state-produced movies must have some ulterior source. He concluded, therefore, that the Africans manning the cinema units were the cause of the trouble at film shows. In September 1964 he told the legislative assembly, "Reports have been coming in to me from members of the Police Force and from officials of the Ministry of Internal Affairs, and District Commissioners, and others, that at the moment these mobile cinema units are doing more harm than good. . . . They have been infiltrated by the African nationalist propaganda and African nationalist intimidation." He claimed that "a strong determined subversive element has made itself manifest in the personnel of these units." Van Der Byl then promised, "Those who have become indoctrinated will, of course, have either to go through some period of rehabilitation or have to be got rid of."[8] Shortly thereafter, virtually all members of the mobile cinema corps were sacked.[9]

With a new staff manning the mobile cinemas, the RIS embarked on a modest program of film production. Despite the liquidation of CAFU and its assets, RIS still had filmmaking facilities: the Southern Rhodesian government had maintained a small film unit throughout the federal period. In the late 1940s, before CAFU began operations, this unit had produced a few films for African audiences,[10] and in the early 1960s SRIS had produced a few films in Chishona and Sindebele.[11] These films were simple newsreels and documentaries designed to inform audiences about the changing political situation in the colony. When federation ended, RIS expanded its film production in order to partially compensate for the loss of the CAFU films.

However, the ministry found that sacking the staff had little effect on audience reaction. Opposition to the cinema shows, which had grown in the final days of federation and had become more pronounced in the postfederal era,[12] was in part the result of emerging nationalist sentiment in the colony, which was undoubtedly accentuated by the independence of Malawi and Zambia. But it was also exacerbated by the heavy-handedness of some of the new RIS films.

Many of the ministry's films dealt with subjects familiar to Southern Rhodesian audiences—hygiene, animal husbandry, agriculture, and so on. Since RIS had only a small staff, the production of these films was subcontracted to Eagle Films, a Salisbury-based company that employed several former CAFU directors.[13] Typical productions included *More Cash for Cattle*, a Chishona-language film encouraging the dipping of livestock, and *The Good Life*, a simple drama that extolled the benefits of wage-labor employment at the Shabani mine. These didactic films utilized the simplified techniques and didactic approach that had been the hallmark of CAFU and other colonial film units, and in content, too, they were similar to the CAFU films—all of which is unsurprising since former CAFU directors produced most of them. New newsreels and documentaries, too, were similar.

The same assumptions about African audiences that had governed colonial filmmaking since the late 1920s continued to guide Rhodesian directors. For example, Anker Atkinson, who had joined RIS after his long tenure with CAFU, later remembered that the filmmakers reckoned that their audiences had a twenty-to-thirty-minute attention span, beyond which they should not be taxed.[14] Atkinson and his department also assumed that audiences could not absorb a film's message on the first showing, believing that repeated viewings were required to plant the message.[15] Indeed, some RIS officials believed that government information would be communicated more effectively in slide shows because that medium provided much simpler images. In the opinion of one RIS official, "An illiterate audience needs roughly 30 seconds to absorb what has been said on the commentary and associate it with what they see on the screen."[16] Mobile cinema operator Lovermore Mahlahla, who showed these films throughout Southern Rhodesia, summed up the RIS attitude: "Producers regarded viewers as very low people."[17]

In much the same way that CAFU productions had aroused significant audience criticism, RIS films met with widespread dissatisfaction. A cinema officer working in Chipinga reported, "There was some criticism of the film 'Protect Your Cattle.' Handouts issued to people at Mt. Selinda were torn up."[18] In Nuanetsi, "People were resistant to agricultural films. Some people were shouting 'The Demonstrators are no longer wanted in the Reserves.'"[19] In Chinoy, the audience expressed skepticism toward a film encouraging Africans to put their money into savings banks: "One man commented on 'No Place to Hide It' as being 'treachery as government is looking for money to feed political restrictees.'"[20] The only films to receive positive reviews from audiences were those not produced by the government; thus, an operator in Marandellas reported that the film *Japan, 80 Million Mouths to Feed* "made the most impact" and was probably responsible for the widespread adoption of fertilizer in the region.[21]

Audiences reserved their strongest criticisms for the handful of films produced by RIS itself. These productions carried pointed messages regarding the political situation in the colony. In content, the films were similar to CAFU productions (such as *Free from Fear*) that had elicited violent reactions from audiences in the final days of federation. Not surprisingly, they inspired similar reactions. RIS prepared several films to be shown as part of a mobile cinema campaign launched in March 1964. This program consisted of a multimedia demonstration that included films, slides, and still pictures intended to encourage Africans in the colony to respect their chiefs and colonial rulers. According to the report of the minister of information, the program "consisted of films of the chiefs' 1964 overseas tour . . . slide shows were arranged of brutality in other African countries, where political excesses were not restrained by the normal processes of law and order."[22]

Two films were prepared to underscore these messages: *Freedom?* and *Chiefs' Tour.* The former, a documentary, is narrated by Ben Musoni, a cinema operator who had joined RIS as a young man in 1963. The film opens with Musoni sitting at a desk speaking to the camera. He was made up to look elderly: his hair was lightened and he wore glasses and a false beard.[23] The film, a montage of still black-and-white pictures, in its first half shows the rioting and civil unrest that accompanied the independence in the Belgian Congo in 1960. The sequence includes several gruesome close-ups of mutilated corpses. The second half of the film presents photographs of black and white members of the Rhodesian army and air force. Musoni's narration emphasizes the discipline and power of this force and dwells in particular on the sophisticated military technology, such as the tank and air corps, at the government's disposal.[24]

The approach to production in *Freedom?* reflects the continuation of the trend toward audience intimidation that had begun with CAFU productions like *Free from Fear* in the waning days of the federation. Abandoning the storytelling format of traditional colonial cinema, RIS replaced it with a documentary style that relied on graphic images intended to intimidate rather than educate. Such films would become a staple of Rhodesian Front propaganda during the 1970s. For *Chiefs' Tour,* RIS used a well-tried CAFU approach—the newsreel. *Chiefs' Tour* chronicles the travels of several prominent Rhodesian chiefs to Europe in 1964 and is similar in style to CAFU's *Rhodesian and Nyasaland News.* It depicts the

chiefs being greeted respectfully in several European countries. However, both of these new RIS productions became
lightning rods for dissent and violence among African audiences. In the case of *Chiefs' Tour* the sore nerve touched was
that chiefs were widely seen as collaborators with the state,
but it was *Freedom?* that particularly infuriated Africans. One
operator said of the film, "People said the government was intimidating them. People threatened to boycott such films."[25]
Another report stated, "*Freedom* brought many adverse comments. One man said 'This did not happen in Rhodesia. You
are employing clever tactics to do down the African cause of
freedom.'"[26]

Audiences watching *Freedom?* resented the denigration of
African leaders and the film's intimidating tone. Many of the
recorded comments suggest that Musoni was wise to disguise
himself: "At Penhalonga some said the commentator in Freedom should be killed if he is known."[27] At a nearby showing, a
cinema officer reported, "After the show many people demanded to know the man who speaks in the Freedom film. I
said I did not know his name. They threatened to beat me. At
this venue the adult males carried axes and said that killing
was a simple matter for them."[28]

*Chiefs' Tour* was similarly reviled, and one of the chiefs featured, Chief Chirau, became a reviled symbol of collaboration
for many Africans in Rhodesia over the next two decades. In
the Ngkai area, a cinema operator was told, "You are agents of
the Chiefs trying to step up the power of the chiefs by dis-
couraging Nationalist movements." At another performance, a
viewer complained, "Chiefs have sold the country. The information in the film is false. They have not the brains to understand
the things they were shown on tour were useless." After a later
showing, a spectator observed, "Look at them, old people deceived by sweets."[29] And in the Melsetter region, audiences

"said they did not want to see Chief's Tour but would like to see films of independent African states like Tanganyika and Kenya. They added it was time for majority rule in Rhodesia."[30]

Resistance to these films was not confined to verbal complaints. In many cases audiences threatened mobile cinema crews, vandalized their equipment, and obstructed their travel.[31] The hazards of these performances drove some crews to reroute their tours. As the cinema officer working in the Matombo region reported, "It was decided that the centres where politics are to the fore should not be included in future itineraries."[32] The protests had little impact on the Rhodesian authorities. The ministry declared the campaign a success, observing, "Reception was generally good, except in the areas where there was extremist political activity."[33]

In 1965, responsibility for the dissemination of information to Africans was taken out of the hands of the Native Affairs Department and transferred to the Internal Services Department (IS), part of the newly created Ministry for Information, Immigration, and Tourism. The new ministry decided to reduce reliance on mobile cinemas. The ministry report for 1965 said the new year would see "a change of emphasis from the visual to the written medium by the reduction of the number of mobile cinema units and by utilizing the medium of a newspaper, specially designed for Africans, which had been introduced by a private publishing company."[34]

However, the ministry continued to show the existing catalog of films despite reports that they were antagonizing Africans.[35] A study prepared in 1967 reflected both the optimism of the Internal Services Department and the smoldering resentment of the audiences. The author of the document was R. C. Haw, principal information officer for the Department of Internal Services. Haw had been in the audience at

CAFU's first film shows in 1948 and was an early supporter of their approach to African audiences. In his report, he cited comments that praised all of the films shown at recent cinema shows. Audiences viewing films on agriculture are quoted as saying, "This has been a thrilling film show" and "This is a school in itself." Similarly "Films on Chiefs" met widespread approval as well. Though the report does not consider reactions to *Freedom?* it does discuss audience reactions to a similar film, *The Sword* (described in the report as "a film on Rhodesia's Armed Forces").[36] According to Haw's report, the film was watched in almost complete silence by stunned audiences. As one cinema operator's report explained, "Rhodesian Army film really discouraged the people not to misbehave because they would get shot. Everyone kept very quiet when they saw people being shot, and this terrified the audience."[37]

The new ministry's change in policy may have resulted in part from a recognition that the RIS films had been provoking audiences. It was also apparent that replacing the entire mobile cinema corps had not solved this problem. However, once again colonial officials determined that the fault lay with the limitations of the audience. A memo circulated by an official of the Internal Services Department in 1967 reflects this view: "It has been known for some time that many film productions designed for African audiences were, in fact, not getting across, mainly because the story was too fast-moving and the techniques used tended to confuse."[38] This view was supported by the new mobile cinema operators, several of whom had informed their superiors in IS that the audiences were failing to understand their productions properly.[39] Musoni, the star of *Freedom?*, suggested that the department could end audience confusion if future films did not involve complicated plots and messages. As an alternative, he suggested that the colony's information officers be equipped with cameras and instructed to make films of local events. These would be shown only within communities where the actors and settings of the films were familiar. The IS adopted Musoni's suggestion in 1967. The filmmakers thereafter adopted the "home movie" approach, which they believed would make the films more comprehensible for audiences.

This new approach saw IS employees making simple films of rural audiences and then playing the films back to them. The idea was to draw audiences for the shows and then have colonial officers disseminate materials at the meetings. The new films proved extremely popular. By July 1967, IS reported that the new films were having a significant influence on audiences. As one IS official explained it, "Because of the local colour or 'home movie' content of the film, it was accepted as truth."[40] As the minister announced the following year in the legislative assembly, "I have heard of people walking 10, 15, 20 miles looking at the same film 19, 20, or 25 times because of the popularity of the films."[41] He conceded that this had not formerly been the case: "Almost three years ago all the cinema vans were removed from service because the films then being shown and the popularity of the scheme at that time indicated that the people did not want them. Now an entirely different picture arises. They are seeing films that interest them within a time that the film means something to them."

The switch to "home movies" after 1967 was part of IS's new media strategy. Film no longer played a central role in imparting information; rather, it became a source of entertainment that would draw audiences to the mobile cinema. There they would receive government information such as the *African Times*. As a part of this strategy, IS began making brief entertainment films to accompany the "home movie" shows. These included films of current events, sports, musical performances, and short comedies. As Van Der Byl explained it, "The mobile cinema units concentrate primarily on showing films of general interest and entertainment . . . [including] numbers of comedies . . . and films of the popular variety type as well as musicals."[42]

The most memorable films produced during these years were the *Tickey* series—slapstick comedies inspired by a character created by a settler from Que Que. Though no copies of these films are now available, they appear to have been similar to the Films of Africa *Pikki* series, which was popular during the 1950s, and the Roman Catholic Church's *Matamata and Pilipili* comedies that were popular in Congo. The *Tickey* films were popular with rural audiences and helped the mobile cinemas regain some of the status they had enjoyed in the earliest years of the federation.[43] In addition to the "home movies" and *Tickey* films, government cinema vans also carried newsreels and short films of sporting events.[44]

The new cinema program was accompanied by an expansion of the government's other media services. A key component was the *African Times*, a government newspaper for Africans that was distributed by the mobile cinemas. The mobile cinema shows became important locations for the distribution of this paper, cinema officers handing out the paper free of charge.[45] The *African Times* came to be widely criticized by educated Africans in the colony. African members of the legislative assembly called for the government to stop its publication. They repeatedly insisted that many Africans were intimidated into taking the paper and that most copies ended up being used for wrapping merchandise in rural stores. Despite their repeated protests, government ministers insisted that the paper was popular and influential. They continued to print it despite the opposition.

The government also expanded its radio services for

Africans. This was made a priority when the nations on Rhodesia's borders began broadcasting propaganda that was hostile to the settler regime. Initially, IS produced a program called *Padare* that was intended to keep Rhodesian Africans abreast of political developments in the colony. Again, the African members of the legislative assembly criticized the program, insisting that it was aggravating rather than reassuring audiences.[46] There is evidence to suggest that this program was widely disliked by African audiences. Once again, despite the objections of the audience, the members of IS and their employers in the Rhodesian legislative assembly refused to recognize the widespread unpopularity of its media.[47]

The Rhodesian government adopted its "bread and circuses" approach to film during the late 1960s in part as a cost-cutting measure. As a departmental memo explained, "The method of production of the new type of films is comparatively simple, quick, and cheap. This last is most important as in the past film production costs have been high."[48] The cut-the-costs decision was possible only because of a lull in nationalist activity in the colony. As political tension subsided in the wake of the collapse of the federation, the need to continue disparaging the nationalist cause on film diminished as well. This situation changed suddenly in 1972. During 1971, ZANLA (the Zimbabwe National Liberation Army) had been training in neighboring Mozambique. In the final months of 1972 they launched their first well-organized incursion into Rhodesia.[49] This was the beginning of the final phase of a guerrilla war that would end white rule in the colony.

Most government officials disparaged the efforts of the insurgents during this initial stage of the war. However, many expressed concern that too little was being done to discourage Africans from aiding the guerrillas, and some officials attributed this failure to the change in cinema policy. A memo

202 / Flickering Shadows

from the provincial commissioner in Mashonaland South from summer 1973 expresses this concern: "I have read through most of the June reports and quite frankly I am disappointed. Most of the films are of entertainment value only and have no lasting effect at all." He provided a list of films from the show—*Rufaro Stadium Opening, Tickey Takes a Ride, Marimba No. 1, Gatooma Cotton Pickers, See How It Is Made*—and lamented their apolitical nature: "I noticed very little propaganda and what is shown appears to lack a direct message." He believed such an approach was no longer justifiable in light of the changing political situation: "To win the 'hearts and minds' of the people we must utilise this very excellent medium to broadcast our own propaganda."

The commissioner went on to outline a series of points that should be made through film propaganda:

1. Show just how bad communism is—some viewers think [it's] good.
2. Acts of terrorism and what is being done by the terrorists.
3. Show life in other countries—and emphasis[e] how well off Rhodesians are.
4. Interviews with terrorists—get them to confess just what they intend doing.
5. Women's clubs—councils can provide funds.
6. Interviews with R.A.R. soldiers—why they're in the Army, what they're doing, conditions of service.
7. Effects of over population—methods of control.
8. Farming methods in other countries.

Finally, the provincial commissioner insisted that closer attention should be paid to the influence of films on viewers: "How many of the films impart the message they are supposed to convey. From some I see that each audience receives a different message. Somehow audience reaction must be better gauged."[50] Here again we see the constant fear of alternative, subversive, readings that plagued white Rhodesia for decades.

The guerrilla campaign grew steadily after 1972 as soldiers infiltrating into the colony from neighboring Zambia and Mozambique found support among the rural peasantry in the border regions. The growing threat encouraged a revision in film policy along the lines suggested by the commissioner. Despite the government's insistence that the insurgents posed no threat to public order, new plans were drawn up to double the number of cinema units by the end of 1972 and to expand the fleet by 50 percent the following year.[51] The new units would also have new films to show. The "home movies" would continue to provide entertainment and the *Tickey* films would likewise remain a fixture of the mobile cinema programs; however, they would become a draw for a series of government films that, in the event, would encourage an unprecedented degree of criticism and violence.

The new films focused on the strength of the Rhodesian army and its successful prosecution of the guerrilla war. They were remarkable for the brutality and violence they depicted. While earlier RIS productions (such as *Freedom?*) had shown photographs of dead and injured bodies, the new films staged combat scenes and often showed graphic images of slain guerrillas. The filmmakers employed a psuedodocumentary style that combined interviews with soldiers and newsreel footage with staged scenes of combat.

A film that typified the RIS new approach to audiences was *Vigil*, which was produced some time after 1972.[52] The film begins with scenes of a burning car in a Rhodesian city: a narrator declares, "While the people of Rhodesia go quietly about their business the pressures of the communist world against this little country grow stronger every day." Scenes of African guerrillas training follow, and the narrator explains, "Lured by promises of free education, unsuspecting Africans make their way to hostile camps behind the iron curtain." The recruits are next depicted being shown a map of Mozambique and Rhodesia by their officers as the voice-over confidently explains, "The only thing over looked by these instructors is that Rhodesia has an army." The rest of the film is a reenactment of a Rhodesian army raid on a guerrilla base, with emphasis on the advanced military technology available to the Rhodesian forces, particularly high explosives, helicopters, airplanes, and tanks. The guerrillas quickly retreat and surrender. Several are killed during the raid and the camera lingers on their dead bodies. One dead guerrilla is shown clutching a book by Chairman Mao to his chest. *Vigil* was one of several films on similar themes produced by the government after 1972; others included *Contact, Hurricane,* and *War on Terror.*

Resistance to these films was unprecedented. Mobile cinema operators who worked during the middle and late 1970s lived in constant fear of attack and reprisals for showing them. Rhodesian audiences objected in particular to the scenes of dead soldiers.[53] Mobile cinema operator Lawrence Moringay believed the films did nothing to persuade the audiences to oppose the guerrillas. "The people didn't want to see things like that—guerrillas being killed . . . they knew that the purpose of the war was that the Africans were in the majority, and they were going to govern the country one day, and the rest was propaganda."[54] In the border regions of the colony, which had the heaviest incidents of guerrilla infiltration, freedom fighters often attended the shows.[55] They made their preferences clear, and cinema officers would shelve the more inflammatory films and show *Tickey* instead.[56]

In addition to the anger of audiences there was also widespread skepticism about the government's version of the guerrilla war. According to mobile cinema operators, the films did not convince many people that the security forces were firmly in control. Part of the reason was that viewers had their own sources of information about the war. But equally important was audiences' clear recognition of the "staged" nature of the films.[57]

In the final years of Rhodesian Front rule, officials in the ministry began to suspect that some officers were fraternizing with the guerrillas. It was perhaps in response to this development that the government began producing films of such a violent and graphic nature that they did not trust the mobile cinema operators to carry them. Instead, in the regions most affected by the war the films were shown by cinema vans run by the Rhodesian army. These films and the documents about their production and distribution are among the mountains of materials destroyed by the archivists of the Rhodesian Front in the waning days of white rule. It seems apparent that the production of these films reflects the government's abandonment of the hope of persuading audiences, and the films appear to have constituted a final desperate attempt to intimidate Africans into obedience.[58]

White Rhodesia ended in 1980 as Robert Mugabe and his ZANU party swept the first democratic elections in the colony's history. Government films intended to discredit Mugabe had only increased his popularity, audiences apparently assuming that such a bitter enemy of the regime was worth supporting.[59] For many whites in the colony, Mugabe's victory was a tremendous shock. They had been led to believe that they were winning the war against his forces and that the average African voter would undoubtedly support the continuation of white rule.

In the end, it was the white settlers of Rhodesia who proved the most susceptible to the government's propaganda. The Rhodesian Front, like several colonial regimes before it, placed a significant degree of faith in the ability of motion pictures to influence Africans. They were among the last of the colonial regimes to realize that their confidence in the medium was misplaced.

The films-for-Africans program was based on the conviction that Africans were particularly vulnerable to motion-picture propaganda. The regime therefore continued to produce films emphasizing the power of the state and highlighting the good fortune of Rhodesia's Africans to be ruled by whites. What happened instead was that for seventeen years government cinema shows served as a constant reminder to audiences of the inequities of life in a colonial state. The ineffectiveness of the government's propaganda efforts was not exposed until the election of 1980. But two decades of evidence of audience dissatisfaction, largely ignored by the settler regime, pointed the way to the sweeping victory of Mugabe and his ZANU party.

# Conclusion

Blacks don't understand film language. This means that if you show a guy going into a house, you have to show him coming out as well. If you cut from the house to a car on the highway, your audience won't know what the hell's going on.[1]

Assumptions like the above—the 1986 opinion of a South African film director—that African cinema audiences were particularly credulous and impressionable died hard in Southern Africa. Though it was dispelled in Zimbabwe soon after independence, it continued to influence film production in the Republic of South Africa, the continent's last settler colony, for another decade. Indeed, several filmmakers who lost their jobs when the Mugabe regime took power in 1981 found work in South Africa's dynamic commercial film industry. They took with them a condescension toward African audiences that was seventy years in the making.

Today most Zimbabweans who lived through the 1960s have only a dim memory of CAFU and Rhodesian Information Service movies. Few rural people recall the shows of the federal period, though the more notorious production of the

1970s still loom large in the minds of many. Ask Zimbab-weans over fifty about the "bioscope" and they often smile and begin telling you about "cowboy" films. Thus these colonial film projects are significant if only for the ephemeral nature of their influence. For all of the effort that went into producing and distributing these films, they remain forgotten by those whose lives they were supposed to transform.

But that is not to say that the study of them is insignificant. Rather, such an examination provides insight into the compli-cated relationship between ruler and ruled in the region. Film arrived in Rhodesia as a diversion for the settler community. Whites saw it as a "complicated" technology, which in fact it did prove to be. It was expected to shock and unnerve audi-ences, and it seems to have done so on occasion, particularly in its early days, though never to the degree that whites antici-pated. It was expected to transform the behavior of Africans. It did, but again not in the way the state had hoped. It was as-sumed to lend itself to resistant and alternative readings, and it often did, though again rarely in the way whites had antici-pated. From the arrival of cinema in Southern Rhodesia, colo-nial observers feared its influence. Perhaps they were right to do so. Though it never inspired the crime, violence, and politi-cal disorder of the imperial imagination, the spread of the cin-ema had important, if unintended, consequences. It provided the peoples of Central and Southern Africa with novel views of their colony, their continent, and their world. In rural areas, it reminded audiences that they lived in a despotic state that was either unwilling or incapable of making good on its own propaganda. In the cities and mining compounds, it allowed workers to develop tastes that no amount of official pressure could influence.

The story of how African communities, in all of their di-versity, came to embrace, reject, comprehend, and enjoy the movies is an important one. It was through the cinema that many Africans first saw the world outside of the village and began to construct their own vision of the occidental "other." The cinema became to some extent what Bennedict Anderson has said of print capitalism: a technology that made people aware of their participation in a larger "imagined community."[2] In this case, the cinema created a community that was given coherence and boundary by the common experience of colonialism.

The idea of a cinema for Africans has not disappeared. In Zimbabwe, the government has continued to produce films for rural peoples and has even hired some former CAFU directors to produce them.[3] There are rumors that the Mugabe regime has followed in the footsteps of its predecessor by using "intimidating" films during elections.[4] However, in general the mobile cinema program in Zimbabwe has become moribund over the past decade due to the high cost of manning the mobile units. The Zimbabwean government has also carried on the country's time-honored tradition of censorship by trying to ban the 1996 film *Flame* because it presented an unflattering version of the nation's history.[5]

Elsewhere in Africa, the promise of a cinema for Africans lives on. In the decades following independence, African cineastes promised to replace colonial cinema, and the Hollywood hegemony, with an indigenous film industry that would produce motion pictures by Africans, starring Africans, for Africans. However, these directors suffer from many of the problems that plagued their colonial predecessors. They are poorly financed, often didactic, and frequently humorless. The popular view of today's African cinema is satirized in Jean-Pierre Bekolo's film *Aristotle Plot*, in which African audiences are addicted to the most recent American action movies, while African cinema is dismissed as, in the estimation of one character, "goats chasing chickens, and chickens chasing goats." Thus, though they have impressed observers overseas, they play to empty theaters in their country of origin. Of course, such an argument should not be taken too far. African directors are mercifully free of the prejudices and condescension of their predecessors. But otherwise the parallels with colonial cinema are ironic and striking.

The history of the cinema in colonial Zimbabwe reveals the settler state's phenomenal capacity for self-deception. For seventy years, whites in the colony ignored all evidence that suggested their subjects were no different from them when it came to watching movies. Any experiment that seemed to intimate otherwise was ignored or disparaged: any anecdote or rumor that seemed to support it was believed and recirculated.

Today Zimbabwe's tiny white population still retains its control over the levers of the nation's economy. Many members of this minority community continue to refer to themselves proudly, in private, as "Rhodies." Nostalgia for white rule is widespread, as evidenced by the popularity among white Zimbabweans of the recent autobiography of Rhodesian Front Prime Minister Ian Smith. The remnants of the settler community delight in relating to American visitors to Zimbabwe the shock they felt when Mugabe's ZANU party won the 1980 elections in the country, effectively ending white rule in the colony forever. "How," these people ask rhetorically, "could we have been so deceived?" The answer, this study suggests, is that they had an enormous amount of practice.

# Notes

## *Abbreviations Used in Notes*

| | |
|---|---|
| BFI | British Film Institute |
| BSAP | British South African Police |
| CAC | Central African Council |
| CAFU | Central African Film Unit |
| CFU | Colonial Film Unit |
| CID | Criminal Investigations Department |
| CIO | chief information officer |
| CNC | chief native commissioner |
| corr. | correspondence |
| FID | Federal Information Department |
| INF | Information Ministry |
| IO | Information Office |
| MOI | Ministry of Information |
| NA | native affairs |
| NR | Northern Rhodesia |
| PM | prime minister |
| PR | public relations |
| PRO | Public Records Office |
| RCofM | Rhodesian Chamber of Mines |
| sec. | secretary |
| SR | Southern Rhodesia |
| supt. | superintendent |
| ZNA | Zimbabwe National Archive |

# *Preface*

1. Zimbabwe National Archive (ZNA) S926/F54 1949–53, Native Dept., Salisbury, corr., mobile cinema report, 1952.

2. See Manthia Diawara, *African Cinema: Politics and Culture* (Bloomington: Indiana University Press, 1992), p. 4.

3. For a discussion of audience research in Hollywood, see Robert C. Allen, "From Exhibition to Reception: Reflections on the Audience in Film," *Screen* 31, no. 4 (1990): 347–56. Allen points out that Hollywood began conducting systematic audience research only after World War II. See also Janet Staiger, "The Handmaiden of Villainy: Method and Problems in Studying the Historical Reception of a Film," *Wide Angle* 8, no. 1 (1986): 20–27.

4. For a discussion of the search for evidence of hegemony, see James Scott, *Domination and the Arts of Resistance: Hidden Transcripts* (New Haven: Yale University Press, 1990).

5. See, for example, Andrew D. Roberts, *The Cambridge History of Africa*, vol. 3 (New York: Cambridge University Press, 1990).

6. See Rosaleen Smyth, "The Development of British Colonial Film Policy, 1927–1939, with Special Reference to East and Central Africa," *Journal of African History* 20, no. 3 (1979): 437–50; "The British Colonial Film Unit and Sub-Saharan Africa, 1939–1945," *Historical Journal of Film, Radio, and Television* 8, no. 3 (1988): 285–98; and "The Central African Film Unit's Images of Empire, 1948–1963," *Historical Journal of Film, Radio, and Television* 3, no. 2 (1983): 143.

7. See David Kerr, "The Best of Both Worlds: Colonial Film Policy and Practice in Northern Rhodesia and Nyasaland," *Critical Arts: A Journal of Cultural Study*, no. 2 (1993). Smyth's excellent, though brief, article on CAFU, "Development of British Colonial Film Policy," constructs a useful outline of the unit. Kedmon Hungwe, "Southern Rhodesian Propaganda and Education Films for Peasant Farmers, 1948–1955," *Historical Journal of Film, Radio, and Television* 11, no. 3 (1991), and Kerr provide useful observations on narrow aspects of the unit's work.

8. One important exception is Professor Kedmon Hungwe, who interviewed two retired cinema officers and graciously shared the transcripts of these conversations with me.

9. See Elaine Windrich, *The Mass Media in the Struggle for Zimbabwe: Censorship and Propaganda under Rhodesian Front Rule* (Gwelo,

Zimbabwe: Mambo Press, 1981), and Julie Frederikse, *None but Our-selves: Masses vs. Media in the Making of Zimbabwe* (New York: Penguin Books, 1984).

10. For an illuminating elaboration on this question, see Mahmood Mamdani's *Citizen and Subject: Contemporary Africa and the Legacy of Late Colonialism* (Princeton, N.J.: Princeton University Press, 1996).

11. Frank Ukadike, *Black African Cinema* (Berkeley: University of California Press, 1994).

## Chapter 1

1. Lizbeth Malkmus and Roy Armes, *Arab and African Film Making* (London: Zed Books, 1991), p. 4.

2. See Brian Larkin, "Uncertain Consequences: The Social and Religious Life of Media in Northern Nigeria," Ph.D. diss., New York University, 1998.

3. See Prem Chowdhry, *Colonial India and the Making of Empire Cinema: Image, Ideology, and Identity* (Manchester: Manchester University Press, 2000).

4. Jock McCulloh, *Scientific Racism in Modern South Africa* (Cambridge: Cambridge University Press, 1995), p. 203.

5. Ibid., p. 204.

6. Dane Kennedy, *Islands of White: Settler Society and Culture in Kenya and Southern Rhodesia* (Durham, N.C.: Duke University Press, 1987).

7. George Henry Tanser, *A Scanting of Time: The Story of Salisbury, Rhodesia, 1890–1900* (Salisbury: Pioneer Head Press, 1974), p. 220.

8. ZNA S2784/3/A-Z, 1917, 5 June 1914.

9. ZNA S2784/3/A-Z, 1917, cinematographic censorship.

10. See Larkin, "Uncertain Consequences."

11. See Poonam Arora, "Imperilling the Prestige of the White Woman: Colonial Anxiety and Film Censorship in British India," *Visual Anthropology Review* 11, no. 2 (1995).

12. See Thelma Gutsche, *The History and Social Significance of the Motion Picture in South Africa* (Cape Town: H. Timmins, 1972), p. 284.

13. The standard work on the rising of 1896 is T. O. Ranger, *Revolt*

*in Southern Rhodesia, 1896–97: A Study in African Resistance* (London: Heinemann, 1967).

14. ZNA A3/21/10–13, cinematograph ordinance, Mr. Stewart to administrator, Salisbury, 9 Nov. 1916.

15. Ibid. For a discussion of the violence associated with this film, see Peter Davis, *In Darkest Hollywood: Exploring the Jungles of Cinema's South Africa* (Athens: Ohio University Press, 1996), pp. 128–31.

16. ZNA A3/21/10–13, cinematograph ordinance, administrator to attorney general, 11 Nov. 1916.

17. ZNA A3/21/10–13, cinematograph ordinance, from Tregold, attorney general, to administrator, 16 Nov. 1916.

18. ZNA A3/28/10–12, cinematograph ordinance, BSAP Bulawayo to sec., Admin. Dept., 8 June 1917.

19. ZNA S2784/3/A-Z, 1917, cinematographic censorship, BSAP Bulawayo to supt., CID, Bulawayo, 15 July 1917.

20. ZNA A3/28/10–12, cinematograph ordinance, "African Films Trust Ltd.," to administrator, Southern Rhodesia (SR), 22 May 1917.

21. ZNA A3/28/10–12, cinematograph ordinance, Fred H. Barlmann, sec., African Political Association, to F. D. P. Chaplin, 18 May 1917.

22. Quoted in Tim Couzens, "Moralizing Leisure Time: The Transatlantic Connection and Black Johannesburg, 1918–1936," in *Industrialisation and Social Change in South Africa: African Class Formation, Culture, and Consciousness, 1870–1930*, ed. Richard Rathbone and Shula Marks (New York: Longman, 1982).

23. Ibid.

24. Charles van Onselen, *Chibaro: African Mine Labour in Southern Rhodesia, 1900–1933* (London: Pluto Press, 1976), p. 89.

25. Gutsche, *History and Social Significance*, p. 374.

26. Cited in M. Beiel, "Mapantsula: Cinema, Crime, and Politics on the Witwatersrand," *Journal of Southern African Studies* 16, no. 4 (1990).

27. African Education Commission, *Phelps-Stokes Commission on Education in Africa* (New York: Phelps-Stokes Fund, 1922), p. 216.

28. Gutsche, *History and Social Significance*, p. 374.

29. Ibid., p. 379.

30. Stephen Bottomore, "The Coming of the Cinema," *History Today* 46, no. 3 (1996): 14–21.

31. Quoted in Rex Stephenson, "Cinema and Censorship in Colo-

nial Malaya," *Journal of Southeast Asian Studies* 5, no. 2 (1974): 209–24.

32. ZNA A3/28/10–12, chairman, Globe and Phoenix Mining Co., Que Que, to sec., Admin. Dept., 3 Sept. 1918.

33. Ibid.

34. By 1925 the police were also anticipating the introduction into the colony of subversive films intended to incite violence against the state. In March 1925, the CID in Bulawayo received a warning from the authorities in Northern Rhodesia that a German group was trying to smuggle films into the territories "depicting oppression suffered in Colonial countries by the native population . . . for the purpose of display to negroes," ZNA S2784/3/A-Z, 1917, cinematographic censorship, from E. N. Carlton, assistant sec., Chief Secretary's Office, Livingstone, NR, to OIC, CID, Livingstone, 25 Mar. 1925, copy to supt., CID, Bulawayo.

35. ZNA S2784/3/A-Z, 1917, cinematographic censorship, OIC, CID, NR, from chief supt., CID, BSAP, 9 Apr. 1927.

36. ZNA S2784/3/A-Z, 1917, cinematographic censorship, T. H. Brycard to chief supt., CID, Bulawayo, 3 June 1927.

37. ZNA S2784/3/A-Z, 1917, cinematographic censorship, A. Harris, CID Que Que, det.-sgt., CID SR, to chief supt., CID, Bulawayo, "Native Bioscopies: Southern Rhodesia," 10 June 1927, "The Rhodesian Native Bioscope Circuit."

38. Ibid.

39. Ibid.

40. Ibid., Det.-sgt. Riddell to supt., CID, Bulawayo, 6 June 1927.

41. Ibid., Carbutt, supt. of natives, Bulawayo, chief native commissioner (CNC), Salisbury, 10 Jan. 1930.

42. Ibid., CNC, H. M. Jackson, to supt. of natives, Matabeleland, 13 Jan. 1930, "Bioscope: Bulawayo Municipal Location."

43. Ibid., Carbutt, supt. of natives, Bulawayo, to CNC Salisbury, 10 Jan. 1930, "Bioscope: Bulawayo Municipal Location."

44. Ibid., to Major Brundell, Bulawayo CID, 26 Sept. 1931.

45. Ibid., cinema report by L. Thornton (n.d.). The next several quotes are all from this report.

46. ZNA S246/73, "Censorship of Films Intended for Exhibition to Native & Coloured Audiences," L. E. Friff to Attorney General Dept., 1932.

47. Ibid., draft speech prepared by W. Thomas, n.d.

48. Ibid., draft speech.

49. Ibid.

50. Ibid.

51. Ibid., from office of commissioner, BSAP, to sec., Dept. of the Colonial Secretary, 1 Apr. 1932.

52. Ibid., draft speech.

53. *Debates of the Southern Rhodesian Legislative Assembly*, Entertainments Control and Censorship Bill, 2nd reading, 2 Apr. 1932, col. 94.

54. Ibid., col. 95.

55. Ibid., col. 96–97.

56. Ibid., col. 101.

57. Ibid.

58. ZNA S2784/3/A-Z, T. H. Brycard to CID sgt., 1917.

59. ZNA S1542/S12, 1934–36, social and moral development, Dec. 1934-Dec. 1936, sec., RCofM, to African Consolidated Films Ltd., 1 Nov. 1935, "Re Bioscopes in Native Mine Compounds."

60. Ibid.

61. Ibid.

62. Ibid., E. Watson, general manager, African Consolidated Films, to sec., RCofM, 7 Nov. 1935.

63. Ibid.

64. Ibid., CNC to sec., RCofM, 4 Nov. 1935.

65. See note 52 above.

66. ZNA S1542/S12, 1934–36, social and moral development, Watson to Morton.

67. Ibid., CNC to sec., RCofM, re bioscopes in native mine compounds, 4 Nov. 1935.

68. *Report of the Colonial Films Committee* (London: HMSO, 1927), p. 23.

69. Ibid.

70. Ibid.

71. Ibid.

72. Ibid., p. 6.

73. Ibid., p. 32.

74. *The Film in National Life* (London: HMSO, 1932).

75. Ibid., p. 136.

76. Ibid., p. 126.

77. Julian Huxley, "Report on the Use of Films for Educational

Purposes in East Africa," 1930; typescript copy, ZNA S1542/S12, 1934–36, social and moral development, 1934–36.

78. L. A. Notcutt and Geoffrey Latham, *The African and the Cinema* (London: Edinburgh House Press, 1937).

79. J. Merle Davis, *Modern Industry and the African* (London: Macmillan, 1933).

80. Notcutt and Latham, *African and Cinema*, p. 32.

81. ZNA S154/S12, G. C. Latham, "Memo: A Bantu Educational Cinema Experiment," 3 Dec. 1935.

82. Notcutt and Latham, *African and Cinema.* For a list of BEKE productions see Notcutt and Latham chapters 2 and 3.

83. For more on the BEKE see Rosaleen Smyth, "The Development of British Colonial Film Policy, 1927–1939, With Special Reference to East and Central Africa," *Journal of African History* 20, no. 3 (1979).

84. ZNA S1542/S12, 1934–36, "Social and Moral Development, Dec. 1934-Dec. 1936," 26 July 1934, sec., International Congress of Educational and Instructional Cinematography, Rome.

85. Ibid., medical director to sec., internal affairs, 4 Sept. 1934. The Kenya reference is to the work of Dr. Patterson.

86. Ibid.

87. Ibid., Charles Bullock to sec. to PM (native affairs), 13 Apr. 1935.

88. Ibid., to CNC, 12 Aug. 1937, "Films For Instruction of Natives."

89. Ibid.

90. Ibid., CNC to sec. to PM (native affairs), "Bantu Educational Kinema Experiment."

91. ZNA S482/240/39, PM, "Films of Rhodesian Interest," Gordon Cooper, president, Rhodesian Film Productions, to PM Godfrey Huggins, 25 Feb. 1936.

92. Ibid.

93. ZNA S1542/S12, 1934–36, social and moral development, Dec. 1934–Dec. 1936, from Charles Bullock, CNC, to sec. to PM (native affairs), "Film Production," 13 Apr. 1935.

94. See Cooper's autobiography *Life's a Short Summer: The Tale of One Man's Life* (London: Jarrolds, 1958).

95. ZNA S1801/4920, Rhodesian Film Productions, "The Poison Ordeal." Perhaps the only existent copy of this film is held in the

National Film Archives, London. Cooper published "Filming the Matabele," an article about the making of the film, in the 1934 issue of *N.A.D.A.: The Southern Rhodesian Native Affairs Department Annual.*

96. Martin Meredith, *The Past Is Another Country: Rhodesia, 1890–1979* (London: Deutsch, 1979), p. 21.

97. Ibid.

98. ZNA S935/10, "Rhodesian Film Institute," Oliver Bell, BFI, to S. M. Lanigan O'Keefe, high commissioner SR, 9 Oct. 1941.

99. Ibid., "Article for Sight and Sound," n.d., "Film Institute Plans in Southern Rhodesia."

100. Ibid.

101. Ibid., Bell to Gale, 9 June 1942.

102. ZNA S935/10, Gale to Bell, 3 Aug. 1942.

103. Ibid.

104. Ibid.

105. Indian Office report, cited in Chowdhry, *Colonial India and the Making of Empire Cinema*, p. 17.

106. See Larkin, "Uncertain Consequences," on the end of the "moral panic" in Nigeria, Malaysia, and India.

## *Chapter 2*

1. William Sellers, "Making Films in and for the Colonies," *Journal of the Royal Society of the Arts* 101 (1953): 829–37.

2. Rosaleen Smyth, "The Development of British Colonial Film Policy, 1927–1939, with Special Reference to East and Central Africa," *Journal of African History* 20, no. 3 (1979): 437–50.

3. Sellers, "Films for Primitive Peoples," *Documentary Newsletter*, Sept. 1941, p. 221.

4. Ibid., p. 222.

5. Ibid.

6. Sellers, "Making Films," p. 831.

7. Sellers, "Films for Primitive Peoples," p. 223.

8. Sellers, "Making Films," p. 831.

9. Ibid.

10. Ibid.

11. Sellers, "Films for Primitive Peoples," p. 222.

12. Ibid.

13. L. M. Ross, "Africans and Propaganda Films," *United Empire* 30 (Feb. 1940): 65.

14. Ibid.

15. Ibid.

16. During World War II, when the Colonial Film Unit showed *Machi Gaba* throughout Africa, it was much criticized by information officers. The information officer in Kenya remarked on its poor acting (ZNA S935/36/2, Information Office [IO]: Kenya file 2. Kenya IO: History of Activities, 1 Jan. to 31 Mar. 1944). An information officer in Northern Rhodesia reported that Africans there found the Islamic dress in *Machi Gaba* "amusing and instead of being taught that clean village life makes for healthier living" formed the impression "that Nigerians are funny people"—quoted in Rosaleen Smyth, "The British Colonial Film Unit and Sub-Saharan Africa, 1939–1945," *Historical Journal of Film, Radio, and Television* 8 (1988): 292.

17. Quoted in "Comments on Work with Film Preliterates in Africa," ed. Louis Forsdale, *Studies in Visual Communication* 9 (winter 1983): 31.

18. Ibid.

19. Interview with Nell in Borrowdale, Zimbabwe, 14 Mar. 1997.

20. See chapter 1.

21. *Report of the Colonial Films Committee* (London: HMSO, 1930), p. 23. Sellers's first films were made in 1929, but he was already experimenting with films in 1926 and this may have been the inspiration for this comment.

22. L. A. Notcutt and Geoffrey Latham, *The African and the Cinema* (London: Edinburgh House Press, 1937).

23. "Putting Film to Work in the Colonies," *Colonial Development: A Magazine Devoted to Development in the Colonies* 2, no. 1 (1956): 16–18.

24. George Pearson, "Health Education by Film in Africa," *Colonial Cinema* 7, no. 1 (1949): 17.

25. George Pearson, *Flashback: The Autobiography of a British Film Maker* (London: G. Allen and Unwin, 1957), pp. 211–12.

26. Timothy Burke, "Our Mosquitoes Are Not So Large," paper presented at Yale Conference on Colonial Representation, Jan. 1997, p. 3. Cited with the author's permission.

27. This story appears in, among other places, Louis Nell, *Images*

*of Yesteryear* (Harare: Harper Collins, 1998), and Harry Franklin, "The Central African Screen," *Colonial Cinema* 8, no. 4 (Dec. 1950): 86.

28. See *Nyasaland Herald* for one example of this story. Cameroonian director Jean-Pierre Bekolo playfully explores this trope of African credulity in his film *Aristotle's Plot*, in which an African police officer is sent to investigate the question of how a man who dies in one film can appear alive in another.

29. For more on the Tanganyikan audience, see Vernon Brelsford's article "Analysis of African Reactions to Propaganda Film," *N.A.D.A.: The Southern Rhodesian Native Affairs Department Annual*, no. 24 (1947), where the newspaper editorial that commented on the incident is cited at length.

30. "Laughter," *Colonial Cinema* 8, no. 1 (1950): 22.

31. Steven Bottomore has collected several of these stories from the non-Western world in his article "The Coming of the Cinema," *History Today* 4, no. 3 (1996): 14.

32. Quoted in Francis Ramirez and Christian Rolot, *Histoire du cinéma colonial au Zaïre au Rwanda et au Burundi* (Tervuren, Belgium: Musée Royal de l'Afrique Centrale, 1985).

33. Megan Vaughan, *Curing Their Ills: Colonial Power and African Illness* (Stanford, Calif.: Stanford University Press, 1991), p. 191.

34. Interviews with Lovermore Mhlahla, 18 Mar. 1997; Lawrence Moringay, 7 May 1997; and Ben Musoni, 17 Mar. 1997, in Harare. For an interesting discussion of the dissemination of similar tales of audience credulity in the early cinema in Europe and the United States, see Stephen Bottomore, "The Panicking Audience? Early Cinema and the 'Train Effect,'" *Historical Journal of Film, Radio, and Television* 19, no. 2 (1999): 177.

35. See Bottomore, "Panicking Audience?"

36. Tom Gunning, "An Aesthetic of Astonishment,' *Art and Text* 34 (spring 1989).

37. Quoted in Bottomore, "Panicking Audience?" p. 6. On at least one occasion, European observers related the influence of the "train effect" on African audiences. See the interview with Belgian missionaries in Tristan Boulard's film *Matamata and Pilipili* (First Run/Icarus Films, 1996).

38. Bottomore, "Coming of the Cinema," p. 14.

39. Yuri Tsivian, *Early Cinema in Russia and Its Cultural Reception*, trans. Alan Bodger, foreword by Tom Gunning (New York: Routledge, 1994), p. 145.

40. See Bottomore, "Coming of the Cinema."

41. Brian Larkin, "Uncertain Consequences: The Social and Religious Life of Media in Northern Nigeria" (Ph.D. diss., New York University, 1998), p. 121.

42. Notcutt and Latham, *African and Cinema*, p. 11.

43. See J. Merle Davis, *Modern Industry and the African* (London: Macmillan, 1933), p. 381.

44. Notcutt and Latham, *African and Cinema*, p. 146.

45. Ibid., p. 167.

46. Ibid., p. 34.

47. Ibid., p. 100.

48. Ibid., p. 183.

49. ZNA S935/37/1, 24 Oct. 1939.

50. ZNA S935/24, Ministry of Information Publicity Division, planning section memo 230, "Publicity in the British Empire: General Principles."

51. Rosaleen Smyth, "Movies and Mandarins: The Official Film and British Colonial Africa," in *British Cinema History*, ed. James Curran and Vincent Porter (Totowa, N.J.: Barnes and Noble Books, 1983), p. 132.

52. For the cinema in the Congo and francophone Africa, see Lizbeth Malkmus and Roy Armes, *Arab and African Film Making* (London: Zed Books, 1991), pp. 4–23.

53. L. Van Bever, "The Cinema in the Belgian Congo," *Colonial Review* 13, no. 3 (Sept. 1952). The Belgians conducted a series of experiments that led them to compile a list of rules of colonial cinema that were virtually identical to those developed by Sellers. See Ramirez and Rolot, *Histoire du cinéma colonial.*

54. See David and Peggy Giltrow, "Cinema with a Purpose: Films for Development in British Colonial Africa," paper presented at the African Studies Association (U.K.) meeting, University of Kent, 17–19 Sept. 1986.

55. E. R. Edmetts, 26 Mar. 1942, quoted in Rosaleen Smyth, "The Development of Government Propaganda in Northern Rhodesia up to 1953" (Ph.D. diss., University of London, 1983), p. 364.

56. See Smyth, "Movies and Mandarins," p. 134. According to Captain Dickson, "Practically 100% of films sent out by the Ministry of Information proved quite impossible for Africans. . . . The 'angles' of photography are entirely European, and are either unintelligible or pointless to Africans. How many times in war reels,

does one see heavy guns being fired, the camera leaping from the shell to the breach, from the gun to the muzzle to the Commander's up-stretched hand—and backwards and forwards . . . with demoniacal speed?" Such criticisms were not uncommon. An information officer in Nyasaland found the CFU film *London River* "unsuitable and confusing for the ordinary African audience . . . the picture was generally beyond the comprehension of the average audience": ZNA S935/38 IO, Nyasaland, 1939–45, Jan. to Mar. 1944, R. H. Wisdom.

57. Quoted in UNESCO, *The Use of Mobile Cinema and Radio Vans in Fundamental Education* (Paris: UNESCO, 1949), p. 162.

58. Alan Izod, "Some Special Features of Colonial Film Production," in *The Film in Colonial Development: A Report of a Conference* (London: British Film Institute, 1948), p. 28.

59. On African laughter, see Izod, "Some Special Features," p. 1; on film and crime, ibid., p. 17; on the intellect of African audiences, ibid., p. 19.

60. A. R. Baëta, "The Two Worlds," *Sight and Sound* 17, no. 65 (1948): 5.

61. Ibid.

62. John Grierson, "Film in British Colonial Development," *Sight and Sound* 17, no. 65 (1948): 3.

63. G. Odunton, "One Step Ahead," *Colonial Cinema* 8, no. 2 (1950): 29.

64. Ibid.

65. Ibid., p. 31.

66. George Pearson, "One Step Ahead," *Colonial Cinema* 8, no 2 (1950).

67. Norman Spurr, "Regarding Odunton's Article," *Colonial Cinema* 8, no. 2 (1950): 33. "I think there is valid criticism," Spurr commented. "We are all conscious of the rut into which our films have got themselves, but how to get out of it and yet remain a teacher is one of the problems."

68. Norman Spurr, "The Reactions of Audiences to Films," *Colonial Cinema* 6, no. 3 (1949).

69. Champion is quoted in UNESCO, *Use of Mobile Cinemas*, p. 82.

70. ZNA S3269/61/4 PRO(51)29, 28 June 1951, "Films—Audience Research" (note by CFU).

71. Ibid.

72. Ibid.

73. P. Morton-Williams, *Cinema in Rural Nigeria: A Field Study of the Impact of Fundamental-Education Films on Rural Audiences in Nigeria* (Ibadan: Federal Information Services, 1953).

74. Ibid., p. 44.

75. Ibid., p. 45.

76. Ibid., p. 37.

77. Quoted in Mike Hilary Ssali, "The Development and Role of an African Film Industry in East Africa, with Special Reference to Tanzania, 1922–1984" (Ph.D. diss., UCLA, 1986), p. 87.

78. See, for example, an interview with Rouch in Manthia Diawara's film *Rouch in Reverse*, in which the French filmmaker asserts that Africans who had never witnessed cinema before recognized themselves "in about twenty-five seconds."

79. See W. Sellers, "The Production and Use of Films for Public and Informational Purposes in British African Territories," in *Recontres internationales: Le cinéma et l'Afrique au Sud du Sahara* (Brussels: 1958), pp. 36–38, cited in Smyth, "Movies and Mandarins," p. 138.

## *Chapter 3*

1. Quoted in UNESCO, *The Cinema and Social Science: A Survey of Ethnographic and Sociological Films* (Paris: UNESCO, 1962), p. 42.

2. Some of the films made for white audiences held at the National Archives include *Roads of Rhodesia*, *The Sea Saw Years*, *Farming in the Federation*, and *The Two Salisburies*.

3. Though the films were produced for distribution in British theaters, they found their main audience at Rhodesia House in London, where they played to large crowds of English schoolchildren.

4. See chapter 2 and Rosaleen Smyth, "The British Colonial Film Unit and Sub-Saharan Africa, 1939–1945," *Historical Journal of Film, Radio, and Television* 8 (1988): 135.

5. ZNA S482/41/39, "Ministry of Information & SR Information Officer, 1939–1940," G. Martin Huggins to editor, *Rhodesia Herald*, 15 June 1940; copy to *Bulawayo Chronicle*.

6. ZNA S940, IO, SR, progress reports (1939–40), 9 Sept. 1940, "Native Broadcasts."

7. Ibid.

8. ZNA S935/37/1, IO, NR, 1939–41, Gale, 30 Oct. 1939, to "The Minister," "Information Officers: Co-Operation between Southern Rhodesia, Northern Rhodesia, and Nyasaland: Report on a Conference held at Information Office, Salisbury," 27 Oct. 1939.

9. ZNA S935/37/1, IO, NR, 1939–41, Info. Dept. progress report no. 3, "Broadcasting: Reaction of Africans." The correspondent is passing along the opinion of the provincial governor of the Northwest District.

10. ZNA S935/14, "Natives Propaganda & Broadcasting," J. Blake Thompson, supt., Native Infectious Disease Hospital, 28 Apr. 1940.

11. ZNA S935/40, "Report on tour made with the object of ascertaining to what degree the Governments of the East and Central African Territories would be prepared to participate in the establishment of a central film making unit and other matters concerning cinema propaganda," A. M. Champion, 22 June 1944.

12. See also ZNA S932/34/1, Central African Council (CAC) corr., pt. 1. Gale to sec., CAC, 2 Jan. 1946, joint film unit, "What the Unit Will Do."

13. ZNA S482/239/39, Office of the PM: films: educational, "Summary of correspondence on the establishment of a Film Institute," 11 Apr. 1939, despatch from governor, NR, and 13 Oct. 1941, "Despatch from Governor, N.R., asking what progress had been made in obtaining suitable films for display to Africans on the Copperbelt."

14. ZNA S932/1J, "Film Production Unit, 1945–1954," W. D. Gale, director, public relations, to sec., internal affairs, 30 Jan. 1947, film production unit.

15. ZNA S1812, CAC, minutes, "Summary of Council's Activities between 1945 and 1948 for the Information of Members of the Legislative Assembly of Southern Rhodesia and the Legislative Councils of Northern Rhodesia and Nyasaland," n.d., "Central African Film Unit," H. Nigel Parry, acting chief sec., Salisbury, 9 June 1948.

16. ZNA S1812, CAC, minutes, NR, Central African film production unit, CDWAC, no. 1060.

17. ZNA S932/34/1, CAC corr., pt. 1, Gale to sec., CAC, 2 Jan. 1946, joint film unit.

18. Ibid., CNC, government film production unit, 9 Jan. 1946.

19. Ibid.

20. *Rhodesia Herald,* 12 Feb. 1948.

21. Ibid., 20 Nov. 1951.

22. For the history of broadcasting in the region, see Rosaleen Smyth, "A Note on the 'Saucepan Special': The People's Radio of Central Africa," *Historical Journal of Film, Radio, and Television* 4, no. 2 (1984): 195–201.

23. ZNA S1812, CAC, minutes. For the history of radio in Central Africa, see Peter Fraenkel, *Wayaleshi* (London: Weidenfeld and Nicholson, 1959).

24. "Producer" was the title given to the administrative head of CAFU. Alan Izod, who held this title from 1948 to 1960, did not produce the films but coordinated their production from the unit's headquarters in Salisbury. The films were made by the unit's director-cameramen. When Izod was promoted to head of Federal Information Services in 1960, the title of producer was held briefly by Denys Brown and Louis Nell. The unit was dissolved in 1963.

25. Nell, who worked with the unit off and on from its inception to its demise, remembered that John Grierson, the Canadian film critic, applied for the position. Though Grierson expressed a great interest in colonial filmmaking and visited the unit in its early days of production, his name does not appear on the short list prepared by the CAC. Nell speculated that Grierson probably would have insisted on more control over the unit than the council would have wished and that council members suspected he would not permit them to tell him how to make films; interview with Nell, in Borrowdale, Harare, Zimbabwe, 18 Mar. 1997.

26. For the history of the CAFU personnel, see Louis Nell, *Images of Yesteryear* (Harare: HarperCollins, 1998), p. 200.

27. See chapter 2.

28. ZNA S926/F56, 1947–52, CAFU (précis of work to be circulated to departments), 30 Nov. 1948.

29. Harry Franklin, "The Central African Screen," *Colonial Cinema* 8, no. 4 (Dec. 1950): 86.

30. ZNA S926/F56, 1947–52, Izod to C. Lawrence, re. CFU, 17 Oct. 1950.

31. ZNA S926/F56, 1947–52, director, information, to administrative sec., Lusaka, 25 Oct. 1950.

32. Nell interview, Borrowdale, 18 Mar. 1997.

33. Interview with David Hlazo, Waterfalls, Harare, 3 Mar. 1997.

34. Rosaleen Smyth, "The Central African Film Unit's Images of Empire, 1948–1963," *Historical Journal of Film, Radio, and Television* 3, no. 2 (1983): 143.

35. Nell, interview cited above; Peet's 1988 interview with Izod, transcript in ZNA.

36. Interview with Atkinson, 13 Mar. 1997, Glendale, Zimbabwe.

37. Interviews with Peet appear in Smyth, "CAFU's Images of Empire"; Kedmon Hungwe, "Southern Rhodesian Propaganda and Education Films for Peasant Farmers, 1948–1955," *Historical Journal of Film, Radio, and Television* 11, no. 3 (1991); and David Kerr, "The Best of Both Worlds: Colonial Film Policy and Practice in Northern Rhodesia and Nyasaland," *Critical Arts: A Journal of Cultural Study*, no. 2 (1993). Timothy Burke also interviewed Peet for his monograph *Lifebuoy Men, Lux Women: Commodification, Consumption, and Cleanliness in Colonial Zimbabwe* (Durham, N.C.: Duke University Press, 1996).

38. See interview with Nell, cited above.

39. Kerr, "Best of Both Worlds," p. 24.

40. ZNA S926/F34/2, S. Peet, director-cameraman, 1951–54, 3 Apr. 1954, "Blantyre and Zomba Districts."

41. Kerr, "Best of Both Worlds," p. 23.

42. ZNA S926/F35, "Film Shows and Reports Thereof," E. D. Alvord questionnaire.

43. For white critiques of Peet's *Mujenji Builds a Bridge*, see chapter 4.

44. See Nell, *Visions of Yesteryear*, for Atkinson's subsequent career working for Rhodesian Information Services.

45. Cited in transcript of Kedmon Hungwe's interview with Hlazo.

46. ZNA S2791/19, 25 Oct. 1962, G. Mangin, "Associated Rhodesian Telefilms," to H. J. Quinton, minister, native affairs (NA).

47. ZNA S926/F22, "Central African Film Unit," Izod memo, 30 November 1948.

48. See, for example, ZNA S926/F56, 1947–52, Izod to Brelsford, 31 July 1948, thanking him for ideas, and ZNA S926/F56, 1947–52, Izod to Franklin, 13 Oct. 1948, describing the film *Mulenga Goes to Town*, "based very closely on your original script."

49. ZNA S926/F35, "Film Shows and Reports Thereof," draft of Izod's speech for opening night.

50. Uncataloged CAFU material, [CAFU box] ZNA. Izod broadcast "The Film in Native Development," 23 Mar. 1950.

51. Izod interview, 1988.

52. ZNA CAFU box, "Making films in Central Africa," 18 Dec. 1951.

53. ZNA S2961, CNC annual report vol. 2, Information Services Branch, 1951, 1st report: films.

54. Ibid.

55. ZNA S1812, CAC minutes, annex A: CAFU—summary progress report, 31 Dec. 1949.

56. ZNA S926/F34/1, S. Peet, director-cameraman, general corr., 1949–54, Izod to Peet, 5 Oct. 1950.

57. Ibid., Izod to Peet, 26 Sept. 1950.

58. ZNA S927/17, production files—scripts, 1949–52, "The Three Men," submitted by teacher John Moses to *African Weekly* short-story competition, 9 Oct. 1950.

59. One result of this arrangement was that CAFU directors rarely had the opportunity to see one another's films. Thus Nell, when interviewed in 1996, had little knowledge of any but a handful of his colleagues' films and he assumed that they were equally ignorant of his work. The director-cameraman initially traveled in a truck equipped with a mobile cinema and showed films while on tour; however, this practice seems to have lasted only briefly. For most of the unit's history, the filmmakers seem to have gained little first-hand experience of audience reception of their films.

60. ZNA S927/17, production files—scripts, 1949–52.

61. For a discussion of the "wise and foolish" format, see Megan Vaughan, *Curing Their Ills* (Stanford, Calif.: Stanford University Press, 1991).

62. Ibid.

63. Ibid.

64. Ibid.

65. Ibid.

66. Ibid.

67. And in doing so, perpetuating a time-honored theme of colonial cinema. See Vaughan, ibid., for a discussion of the "witchdoctor" in colonial film.

68. ZNA S927/17, production files—scripts, 1949–52.

69. Other films in this genre held at ZNA include *Feniasi and*

*Timoti*, pt. 1, 1948; *Building Barns*, 1949; *Kilyoni, Peasant Farmer*, 1949; *Africans in Action: Kachesa Farmer*, n.d.; *Ncube Plows a Slope*, n.d.; *Ncube Cultivates His Land*, 1951; *Farmers of Mshawasha, Harneck's Cotton*, 1953; *Land Development Officer*, 1953; *Magodi and the Dairy*, 1949; *Mangwende and the Trees*, 1949; *Marimo Finds a New Life*, 1949; and *Master Farmer*, 1955.

70. The rapidity with which the driver becomes ill alarmed African audiences, several of whom apparently believed that his illness was the direct result of a spell cast on him by the cyclist he almost hit.

71. Given the BSAP's reputation for brutality, this scene was likely greeted with skepticism and derision by the audience.

72. Peet's interview of Izod, 1988.

73. ZNA S926/F35, "Film Shows and Reports Thereof," R. C. Haw questionnaire.

74. ZNA S927/17, production files—scripts, 1949–52, the thief story outline, for commentators production 10. The chief's beard is so apparently and comically false that Nell remembered this detail five decades after first seeing the film. Nell believed (interview with Nell, 16 Mar. 1997) that the effect inevitably undermined the influence of the film, despite Peet's efforts to integrate it into the narrative.

75. Thief story outline.

76. Other films with a crime-doesn't-pay message available at ZNA, Harare, include *The Five Messengers*, 1948; *The Box*, 1948; *The Story of Petale*, n.d.; and *Mapolisa*, n.d..

77. Such films, which emphasized the benefits conferred on Africans from the federal government became a priority of the federal government after 1954. The time-honored image of Africans staring in wonderment at sound recordings dates back to the earliest films made about Africa. As a film critic noted in the *New York Times* in 1929, "To show a film of Africa the following ingredients must be incorporated: A shot of natives listening to a phonograph," quoted in Kenneth M. Cameron, *Africa on Film: Beyond Black and White* (New York: Continuum, 1994), p. 49.

78. Though she does refer to the film as "highly successful": see her "The Development of Government Propaganda in Northern Rhodesia up to 1953" (diss., University of London, 1983), p. 359.

79. Jean Rouch, "The Situation and Tendencies of the Cinema in

Africa," trans. Steve Field, *Studies in the Anthropology of Visual Education* 2, no. 1 (1975): 112–20.

80. ZNA S2827/2/2/2, annual district reports, 1952–53, Goromonzi.

81. A letter from the chief information officer (CIO), SR NA Dept., to Izod highlights this emphasis. ZNA F158/F54a, NA Dept. mobile cinema officers' reports, Mar. 1953–Dec. 1957, Bowles, CIO, NA Dept., to Izod, 7 Jan. 1954.

82. The failure to cast women in CAFU films can also be attributed in part to the widespread belief that female actors were unreliable and difficult to work with. Both BEKE and CFU avoided casting women whenever possible. CAFU production notes clearly indicate that the unit used women actors only when absolutely necessary.

83. It is worth noting that this film was cited as one of the unit's biggest successes. Its influence on the development of women's clubs was proffered as proof of film's effect on African audiences. However, it is likely that its influence stemmed from its being unique among CAFU films in presenting strong female protagonists, which would undoubtedly have held great appeal for their predominantly female audiences.

84. The quote is taken from the film's narration, stored with the film in the audio-visual library, ZNA.

85. ZNA S926/F56, 1947–52, Christie Lawrence to Izod, 4 Oct. 1950.

86. Ibid. Izod to Christie Lawrence, Information Dept., 11 Oct. 1950.

87. Ibid. Christie Lawrence to Izod, 13 Oct. 1950.

88. See chapter 2.

89. Izod interview, 1988.

90. ZNA S926/F43, 1948–53, "Some notes about the unit," memo, n.d. (1952).

91. ZNA S926/F34/2, S. Peet, director-cameraman, 1951–54. It is worth noting that these views were shared with Peet, his fellow Englishman.

92. Ibid.

93. See ZNA S926 on Izod's attempt to "unseat" Sellers, the head of the CFU, during the war.

94. Ibid., 8 Apr. 1954 .

95. ZNA S926/F43, press cuttings, 1948–53, *Rhodesia Herald*, 12 Feb. 1948.

96. Ibid.

97. ZNA F158/F54a, NA Dept. mobile cinema officers' reports, Mar. 1953–Dec. 1957.

98. Ibid.

99. *Federation of the Rhodesias and Nyasaland Parliamentary Debates*, vol. 8, 1958, 12 Aug. 1957, Capt. Robertson, col. 1177.

100. ZNA F128/INF/16/G, CAFU, general administration, 1953–57, films officers conference, 16 Oct. 1957, Cabinet Information Committee.

101. ZNA F121 H3/32, Information Dept., propaganda by films, mobile cinema vans, 1 Mar. 1959 to Dec. 1963.

102. ZNA F128/HAF/127/17, Home Affairs propaganda meetings, 1959–60, to Mr. Foot, film program, 1959/60.

103. ZNA F128/HAF/25/6, tours and tour reports: Federal Information Dept. officers, Apr. 1954–Dec. 1958, vol. 1, Milner Erlank tour report, re. SR, Nyasaland, 19 June 1958.

104. ZNA F158/F39, treatments and suggested subjects for films, corr. and scripts, Izod to Dr. Ashton, "Films for Africans," 26 July 1957.

105. See ZNA F121/H103, CAFU monthly reports/newsletter, vol. 2 (1957–62); Nell comments in newsletter no. 74 (2 Sept. 1958), "I can claim that this section shot over two thousand feet on the Copperbelt Emergency—and not a single foot was used! (Mostly for security reasons, of course!)."

106. ZNA F121/H103, CAFU monthly reports/newsletter, vol. 2 (1957–62), 2 Feb. 1960, "Rhodesia and Nyasaland News."

107. On censorship of the drought in Matabeleland in 1960, see ibid.

108. ZNA F128/H2/50, public relations (PR), National Film Library, "Federal National Film Services: A Preliminary Report concerning a National Film Library leading to a National Film Board," 23 Apr. 1958, H. C. Butler, Educational Aids Office, Federal Ministry of Education.

109. ZNA F121/H3/10, Information Dept., propaganda suggestions, 1959–63 (n.d.), "Steps Taken by the Federal Information Department to put over Federation and to allay Fears."

110. ZNA F121 H3/32, Information Dept., propaganda by films,

mobile cinema vans, 1 Mar. 1959 to Dec. 1963, 29 June 1959, "Film Distribution for African Audiences," by Brelsford, to sec., Home Affairs. By the late 1950s, the FID's main vehicle of rural propaganda had become the FACT publications—propaganda booklets distributed free in rural areas. Though the home-affairs minister maintained that they were much sought after throughout the federation, an article in Rhodesia's *Sunday Mail* in July 1962 suggested otherwise. Thereafter, parliamentary critics of the department's laissez-faire attitude toward African services greeted discussion of the pamphlets with the cry "Fish and Chips!" See *Federation of the Rhodesias and Nyasaland Parliamentary Debates*, 30 July 1962, col. 1237.

111. See, for example, Mr. Birch, 30 July 1962, regarding his "criticism concerning our African film services as being insufficiently active. . . . I have seen the impact of film shows on people who have little or no contact with the outer world and I have no hesitation in saying that suitable film shows are likely to go a long way towards countering subversive propaganda which is undermining the stability of the country at the present time and receiving very little opposition in the way of publicity of the general situation in the country to-day"; col. 1239.

112. Though some of them did become quite accomplished filmmakers in their own right. For example, CAFU veteran Tony Pierce Roberts went on become an accomplished cinematographer, earning two Academy Award nominations for the Merchant Ivory films *Howard's End* and *Room with a View*. Peet went on to produce the BBC series *Yesterday's Witness*.

113. Francis Ramirez and Christian Rolot, *Histoire du cinéma colonial au Zaïre au Rwanda et au Burundi* (Tervuren, Belgium: Musée Royal de l'Afrique Centrale, 1985), pp. 137–38.

114. Ibid., p. 273, "Elle est relativement simple et consiste en quelque sorte à utiliser la technique du film pour enfants." [It is relatively simple and consists for the most part in utilizing a film technique for children.] The priest continued to invoke another axiom of colonial cinema, "Tout d'abord, peu de personages et qui soient de preferences des Congolais." [Above all, not many characters, and let them be ones Congolese people prefer.]

115. Quoted in Manthia Diawara, *African Cinema: Politics and Culture* (Bloomington: Indiana University Press, 1992), p. 17.

116. See Tristan Bourland's film *Matamata and Pilipili*, First Run/Icarus Films, 1996, in which the director interviews members of the film's original audiences. The popularity of the films was also attested to by historian Victory Bachy, who believed "the films spoke a simple language which was direct, received, understood, appreciated, and requested"; quoted in Diawara, *African Cinema*, p. 23.

117. Ibid. It is unclear how many Africans in Congo actually saw these films, although in 1957 the Belgian government boasted that they were showing state-produced films to more than 8 million people annually, at 15,000 shows. See Lizbeth Malkmus and Roy Armes, *Arab and African Film Making* (London: Zed Books, 1991), p. 22.

## Chapter 4

1. See Manthia Diawara, "Black Spectatorship: Problems of Identification and Resistance," *Screen* 29, no. 4 (1988).

2. See Louis Nell, *Visions of Yesteryear* (London: Macmillan, 1999).

3. ZNA S927/17, production files—scripts, 1949–52, 26 May 1949, Izod to Powys-Jones, CNC.

4. Ibid., Nielsen to Izod, 14 June 1949.

5. Ibid.

6. ZNA S926/F34/1.

7. ZNA S926/F34/2, S. Peet, director-cameraman, 1951–54, Peet to Izod, 29 Aug. 1953. The DC in Katete told Peet that he enjoyed the films but that audiences found them hard to follow because he was not supplied with story outlines.

8. ZNA S926/F54, 1949–53, Native Dept., Salisbury, corr., memo (Dec. 1952), "Commercial Film Shows at Native Reserves and Areas," CIO.

9. David Kerr, "The Best of Both Worlds: Colonial Film Policy and Practice in Northern Rhodesia and Nyasaland," *Critical Arts: A Journal of Cultural Study*, no. 2 (1993): 16.

10. ZNA S1812, CAC minutes, paper INF/12/49, PR committee review of film-unit work as at 1 Dec. 1949.

11. ZNA S926/F54, 1949–53, Native Dept., Salisbury, J. Stakesby-Lewis, mobile cinema officer, June 1952.

12. ZNA F121 H3/32, Information Dept., propaganda by films, mobile cinema vans, 1 Mar. 1959 to Dec. 1963, PM's confidential report on trip to Nyasaland, 12–16 Feb. 1962, "Cinema Unit Staff."

13. *Debates of the Southern Rhodesian Legislative Assembly*, 22 July 1959, Mr. Grey, p. 547.

14. ZNA S2961, CNC annual report, vol. 2, "Report of the Information Services Branch," 1951, 1st report.

15. ZNA S927/14, PR Dept., film production, 1947–54, synopses of films held by Rhodesia House Film Library.

16. ZNA S932/34/1, CAC corr., pt. 1, memo by SR sec. for NA, 31 Jan. 1946, H. H. D. Simmonds, "Lusaka Broadcasts for Africans."

17. Ibid. The report does not explain what problems broadcasting supposedly caused in South Africa during the war.

18. NA Dept., annual (SR) vol. 37, 1960, "The Information Services Branch," by division of NA, SR. p. 56.

19. ZNA S926/F35, "Film Shows and Reports Thereof."

20. Ibid., Lengthy report by M. Ngulumbra from Fort Jameson.

21. Ibid., report of J. J. Moyo.

22. Ibid., questionnaire for September 1949 Matopos show, report of Shadrock Humeme.

23. Ibid., report of J. K. Dawinga.

24. Ibid., report of R. R. Jack.

25. Ibid., response to films at Matopos, September 1949.

26. Ibid.

27. ZNA S927/17, production files—scripts, 1949–52, Izod to Franklin, 26 May 1949. Izod went on to remark, "I am completely in sympathy with one of the points made—that it is unnecessary for the policemen to upset Mulenga's porridge, but unfortunately this is impossible to alter without spoiling the continuity of the film. The second point, the imprisoning of Mulenga, is I feel open to argument; surely it is up to us to show that if people keep behaving stupidly they'll run foul of the law."

28. ZNA S926/F35, "Film Shows and Reports Thereof." Vambe himself was an employee of the federal government and a keen supporter of federation. He was also a film enthusiast and briefly ran his own commercial cinema in Salisbury. Author interview, Harare.

29. ZNA S926/F54, 1949–53, Native Dept., Salisbury, corr., report of the mobile cinema van (Mashonaland).

30. Ibid., mobile cinema report, 1952.

31. ZNA S3269/61/29, minister's publicity campaign, rural areas, vol. 2, "Report from Mobile Cinema Units Reactions to Minister's Address in Rural Areas," Fort Victoria, A. Felix, 11 Oct. 1962, Solomon Bajilla.

32. This was a common concern among colonial audiences. Norman Spurr, in "The Reactions of Audiences to Films," *Colonial Cinema* 7, no. 1 (1949): 15, noted of his experience showing films to Africans, "It soon became evident that the system of finding out what an audience thought of the films was completely inadequate: there was far too much opinion, too little fact, and sometimes we were deliberately misled . . . 'for,' argued the Africans 'we like these films shows, and they will continue as long as we say they are good'—a most understandable sentiment but not much use to us."

33. Interview with Nell, 15 Mar. 1997, Borrowdale.

34. ZNA S926/F54, 1949–53, Native Dept., Salisbury, corr., mobile cinema report, 1952.

35. Ibid., letter, Izod to CIO, 23 Feb. 1953, re. 1952 Mashonaland officer's report. This refers to "Mr. Hausbrook's report"; Izod commented on the report, "Certainly it is a mistake to permit the camera to show unwanted detail, such as that described in the film, 'The Wives of Nendi.' However, that film was made in 1949, and we claim to have learnt a lot since then."

36. ZNA IS 327B/1367, letter from CIO to producer, CAFU, 15 Sept. 1961, re. extracts from cinema unit reports, Aug. 1961.

37. ZNA S926/F54, 1949–53, Native Dept., Salisbury, corr., mobile cinema officer's report, Oct. 1952. The report stated that approximately 85 percent of the people in the audiences had never seen film before.

38. Ibid., mobile cinema report, 1952.

39. For a discussion of the ethnic particularism of African audiences, see Megan Vaughan, *Curing Their Ills: Colonial Power and African Illness* (Stanford, Calif.: Stanford University Press, 1991).

40. ZNA F 158/F54a, NA Dept., mobile cinema officer's reports, Mar. 1953–Dec. 1957, "Central African Film Unit," 28 Jan. 1954, annual report, mobile cinema unit, Mashonaland South, Aug.–Dec. 1953; *Three Wives*, shown at nine meetings.

41. Southern Rhodesian authorities would later play on audience revulsion at the sight of corpses, making close-ups of dead bodies a fixture of propaganda films made during the 1970s. See Frederikse, *None but Ourselves*, for an account of the infamous "hyena" film in which the camera apparently lingered on the image of a dead guerrilla being eaten by a wild animal.

42. ZNA S926/F54, 1949–53, Native Dept., Salisbury, corr., report of the mobile cinema van (Mashonaland).

43. ZNA S2827/2/2/2, annual district reports, 1952–53.

44. ZNA S926/F54 1949–53, Native Dept., Salisbury, agricultural education in Native Areas, 4 Oct. 1950, memo from provincial native commissioner, Southern Mashonaland, Fort Victoria.

45. ZNA S926/F23, PR Dept., Zomba D. E. Lehman, PRO, to Izod, 8 Dec. 1951.

46. ZNA S926/F56, 1947–52, scriptwriter [Denys Brown] to Nell, 22 Mar. 1954.

47. David Martin and Phyllis Johnson, *The Struggle for Zimbabwe: The Chimurenga War* (Boston: Faber and Faber, 1981), p. 54.

48. Report of the CIO, SR Information Service (Native Affairs), 1961 (Salisbury, 1962).

49. ZNA F121/H103, CAFU monthly reports/newsletter, vol. 2 (1957–62); E. O. Mwasi, federal information assistant, monthly report, films, Oct. to 11 Nov. 1958.

50. CIO Report, SR Native Affairs, 1960.

51. ZNA S926/F54, 1949–53, Native Dept., Salisbury, corr., mobile cinema officer's report, Oct. 1952.

52. Hortense Powdermaker, *Copper Town: Changing Africa: The Human Situation on the Rhodesian Copperbelt* (New York: Harper and Row, 1962), p. 269.

53. ZNA F121/H103, CAFU monthly reports/newsletter, vol. 2, 1957–62, CAFU monthly progress report, Jan. 1961, 3 Feb. 1961.

54. Ibid., "Report on Rhodesia and Nyasaland News Films."

55. ZNA F121 H3/32, Information Dept. propaganda by films, mobile cinema vans, 1 Mar. 1959 to Dec. 1963. This report offers an interesting inversion of Phillips's account of using *Felix the Cat* to stop a riot in South Africa in 1922 (see chap. 1).

56. ZNA F121/H103, CAFU monthly reports/newsletter, vol. 2, 1957–62, "Report on Films," [stamped 2 Oct. 1958] from federal government IO.

57. ZNA IS 327A/236, 10 May 1962, W. T. Nesham to acting sec. to PM and Cabinet Office, re. voting at general elections film.

58. Ibid., Urungwe District 25, Nov. 1963 report by Hahlahla Karoi, Location 27, Nov. 1963.

59. ZNA F163/21/1, "Central African Film Production," K. D.

Leaver, CIO, 2 Jan. 1959, "Historical Film," to director, F. Information Dept., and producer, CAFU.

60. Ibid.

61. ZNA IS 327B/1367, letter from CIO to producer, CAFU, 15 Sept. 1961, re. extracts from cinema unit reports, Aug. 1961.

62. ZNA F327B, corr. from B. Tozer to SIOCIO, n.d.

63. ZNA IS 327B/1367, Gwanda Makobano Store, 22 June 1963.

64. ZNA F121/H11, information: tours by PR staff, Sept. 1958 to 3 Aug. 1961, vol. 1, confidential report on visit to Nyasaland, signed W. V. Brelsford, DOI, 1 July 1960.

65. Sir Roy Welensky, prime minister of the federation.

66. ZNA F121 H3/32, Information Dept., propaganda by films, mobile cinema vans, from 1 Mar. 1959 to Dec. 1963, mobile cinema van report, Southern Province, 19 Feb. 1962, Mikolongwe Veterinary Station.

67. Ibid., from 1 Mar. 1959 to Dec. 1963, mobile cinema van report, Southern Province, 2–7 Apr. 1962, D. Coyle.

68. Ibid., mobile cinema van report, Southern Province, Apr. 18.

69. Ibid.

70. ZNA S927/17, production files—scripts, 1949–52, "The Settlement of the Enswazi Area Report," "History of the Scheme," stamped 17 Dec. 1950 (emphasis in the original).

71. Ibid., unsigned, stamped D. E. Brown, 17 Dec. 1950.

72. Ibid.

73. See discussion of the use of the mobile cinemas in the campaign to impose destocking in Matabelaland, *Debates of the Southern Rhodesian Legislative Assembly*, vol. 42, 1958–59, cols. 377–79, 22 July 1958.

74. ZNA IS 327B, L. Beck, Office of Native Agriculture and Lands, to CIO, 27 Sept. 1961, "Film: New Acres Operator's Report": "I have discussed this matter with the Director of Native Agriculture and we feel that in view of audience reaction to this film and the present difficulties being experienced in implementation of the Native Land Husbandry Act this film should be withdrawn from exhibition to African audiences for the time being."

75. ZNA IS 327B, CIO to native-agriculture director, 15 Sept. 1961, "Gwelo."

76. Ibid., extracts from cinema unit reports, 1–15 Oct. 1962.

77. Ibid., 1–15 Oct. 1962.

78. Ibid.

79. ZNA 1/5/326/2, report from R. M. Kawenda to DC, Mt. Darwin, 17 Nov. 1963: "'Grain Storage' was received with a very cold reception."

80. ZNA CIO/357/237/63, confidential, DALINFORM, SR Government Information Services daily digest, 22 July 1963, Sigangatsha, 13 July, "The film 'Uncle Mupari' was just not liked at all."

81. Ibid., Dorowa Township, 29 June 1963.

82. Ibid., Nov. 1963, Bundura, Goromonzi, and Salisbury, report by J. C. Mundawarara.

83. See chapter 3.

84. ZNA F121 H3/32, Information Dept., propaganda by films, mobile cinema vans, 1 Mar. 1959 to Dec. 1963, fact-finding tour (Northern Mashonaland), 6–12 June, 15 June 1962, E. P. G. Mbofana, information assistant.

85. ZNA CIO/357/243/63, DALINFORM, extracts from mobile cinema unit reports, July 1963. Such hats were associated with Joshua Nkomo and his Zimbabwe African People's Union. See Nkomo's autobiography *The Story of My Life* (London: Methuen, 1984) for a picture of him wearing the signature hat.

86. ZNA F327B, extracts from cinema unit reports, 1–15 Oct. 1962, Mudenda School, 27 July: "During projecting 'Ngoma No. 2' there were shouts of 'ZAPU; PUZA' because of fur hats worn by actors," SR, Mazoe Gwanda.

87. ZNA IS 327A/236, 10 May 1962, W. T. Nesham to acting sec. to PM and Cabinet Office.

88. Ibid., "Southern Matabeleland."

89. Ibid., "Northern Mashonaland."

90. ZNA CIO/357/243/63, DALINFORM, 8 Aug. 1963; extracts from mobile cinema unit reports, July 1963, Gillingham, 25 July.

91. Ibid., extracts from mobile cinema unit reports, July 1963, Beatrice, 16 July.

92. Ibid., appendix: extracts from cinema reports, June 1963, Mpingure School, 4 June 1963.

93. Scenes showing whites doing manual labor were incidental to these movies, at least in the eyes of the producers. Though colonial filmmakers expressed a desire to improve "race relations" in the colonies, they were hesitant to present any images that might offer

problematic comparisons with the social order in Southern Rhodesia. Audience amazement at the sight of white workers reflected a commonly held assumption about Europeans. See, for example, the memoir *The Calling of Katie Makanya*, in which a South African woman expresses astonishment upon seeing white porters during a trip to England.

94. Ibid., Karoi Location, 26 June 1963.

95. ZNA I.S. 326/5, report by A. K. Nyabuko, "Unit 5 Urungwe/Lomagundi District," Lion's Den, 22 Nov. 1963.

96. ZNA S927/17, production files—scripts, 1949–52. Mwanawina III, paramount chief, to prov. commissioner, Mongu, n.d.

97. ZNA S926/F35, "Film Shows and Reports Thereof," *Film Shows* Apr./May 1950, Gideon Naminesu, 2 May 1950.

98. ZNA S2827/2/2/2, annual district reports, 1952–53, Bulawayo. For a discussion of similar complaints about colonial representations in film, see Peter Hansen, "The Dancing Lamas of Everest: Cinema, Orientalism, and Anglo-Tibetan Relations in the 1920s," *American Historical Review* 101, no. 3 (1996): 712.

99. ZNA F121/H103, CAFU monthly reports/newsletter, vol. 2 (1957–62), 3 Dec. 1959, films officer for Northern Rhodesia reports.

100. According to S. Tutani, CAFU employee interviewed by Kedmon Hungwe. My thanks to Professor Hungwe for sharing the transcript with me.

101. *Federation of the Rhodesias and Nyasaland Parliamentary Debates*, vol. 1, 1954–55, 5 Aug. 1954, col. 2282.

102. *Bantu Mirror*, 11 Apr. 1959, p. 1.

103. ZNA IS 326 A mobile cinema corr., box 53278, file DMN5/2/62, 11 July 1962.

104. ZNA F121/H103, CAFU monthly reports/newsletter, vol. 2 (1957–62), "Film and TV Unit: Monthly Progress Report for Mar. 1961," 10 Apr. 1961: "One other item for RNN was planned for shooting, 'African Car Owners Club, Chingola but the cameraman was boycotted.'"

105. ZNA IS 327A, vol. 1, Hammond to Leaver, 27 Sept. 1963, re. SR theme song.

106. See Stephen Peet's interview with Alan Izod, ZNA, oral history catalog (uncataloged interview), p. 38.

107. Harry Franklin, "Film Production in Central Africa," *Colonial Cinema* 11, no. 3 (1953): 72.

108. See ZNA S926/F35, "Film Shows and Reports Thereof," Huggins to A. H. Benson, CAC.

109. ZNA S926/F54, 1949–53, Native Dept., Salisbury, 13 Mar. 1952, letter from M. Campbell, Native Dept., Matobo, Bulawayo, to J. Bowles. Izod reproduced this letter to send to his superiors to indicate the support of the rank-and-file DCs in Southern Rhodesia, though he replaced the offensive term *"munt"* with the more acceptable *native*.

110. ZNA S2961, CNC, annual report, vol. 2, report, assistant native commissioner, Nkai, year ended 31 Dec. 1953.

111. ZNA S926/F54, "1949–53," "Native Dept. Salisbury," 26 Feb. 1952, D. A. Robinson, native-agriculture director, to CIO, re. mobile cinema unit.

112. ZNA S2827/2/2/3, vol. 3, annual district reports, 1955, Melsetter.

113. See, for example, annual district reports, 1957, Sipolilo.

114. ZNA F128/HAF3, Blake Darymple to PM Huggins, 8 Aug. 1953.

115. For the racism of Darymple's oeuvre, see, for example, his 1948 Lux short *Mary's Lucky Day*, which tells the story of an African domestic who, thanks to Lux soap—which makes her several shades lighter—snares a husband. For deceptive advertising, see *Pikki versus the Gorilla*, produced to encourage Africans to drink tea, which portrays boxer Pikki being saved from a knockout repeatedly thanks to a freshly brewed cup of tea. These, along with a handful of other Films of Africa productions, are held at ZNA.

116. ZNA F128/HAF3, Vernon Brelsford, to sec., internal affairs, Nov. 12, 1953.

117. *Debates of the Southern Rhodesian Legislative Assembly*, vol. 42, 1958–59. See later calls for more cinema units in vol. 49, 1961–62, ibid., Mar. 1962, col. 918, Mr. Van Heerden re. cinema units.

118. *CIO Report, SR Native Affairs, 1961*: "At the beginning of 1961, four new mobile cinema units were put into the field."

119. *Debates of the Southern Rhodesian Legislative Assembly*, 31 July 1962, vol. 51, col. 1117: "Last year we engaged a consultant who came out and advised us and it is as a result of his advice that we are having this big increase in mobile cinema vans."

120. *NHUME* (publication of the SR Information Dept.), Mar. 1962 issue, "Mobile Cinema Units."

121. Jan. 1950, quoted in Smyth, "The Central African Film Unit's Images of Empire, 1948–1963," *Historical Journal of Film, Radio, and Television* 3, no. 2 (1983): 135.

122. ZNA S926/F43, press cuttings, 1948–53, *Cape Times*, "Film Brings Education to Central African Natives," Thelma Gutsche, 3 Apr. 1950.

123. *East Africa and Rhodesia*, 1 Sept. 1953.

124. Ibid.

## *Chapter 5*

1. See chapter 1.

2. ZNA F137 169/J, "Film Censorship N.R. Film Censorship Board 71E," to sec. to the cabinet, "Censorship of Films for European Audiences: Northern Rhodesia," 17 Mar. 1950.

3. ZNA F137 169/J, "Film Censorship N.R. Film Censorship Board 71E."

4. Report of sec., internal affairs, 1950 (Salisbury, 1951), "Censorship."

5. Thelma Gutsche, *The History and Social Significance of the Motion Picture in South Africa* (Cape Town: Timmins, 1972), p. 60.

6. Ibbotson was sec.-general of the African Welfare Society and a confidant of Godfrey Huggins, the federal prime minister. See Joshua Nkomo, *The Story of My Life* (London: Methuen, 1984), pp. 48–49.

7. *African Welfare Bulletin*, Feb. 1948.

8. Ibid., Feb. 1953.

9. Ibid.

10. *African Weekly*, 9 Jan. 1952.

11. "Censorship of Films Shown to Africans," *African Weekly*, Feb. 1952.

12. ZNA F121/E76, Home Affairs annual report, 26 Jan. 1955 to 22 June 1959. Annual report for year ended 31 Dec. 1952.

13. Harry Franklin, "The Central African Screen," *Colonial Cinema* 8, no. 4 (Dec. 1950).

14. In his article "The Coming of the Cinema," Stephen Bottomore notes a similar phenomenon in Honduras in the early era of the cinema, when the popularity of westerns from the United States

inspired audiences "to come to think that the entire population of the United States is made up chiefly of cowboys, Indians, and soldiers, who spend their time chasing each other"; quoted in Bottomore, "The Coming of the Cinema," *History Today* 46, no. 3 (1996): 14.

15. ZNA S926/F35, "Film Shows and Reports Thereof," extract from memo from J. D. Reinhalt-Jones, adviser on native affairs, American Corporation of South Africa, sent in reply to request of 16 July 1948. Keenly interested in "native psychology," Reinhalt-Jones was a leading figure in the South African Institute of Race Relations. See Jock McCulloh, *Scientific Racism in Modern South Africa* (Cambridge: Cambridge University Press, 1995), p. 220.

16. Manthia Diawara, "Black Spectatorship: Problems of Identification and Resistance," *Screen* 29, no. 4 (1988).

17. Quoted in Rob Nixon, *Homelands, Harlem, and Hollywood* (New York: Routledge, 1994), p. 35. Several U.S. scholars have told me they have observed this phenomenon in Africa.

18. JoEllen Shively, "Cowboys and Indians: Perceptions of Western Films among American Indians and Anglos," *American Sociological Review* 57, no. 6 (1992): 725–34. The German playwright Berthold Brecht recounted a similar experience after seeing the 1939 film *Gunga Din*, which employs egregious stereotypes about South Asians. Brecht wrote:

> The Indians were primitive creatures, either comic or wicked: comic when loyal to the British and wicked when hostile. The British soldiers were honest, good-humoured chaps and when they used their fists on the mob and "knocked some sense" into them the audience laughed. One of the Indians betrayed his compatriots to the British, sacrificed his life so that his fellow country-men should be defeated, and earned the audience's heart-felt applause. My heart was touched too: I felt like applauding and laughed in all the right places. Despite the fact that I knew all the time that there was something wrong, that the Indians are not primitive and uncultured people but have a magnificent age-old culture, and that Gunga Din could also be seen in a very different light e.g. as a traitor to his people, I was amused and touched because this utterly distorted account was an artistic success and considerable resources in talent and ingenuity had been applied in making it.

Quoted in Jeffrey Richards, "Boys Own Empire: Feature Films and Imperialism in the 1930s," in *Imperialism and Popular Culture*, ed. John MacKenzie (Manchester: Manchester University Press, 1986), p. 144.

19. ZNA 926/F35, "Film Shows and Reports Thereof," Izod (in NR) to Denys Brown, 2 May 1950.

20. ZNA S926/F34/2, S. Peet, director-cameraman, 1951–54, "First Report on Visit to Copperbelt, Apr. 17, 1951."

21. Ibid.

22. Ibid.

23. Louis Nell, *Visions of Yesteryear* (London: Macmillan, 1999), p. 140. Nell believed that the main reason that the CAFU films could not compete with cowboy films was that most colonial directors tended to present long, monotonous sequences of actors talking or methodically doing simple tasks. Interview, Harare, 17 Jan. 1997.

24. Quoted in the *African Weekly*, 11 Oct. 1951, "Many Centres Use 'CAFU' Films."

25. ZNA 926/F35, "Film Shows and Reports Thereof," report on film show held at Sakubva Township, Umtali, Aug. 1950, Gideon Naminesu.

26. Ibid.

27. ZNA CAFU file (uncataloged material), "History of the CAFU, July 1960."

28. Ibid.

29. ZNA S2827/2/2/2, annual district reports, 1952–53.

30. *Rhodesia Southern Department of Native Affairs Report* (Salisbury, 1951).

31. ZNA S926/F54 1949–53, Native Dept., Salisbury, corr., mobile cinema officer's report, Sept. 1952. Belingwe, Selukwe, and Shabani.

32. *Bulawayo Chronicle*, 24 June 1950, p. 1.

33. Quoted in M. Beiel, "Mapantsula: Cinema, Crime, and Politics on the Witwatersrand," *Journal of Southern African Studies* 16, no. 4 (1990): 75.

34. *Bantu Mirror*, 22 Mar. 1952, "Cinema's Effect on Africans." Audiences in Johannesburg were more likely to see American gangster and film noir movies. See Nixon, *Harlem, Homelands, and Hollywood*.

35. SR, *Report of the Department of Native Affairs* (Salisbury, 1953).

36. *African Weekly*, 4 Feb. 1950.

37. *African Daily News*, 23 Sept. 1956, "Cinema Is Harmful," and the minutes of the federal parliament, particularly the debate of 10 Feb. 1960, vol. 44, 1959–60, cols. 2621–24.

38. *Bantu Mirror*, 4 Apr. 1959, "Our Readers' Views," "Wants Better Films, Westerns Condemned."

39. *African Daily News,* 9 Feb. 1957, "'That midnight kiss' was a hit."

40. *African Weekly,* 4 Mar. 1953, "Western Films Preferred" [clipping in CAFU files, ZNA S926/F43].

41. *African Home News,* 14 Feb. 1959.

42. Ibid.

43. *African Home News,* 21 Feb. 1959, "Cinema at MacDonald Hall" (letter to the editor from Wilson Sedambe).

44. *African Weekly,* 1 Oct. 1959.

45. Ibid.

46. Ibid., 28 Feb. 1959, "Cinema Shows at Macdonald Hall" (letter to the editor).

47. *African Daily News,* 5 Mar. 1957.

48. ZNA F121C5/4, Film Censorship Procedure and Working Party report 1960.

49. *African Weekly,* 28 Oct. 1959.

50. Ibid.

51. *African Daily News,* 10 July 1959.

52. Editorial, "Films that Africans Should See," *African Weekly,* 4 Nov. 1959.

53. Front-page story in *African Weekly,* "Call for Immediate End to 'Racial' Film Censorship," 10 Oct. 1959.

54. *African Weekly,* 25 Nov. 1959.

55. B. W. Gussman, *African Life in an Urban Area: A Study of the African Population of Bulawayo* (Bulawayo: Federation of African Welfare Societies in SR, 1952).

56. Ibid., p. 239.

57. Ibid., p. 240.

58. Hortense Powdermaker, *Copper Town: Changing Africa; The Human Situation on the Rhodesian Copperbelt* (New York: Harper and Row, 1962), p. 254.

59. Ibid., p. 258.

60. Powdermaker's views appear to have been influenced by her training as an anthropologist under Bronislaw Malinowski.

61. Powdermaker, *Copper Town.*

62. Ibid., pp. 261–62

63. *Federation of the Rhodesias and Nyasaland Parliamentary Debates,* vol. 1, 1954–55, col. 2278, 5 Aug. 1954, Mr. Kakumbi.

64. Ibid.

65. Ibid., col. 2281.

66. Ibid., 12 Aug. 1957, col. 1177–78, 2282, Mr. Hove.

67. Ibid., col. 1179, Mr. Joyce.

68. Ibid., vol. 44, 1959–60, 10 Feb. 1959, Mr. Knight.

69. Ibid., col. 2621, Mr. McLean.

70. Ibid., Mrs. Watson.

71. Ibid., col. 2623, Dr. Burrows.

72. Ibid., col. 67.

73. Ibid., col. 69.

74. ZNA F121C5/4, Film Censorship Procedure and Working Party report, 1960.

75. Ibid., A. J. Harris, senior welfare officer, and Stephen Tembo, African welfare officer, Lusaka Municipality.

76. Ibid. Shamuyarira went on to become minister of information in the post-independence Zimbabwean government.

77. Ibid., Paver had close connections with several prominent officials in SR government; his newspaper was subsidized by the SR NA Dept.

78. ZNA F121C5/4, minutes, second meeting of Intergovernmental Film Censorship Working Party, 27 Apr. 1960.

79. Ibid.

80. Ibid., first draft of report.

## Chapter 6

1. A. J. Wills, *An Introduction to the History of Central Africa: Zambia, Malawi, and Zimbabwe*, 4th ed. (New York: Oxford University Press, 1990), p. 345.

2. Izod became the head of the Rhodesian government's Audio-Visual Media Section. He remained in the country for only a few years, then emigrated. Brown, who briefly headed CAFU in its final days, also left the colony shortly after the end of federation, settling in Australia.

3. "Film Industry Shocked by Disposal of Costly Govt. Equipment: No Tenders," *Rhodesian Property & Finance*, Mar. 1964.

4. See Elaine Windrich, *The Mass Media in the Struggle for Zimbabwe: Censorship and Propaganda under Rhodesian Front Rule* (Gwelo: Mambo Press, 1981), and Julie Frederikse, *None but Ourselves: Masses vs. Media in the Making of Zimbabwe* (New York: Penguin Books, 1984). Windrich (p. 15) states that "little had been done thus far"

to use modern media to communicate with rural Africans in Rhodesia.

5. See Louis Nell's *Images of Yesteryear* (Harare: HarperCollins, 1998) for the future careers of several CAFU employees.

6. See, for example, *Debates of the Southern Rhodesian Legislative Assembly*, 27 July 1965, col. 1420.

7. Ibid., 1 Apr. 1964, debate on information policy 1508, Mr. Nicholson.

8. Ibid., Sept. 1964, col. 1623.

9. Retired mobile cinema operator Lovermore Mahlahla confirmed that many of his colleagues were sympathetic to the nationalist cause by 1964. He believed that he avoided being sacked only because he was ill at the time of the crisis. Interview with Mahlahla, 18 Mar. 1997.

10. Its most ambitious film for African audiences was the 1947 production *We Were Primitive.* See chapter 4.

11. See *Debates of the Southern Rhodesian Legislative Assembly*, 15 Mar. 1962. Mr. Quinton, speaking for the government, said that twelve new productions were planned for the coming year.

12. See chapter 4.

13. Another production company, Dragon Films, is credited for several early RIS films. The relationship between the two companies, however, is not clear to me. Geoff Laws, a veteran of the CAFU, directed films for both companies.

14. Interview with Atkinson, 4 May 1997. Atkinson went on to assume an important role in film production in Rhodesia during the 1970s. See Nell, *Visions of Yesteryear.*

15. Ibid.

16. ZNA S3269/61/18/16, Dept. of Internal Services: Ministry of Information, Immigration, and Tourism, "New-Type Films for African Audiences," 17 July 1967.

17. Interview with Mahlahla, 18 Mar. 1997.

18. ZNA F5/20/4/65, letter, Field Services, MOI, to director of information, 19 Aug. 1965, written by E. A. J. Stoner, "Summary of Field Research and Film Reaction Reports," 2 Aug. to 13 Aug. 1965, no. 25.

19. One retired cinema operator remembered that agricultural films demonstrating the planting of contour ridges would be greeted with the call, "Not that film again"—interview with Mahlahla, 18 Mar. 1997.

20. ZNA box 60464, location 42–211F, "Summary of Field Research and Film Reaction Reports," Aug. to Sept. 1965, no. 26, letter from Field Services, H. G. Baldwin, to Principal Information Officer, Ministry of Information, 8 Sept. 1965.

21. Similar results had been observed with the showing of a film about agriculture in India, *Silent Revolution*, in 1963. See ZNA unprocessed document "DALINFORM: Southern Rhodesia Government Information Service," 8 Aug. 1963.

22. Report for 1965 of sec., information, immigration, and tourism, Salisbury, 1966.

23. Musoni did not wear glasses or contact lenses when I interviewed him so presumably these were intended to further disguise him. Interview with Ben Musoni, 17 Mar. 1997.

24. *Freedom?* viewed at audio-visual library, ZNA. The library holds copies in Chishona and Sindebele.

25. Summary of field research and film reaction reports, 21 June to 2 July 1965, no. 22, Belingwe.

26. Ibid., 7–18 June 1965, no. 21, Sinoia.

27. Ibid., 26 Apr. to 7 May 1965, no. 18, Umtali.

28. Ibid., 26 Mar. to 9 Apr. 1965, no. 16.

29. Ibid., 4 Mar. 1965, no. 13, Belingwe.

30. ZNA F3/20, field services report, 19–30 July 1965, no. 24, 6 Aug. 1965.

31. Ibid., 10–21 May 1965, no. 19.

32. ZNA box 60464, location 42–211F, summary of field research and film reaction reports, Aug. to Sept. 1965, no. 26.

33. Report of the sec. for information, immigration, and tourism, 1965 (Salisbury, 1966).

34. Ibid.

35. The government received frequent complaints about the films from the handful of African representatives in the legislative assembly. See, for example, Mr. Mkudu's plea to stop the showing of films denigrating African nationalists in 1966, *Debates of the Legislative Assembly of Rhodesia*, 9 Sept. 1966, col. 1002.

36. ZNA S3269/61/18/16, R. C. Haw, "Reactions to Films Made for Africans by the Division of Internal Services." R. M. Thomson, sec., Security Council, described the film in a memo to Ian Smith, the Rhodesian prime minister: "It deals with security forces, their training and their work in the field. It is designed for showing in

tribal areas and is a substitute for 'showing the flag' exercises." See ZNA S3269/61/18/16, propaganda films, 1967–68 (PM Office), restricted, PM Dept., 9 June 1967, "Showing of Propaganda Films."

37. ZNA S3269/61/18/16, R. C. Haw, "Reactions to Films Made for Africans by the Division of Internal Services."

38 ZNA S3269/61/18/16, Department of Internal Services: Ministry of Information, Immigration, and Tourism, "New-Type Films for African Audiences," unsigned, 17 July 1967.

39. Interview with Ben Musoni, 17 Mar. 1997.

40. Ibid.

41. Info. minister (John Hartley Howman), *Debates of the Legislative Assembly of Rhodesia*, vol. 72, Aug.–Sept. 1968, 15 Aug. 1968, col. 228.

42. Ibid., 22 Aug. 1973, col. 101.

43. The popularity of the *Tickey* films is attested to in many mobile cinema reports. The films are also remembered by most Zimbabweans who saw the mobile cinema shows during the 1960s and 1970s. Virtually all of the mobile cinema operators interviewed for this study remarked on the popularity of the series.

44. For example, the 1976 film *Muhammad Tar-baby versus Kid Power*, held at ZNA, which is simply an unedited amateur boxing match.

45. See ibid., 8 Aug. 1973, col. 1669, Mr. Sadomba, speaking on the unpopularity of *Padare*. On the *African Times*, see col. 1671, "People will write in to have The African Times and in most cases we find hundreds of copies of The African Times in grocery shops, etc., and they are usually used for wrapping bread and the like."

46. Aug. 1967, col. 1680, Mr. Samuriwo: "The people of Southern Rhodesia are really getting tired of this propaganda of 'Padare.'"

47. Dislike of *Padare* was uniform among Africans interviewed for this project. For broadcasting under the Rhodesian Front, see Frederikse, *None but Ourselves*, and James Zaffiro, "Broadcasting and Political Change in Zimbabwe, 1931–84" (Ph.D. diss., University of Wisconsin, 1984).

48. ZNA S3269/61/18/16, Dept. of Internal Services. Ministry of Information, Immigration, and Tourism, "New-Type Films for African Audiences," 17 July 1967.

49. See David Martin and Phyllis Johnson, *The Struggle for Zimbabwe: The Chimurenga War* (Boston: Faber and Faber, 1981), p. 91.

50. ZNA, prov. commissioner, Mashonaland South, monthly report, June, mobile cinema tours, 14 July 1973 (uncataloged material).

51. *Debates of the Legislative Assembly of Rhodesia*, 21 June 1972. P. K. Van Der Byle's reply to a question regarding the future of the mobile cinema service.

52. Viewed at Audio Visual Services Library, ZNA.

53. According to interviews with Anthony Kadyevu, interviewed at Ministry of Information, 23 July 1997, and Lawrence Moringay. Both worked as mobile cinema operators during the 1970s.

54. Quoted in Frederikse, *None but Ourselves*, p. 94.

55. See interview with ZANLA political commissar Comrade Prince, ibid. Though the commissar stated that the guerrillas attended the shows to analyze government propaganda, the mobile cinema operators maintained that they came for the entertainment, and particularly enjoyed the *Tickey* films.

56. Interview with Lawrence Moringay.

57. This had been true of earlier films from the 1960s.

58. See Frederikse, *None but Ourselves*, p. 95, on the notorious "hyena" film.

59. The government had produced several films in 1979 intended to muster support for their candidate Bishop Abel Muzorewa. While there are no reports on the reception of these films, the bishop's anemic showing in the elections suggests they failed to inspire audiences.

## Conclusion

1. South African Film Director Rudy Meyer, in 1986—quoted in Gus Silber, "Dream Factory," *Frontline*, June 1986, p. 31.

2. Benedict Anderson, *Imagined Communities* (London: Verso, 1983).

3. Nell has worked for the Zimbabwean government on and off since independence. See his autobiography *Visions of Yesteryear* (London: Macmillan, 1999).

4. This was hinted at by more than one witness, but I have come across no evidence in support of this contention. Certainly, given the reputation of the regime's military and security forces, the suggestion is not implausible.

5. See the debate on *Flame* in the Zimbabwean press, 1996. 4 February 1996, "The Wrong Flame" in the *Sunday Mail*, or 2 June 1996, "Dousing the 'Flame' with Facts," *Sunday Mail.*

# Bibliography

## Published Works

African Education Commission. *Phelps-Stokes Commission on Education in Africa.* New York: Phelps-Stokes Fund, 1922.

Amery, Leo. *The Empire and Prosperity.* London: Faber and Faber, 1930.

Anderson, Benedict. *Imagined Communities.* London: Verso, 1983.

Arrighi, Giovanni. *The Political Economy of Rhodesia.* The Hague: Mouton, 1967.

Astrow, Andre. *Zimbabwe, a Revolution That Lost Its Way?* London: Zed, 1983.

Bakari, Imruh, and Mbye Cham. *African Experiences of Cinema.* London: British Film Institute, 1996.

Barber, James. *Rhodesia: The Road to Rebellion.* London: Oxford University Press, 1967.

Barnes, John, and David Nicholson. *The Leo Amery Diaries.* London: Hutchinson, 1988.

Beach, D. N. *War and Politics in Zimbabwe, 1940–1960.* Gweru: Mambo Press, 1986.

Bernstein, Matthew, and Gaylyn Studlar. *Visions of the East: Orientalism in Film.* New Brunswick, N.J.: Rutgers University Press, 1997.

Bhebe, Ngwabi, and Terrence Ranger. *Society in Zimbabwe's Liberation War.* London: Currey, 1996.

Blake, Robert. *A History of Rhodesia.* London: Methuen, 1977.

Blumer, Herbert, and Philip Hauser. *Movies, Delinquency, and Crime.* New York: Macmillan, 1933.

Burke, Timothy. *Lifebuoy Men, Lux Women: Commodification, Consumption, and Cleanliness in Modern Zimbabwe.* Durham, N.C.: Duke University Press, 1996.

Burns, Alan. *Colonial Civil Servant.* London: Allen and Unwin, 1949.

Cameron, Kenneth M. *Africa on Film: Beyond Black and White.* New York: Continuum, 1994.

Caute, David. *Under the Skin: The Death of White Rhodesia.* London: Lane, 1983.

Chief Secretary. "The Information Services Branch." *N.A.D.A.,* no. 37 (1960): 56.

Chowdhry, Prem. *Colonial India and the Making of Empire Cinema: Image, Ideology, and Identity.* Manchester: Manchester University Press, 2000.

Comaroff, Jean, and John Comaroff. *Revelation and Revolution: Christianity, Colonialism, and Consciousness in South Africa,* vol. 1. Chicago: University of Chicago Press, 1991.

Cooper, Gordon. *Life's a Short Summer: The Tale of One Man's Life.* London: Jarrolds, 1958.

Curran, James, and Vincent Porter, eds. *British Cinema History.* Totowa, N.J.: Barnes and Noble Books, 1983.

Davis, J. Merle. *Modern Industry and the African.* London: Macmillan, 1933.

Davis, Peter. *In Darkest Hollywood: Exploring the Jungles of Cinema's South Africa.* Athens: Ohio University Press, 1996.

Diawara, Manthia. *African Cinema: Politics and Culture.* Bloomington: Indiana University Press, 1992.

Dickson, Alec. *A Chance to Serve.* Ed. Mora Dickson. London: Dobson, 1976.

Dorman, T. E. *African Experience: On Education Officers in Northern Rhodesia.* London: Radcliffe Press, 1993.

Ellert, Henry. *The Rhodesian Front War: Counter-insurgency and Guerrilla War in Rhodesia, 1962–1980.* Gweru: Mambo Press, 1989.

Fanon, Frantz. *White Skin, Black Masks.* New York: Grove Press, 1967.

———. *The Wretched of the Earth.* New York: Grove Press, 1963.

Flower, Ken. *Serving Secretly: An Intelligence Chief on Record: Rhodesia into Zimbabwe, 1964 to 1981.* London: Murray, 1987.

Fraenkel, Peter. *Wayaleshi.* London: Weidenfield and Nicholson, 1959.

Franklin, Harry. *Unholy Wedlock: The Failure of the Central African Federation.* London: Allen and Unwin, 1963.

Frederikse, Julie. *None but Ourselves: Masses vs. Media in the Making of Zimbabwe.* New York: Penguin Books, 1984.

Freund, Bill. *The Making of Contemporary Africa: The Development of African Society Since 1800.* Boulder: Lynne Rienner, 1998.

Gale, W. D. *Zambezi Sunrises: How Civilization Came to Rhodesia and Nyasaland.* Cape Town: Timmins, 1958.

Gann, Louis. *A History of Southern Rhodesia: Early Days to 1934.* London: Chatto and Windus, 1965.

Godwin, Peter. *Mukiwa: A White Boy in Africa.* London: Picador, 1996.

Godwin, Peter, and Ian Hancock. *Rhodesians Never Die.* Oxford: Oxford University Press, 1993.

Gramsci, Antonio. *Prison Notebooks.* New York: Columbia University Press, 1991.

Gray, Richard. *The Two Nations: Aspects of the Development of Race Relations in the Rhodesias and Nyasaland.* London: Oxford University Press, 1960.

Gussman, B. W. *African Life in an Urban Area: A Study of the African Population of Bulawayo.* Bulawayo: Federation of African Welfare Societies, 1952.

Gutsche, Thelma. *The History and Social Significance of the Motion Picture in South Africa.* Cape Town: Timmins, 1972.

Hughes, Langston. *An African Treasury.* London: Gollanz, 1961.

Huxley, Julian. *African View.* New York: Harper and Brothers, 1931.

Iliffe, John. *Famine in Zimbabwe, 1890–1960.* Gweru: Mambo Press, 1990.

Jahoda, Gustav. *White Man: A Study of the Attitudes of Africans to Europeans in Ghana before Independence.* London: Oxford University Press, 1961.

Kennedy, Dane. *Islands of White: Settler Society and Culture in Kenya and Southern Rhodesia, 1890–1939.* Durham, N.C.: Duke University Press, 1987.

Kileff, Clive, and W. C. Pendleton, eds. *Urban Man in Southern Africa.* Gweru: Mambo Press, 1975.

Kriger, Norma J. *Zimbabwe's Guerrilla War: Peasant Voices.* Cambridge: Cambridge University Press, 1992.

Küster, Sybille. *Neither Cultural Imperialism nor Precious Gift of Civilization: African Education in Colonial Zimbabwe, 1890–1962.* Münster: Lit, 1994.

Lan, David. *Guns and Rain: Guerrillas and Spirit Mediums in Zimbabwe.* Berkeley: University of California Press, 1985.

Low, Rachael. *History of Film, 1929–1939,* vol. 5: *Documentary and Education Films of the 1930's.* London: Allen and Unwin, 1979.

MacKenzie, John M. *Orientalism: History, Theory, and the Effects.* Manchester: Manchester University Press, 1995.

———. *Propaganda and Empire.* Manchester: Manchester University Press, 1984.

———, ed. *Imperialism and Popular Culture.* Manchester: Manchester University Press, 1986.

Maddox, Gregory. *Conquest and Resistance to Colonialism in Africa.* New York: Garland, 1993.

Malkmus, Lizbeth, and Roy Armes. *Arab and African Film Making.* London: Zed, 1991.

Mamdani, Mahmood. *Citizen and Subject: Contemporary Africa and the Legacy of Late Colonialism.* Princeton, N.J.: Princeton University Press, 1996.

Marks, Shula, and Dagmar Engels, eds. *Contesting Colonial Hegemony.* London: St. Martin's Press, 1994.

Marks, Shula, and Richard Rathbone, eds. *Industrialisation and Social Change in South Africa: Africa Class Formation, Culture, and Consciousness, 1870–1930.* New York: Longman, 1982.

Martin, David, and Phyllis Johnson. *The Struggle for Zimbabwe: The Chimurenga War.* Boston: Faber and Faber, 1981.

Martin, Phyllis M. *Leisure and Society in Colonial Brazzaville.* Cambridge: Cambridge University Press, 1995.

Maynar, Richard. *African Film: Myth and Reality.* New York: Bantam, 1974.

McCulloh, Jock. *Scientific Racism in Modern South Africa.* Cambridge: Cambridge University Press, 1995.

Memmi, Albert. *The Colonizer and the Colonized.* New York: Orion Press, 1965.

Meredith, Martin. *The Past Is Another Country: Rhodesia, 1890–1979.* London: Deutsch, 1979.

Mnyanda, B. J. *In Search of Truth.* Bombay: Hind Kitaby, 1954.

Morton-Williams, P. *Cinema in Rural Nigeria: A Field Study of the Impact of Fundamental-Education Films on Rural Audiences in Nigeria.* Ibadan: Federal Information Services, 1953.

Mudimbe, V. Y. *The Invention of Africa: Gnosis, Philosophy, and the Order of Knowledge.* Bloomington: Indiana University Press, 1988.

Mungazi, Dickson A. *Colonial Policy and Conflict in Zimbabwe: A Study of Cultures in Collision, 1890–1979.* New York: Crane Russak, 1992.

Murray, D. J. *The Governmental System in Southern Rhodesia.* Oxford. Clarendon Press, 1970.

Nell, Louis. *Images of Yesteryear.* London: Macmillan, 1999.

Nixon, Rob. *Homelands, Harlem, and Hollywood.* New York: Routledge, 1994.

Notcutt, L. A., and Geoffrey Latham. *The African and the Cinema.* London: Edinburgh House, 1937.

Pauw, B. A. *Xhosa in Town: The Second Generation: A Study of the Family among the Urbanized Bantu in East London.* Cape Town: Oxford University Press, 1963.

Pearce, R. D. *The Turning Point in Africa.* London: Cass, 1982.

Pearson, George. *Flashback: The Autobiography of a British Film Maker.* London: G. Allen and Unwin, 1957.

Phillips, Ray. *The Bantu in the City.* New York: Lovedale Press, 1938.

Phimster, Ian. *An Economic and Social History of Zimbabwe, 1890–1948: Capital Accumulation and Class Struggle.* London: Longman, 1988.

———. *Wangi Kolia: Coal, Capital, and Labour in Colonial Zimbabwe, 1894–1954.* Johannesburg: Witwatersrand University Press, 1994.

Powdermaker, Hortense. *Copper Town: Changing Africa: The Human Situation on the Rhodesian Copperbelt.* New York: Harper and Row, 1962.

Pronay, Nicholas, and D. W. Spring, eds. *Propaganda, Politics, and Film, 1918–45.* London: Macmillan, 1982.

Ramirez, Francis, and Christian Rolot. *Histoire du cinéma colonial au Zaïre au Rwanda et au Burundi.* Tervuren, Belgium: Musée Royal de l'Afrique Centrale, 1985.

Ranger, T. O. *The African Voice in Southern Rhodesia, 1898–1930.* Evanston: Northwestern University Press, 1970.

———. *Dance and Society in Eastern Africa, 1890–1970: The Beni Ngoma.* Berkeley: University of California Press, 1975.

———. *The Invention of Tribalism in Zimbabwe.* Gweru: Mambo Press, 1985.

———. *Revolt in Southern Rhodesia, 1896–97: A Study in African Resistance.* London: Heinemann, 1967.

Rasmussen, R. Kent. *Historical Dictionary of Rhodesia/Zimbabwe.* New Jersey: Scarecrow Press, 1979.

Roberts, Andrew D. *The Colonial Moment in Africa: Essays on the Movements of Minds and Materials, 1900–1940.* Cambridge: Cambridge University Press, 1986.

Rogers, Cyral, and C. Frantz. *Racial Themes in Southern Rhodesia: The Attitudes and Behavior of the White Population.* New Haven: Yale University Press, 1962.

Rotberg, Richard. *The Rise of Nationalism in Central Africa: The Making of Malawi and Zambia, 1873–1964.* Cambridge: Harvard University Press, 1964.

Said, Edward. *Culture and Imperialism.* New York: Knopf, 1993.

———. *Orientalism.* New York: Vintage, 1979.

Schmidt, Elizabeth. *Peasants, Traders, and Wives: Shona Women in the History of Zimbabwe, 1870–1939.* London: Currey, 1992.

Scott, James. *Domination and the Arts of Resistance: Hidden Transcripts.* New Haven: Yale University Press, 1990.

———. *Weapons of the Weak: Everyday Forms of Peasant Resistance.* New Haven: Yale University Press, 1985.

Shamuyarira, Nathan M. *Crisis in Rhodesia.* London: Deutsch, 1965.

Stoneman, Colin, and Lionel Cliffe. *Zimbabwe: Politics, Economics, and Society.* London: Pinter, 1989.

Summers, Carol. *From Civilization to Segregation: Social Ideals and*

*Social Control in Southern Rhodesia, 1890–1934.* Athens: Ohio University Press, 1994.

Tamarkin, M. *The Making of Zimbabwe: Decolonization in Regional and International Politics.* London: Cass, 1990.

Tanser, George Henry. *A Scanting of Time: The Story of Salisbury, Rhodesia, 1890–1900.* Salisbury: Pioneer Head Press, 1974.

Taylor, Charles T. C. *The History of Rhodesian Entertainment, 1890–1930.* Salisbury: Taylor, 1968.

Thomas, Nicholas. *Colonialism's Culture: Anthropology, Travel, and Government.* Princeton, N.J.: Princeton University Press, 1994.

Tomaselli, Keyan. *The Cinema of Apartheid: Race and Class in South African Film.* New York: Smyrna/Lake View Press, 1988.

Tsivian, Yuri. *Early Cinema in Russia and Its Cultural Reception.* Trans. Alan Bodger. Foreword Tom Gunning. New York: Routledge, 1994.

Ukadike, Frank. *Black African Cinema.* Berkeley: University of California Press, 1994.

Vambe, Lawrence. *An Ill-fated People: Zimbabwe Before and After Rhodes.* London: Heinemann, 1972.

———. *From Rhodesia to Zimbabwe.* London: Heinemann, 1976.

Van Onselen, Charles. *Chibaro: African Mine Labour in Southern Rhodesia, 1900–1933.* London: Pluto Press, 1976.

Vaughan, Megan. *Curing Their Ills: Colonial Power and African Illness.* Stanford, Calif.: Stanford University Press, 1991.

Wason, Eugene. *Banned: The Story of the* African Daily News. London: Hamilton, 1976.

Wills, A. J. *An Introduction to the History of Central Africa: Zambia, Malawi, and Zimbabwe.* 4th ed. New York: Oxford University Press, 1990.

Wright, Allan. *Valley of the Iron Woods.* Cape Town: South African Cape and Transvaal Printers, 1972.

## *Journal Articles and Chapters in Edited Collections*

"Africa and the Cinema." *African Society* 37 (1937): 127–28.

"African Educational Cinema Project." *Oversea Education* 6 (July 1935): 189.

Allen, Robert C. "From Exhibition to Reception: Reflections on the Audience in Film." *Screen* 31, no. 4 (1990): 347–56.

Arora, Poonam. "Imperilling the Prestige of the White Woman: Colonial Anxiety and Film Censorship in British India." *Visual Anthropology Review* 11, no. 2 (1995).

Baëta, A. R. "The Two Worlds." *Sight and Sound* 17, no. 65 (1948): 5–8.

Beiel, M. "Mapantsula: Cinema, Crime, and Politics on the Witwatersrand." *Journal of Southern African Studies* 16, no. 4 (1990).

Bishop, T. "Film Making in Udi." *Spectator*, 1 April 1949, p. 431.

Bottomore, Stephen. "The Coming of the Cinema." *History Today* 46, no. 3 (1996): 14–20.

———. "The Panicking Audience? Early Cinema and the 'Train Effect.'" *Historical Journal of Film, Radio, and Television* 19, no. 2 (1999).

Brelsford, Vernon. "Analysis of African Reactions to Propaganda Film." *N.A.D.A.: The Southern Rhodesian Native Affairs Department Annual*, no. 24 (1947): 7–22.

Carstairs, C. Y. "The Colonial Cinema." *Corona* (February 1953): 53.

———. "Information Services as an Aid to Administration." *Journal of African Administration* 5 (1953): 2–7.

Chirgwin, A. M. "Films and the African." *Spectator*, 3 December 1937, pp. 986–87.

Cooper, Gordon. "Filming the Matabele." *N.A.D.A.* (1934): 60–63.

Davis, J. Merle. "The Cinema and Missions in Africa." *International Review of Missions* 25, no. 99 (1936): 378–83.

———. "The Bantu Educational Cinema Experiment." *Africa* 8 (July 1935): 164–69.

Diawara, Manthia. "Black Spectatorship: Problems of Identification and Resistance." *Screen* 29, no. 4 (1988): 66–76.

Dickson, A. G. "Mass Education on Togoland." *African Affairs* 1 (1950): 136–50.

———. "Studies in War-time Organization: The Mobile Propaganda Unit, East Africa Command." *African Affairs* (1945): 9–19.

Dickson, Alec. "Tell Africa." *Geographical Magazine* 11, no. 3 (1946): 456–62.

Donald, R. "Films and the Empire." *Nineteenth Century* 100, no. 596 (1926): 497–510.

Dumont, Lieut. "Mobile Film Units in Morocco." *Fundamental Education* 2, no. 4 (1950): 12–16.

Expatriate. "An African Observer in London." *African Observer* 4, no. 4 (1936): 58.

Feldman, Seth. "Viewer, Viewing, Viewed: A Critique of Subject-Generated Documentary." *Journal of the University Film Association* 29, no. 1 (1977): 23–26.

"Films for Illiterate Peoples." *Empire* 4, no. 4 (1941): 5.

"Films for Primitive Peoples." *Documentary Newsletter* (March 1940): 10.

Forsdale, Louis. "Comments on Work with Film Preliterates in Africa." *Studies in Visual Communication* 9 (winter 1983): 30–35.

Franklin, Harry. "The Central African Screen." *Colonial Cinema* 8, no. 4 (1950): 85–86.

Grierson, John. "Film in British Colonial Development." *Sight and Sound* 17, no. 65 (1948): 2–4.

Hansen, Peter H. "The Dancing Lamas of Everest: Cinema, Orientalism, and Anglo-Tibetan Relations in the 1920s." *American Historical Review* 101, no. 3 (1996): 712–44.

Hawkins, Gerald. "A Travelling Cinema in Malaya." *Overseas Education* 8 (July 1937).

Holbrook, Wendell P. "British Propaganda and the Mobilization of the Gold Coast War Effort." *Journal of African History* 26 (1985): 327–61.

Hungwe, Kedmon. "Southern Rhodesian Propaganda and Education Films for Peasant Farmers, 1943–1955." *Historical Journal of Film, Radio, and Television* 11, no. 3 (1991): 229–41.

Izod, Alan. "Some Special Features of Colonial Film Production." In *The Film in Colonial Development: A Report of a Conference.* London: British Film Institute, 1948.

Jayesinghe, C. "The Imperial Film Project." *Modern Review* (1927): 675–76.

Kellerman, G. "The Cinema in Asia and Africa." *East and West Review* 2 (1936): 295–303.

Kerr, David. "The Best of Both Worlds: Colonial Film Policy and Practice in Northern Rhodesia and Nyasaland." *Critical Arts: A Journal of Cultural Study*, no. 2 (1993): 11–42.

Latham, G. C. "The Use of the Film for Educational Purposes in Northern Rhodesia." *Sight and Sound* 1, no. 2 (June 1932).

———. "Films for Africa." *Sight and Sound* 6, no. 24 (1936–37): 123–25

Lewis, L. J. "Visual Aids in the Mission Field." *International Review of Missions* (October 1945): 421–26.

Little, K. "The Sociological Implications of the Film in Colonial Africa." *Colonial Review* (1948).

"Mobile Film Units Work in Gold Coast." *Africa World* (5 February 1944).

Notcutt, L. A. "The African and the Cinema." *Sight and Sound* (1937): 90.

Odunton, G. "One Step Ahead." *Colonial Cinema* 8, no. 2 (1950): 29.

Pearson, George. "Health Education by Film in Africa." *Colonial Cinema* 7, no. 1 (1949): 17.

———. "One Step Ahead." *Colonial Cinema* 8, no. 2 (1950).

Phillips, Ray. "The African and the Cinema." *Race Relations* 5, no. 3 (1938).

"Presenting the Colonies in Films." *Corona* (March 1959): 104–5.

"Putting Film to Work in the Colonies." *Colonial Development: A Magazine Devoted to Development in the Colonies* 2, no. 1 (1956): 16–18.

Roberts, A. D. "Africa on Film to 1940." *History in Africa* 14 (1987): 189–227.

Ross, L. M. "Africans and Propaganda Films." *United Empire* 30 (February 1940): 63–65.

Rouch, Jean. "The Situation and Tendencies of the Cinema in Africa." Trans. Steve Field. *Studies in the Anthropology of Visual Education* 2, no. 1 (1975): 112–20.

Schauder, Leon. "South Africa, I Presume!" *Sight and Sound* 8, no. 30 (1939): 55–57.

Sellers, William. "Films for Primitive Peoples." *Documentary Newsletter*, September 1941, 173–74.

———. "Making Films in and for the Colonies." *Journal of the Royal Society of the Arts* 101 (1953): 829–37.

———. "The Production of Films for Primitive People." *Oversea Education: A Journal of Educational Experiment and Research in Tropical and Sub-tropical Areas* (October 1941): 221–26.

Shiels, T. Drummond. "The Cinema for Africans." *International Review of Missions* (April 1938): 268–71.

Shively, JoEllen. "Cowboys and Indians: Perceptions of Western Films among American Indians and Anglos." *American Sociological Review* 57, no. 6 (1992): 725–34.

Silber, Gus. "Dream Factory." *Frontline*, June 1986, 30–31.

Smyth, Rosaleen. "Britain's African Colonies and British Propaganda during the Second World War." *Journal of Imperial and Commonwealth History* 14, no. 1 (1985): 66–82.

———. "The British Colonial Film Unit and Sub-Saharan Africa, 1939–1945." *Historical Journal of Film, Radio, and Television* 8 (1988): 285–98.

———. "The Central African Film Unit's Images of Empire, 1948–1963." *Historical Journal of Film, Radio, and Television* 3, no. 2 (1983): 135–43.

———. "The Development of British Colonial Film Policy, 1927–1939, with Special Reference to East and Central Africa." *Journal of African History* 20, no. 3 (1979): 437–50.

———. "Movies and Mandarins: The Official Film and British Colonial Africa." In *British Cinema History*, ed. James Curran and Vincent Porter. Totowa, N.J.: Barnes and Noble Books, 1983.

———. "A Note on the 'Saucepan Special': The People's Radio of Central Africa." *Historical Journal of Film, Radio, and Television* 4, no. 2 (1984): 195–201.

———. "The Post-War Career of the Colonial Film Unit in Africa: 1946–1955." *Historical Journal of Film, Radio, and Television* 12, no. 2 (1992): 163–77.

———. "War Propaganda during the Second World War in Northern Rhodesia." *African Affairs* 83 (July 1984): 337–45.

"South African Developments." *Sight and Sound* 6, no. 21 (Spring 1937): 15–16.

"Southern Rhodesia's First Film." *Saturday Review* 160 (23 November 1935): 508.

Spurr, Norman. "The Reactions of Audiences to Films." *Colonial Cinema* 6, no. 3 (1949).

————. "Regarding Odunton's Article." *Colonial Cinema* 8, no. 2 (1950).

Staiger, Janet. "The Handmaiden of Villainy: Method and Problems in Studying the Historical Reception of a Film." *Wide Angle* 8, no. 1 (1986): 20–27.

Stam, Robert, and Louise Spence. "Colonialism, Racism, and Representation." *Screen* 24, no. 2 (1983).

Stephenson, Rex. "Cinema and Censorship in Colonial Malaya." *Journal of Southeast Asian Studies* 5, no. 2 (1974): 209–24.

Swann, Paul. "The Selling of the Empire: The Empire Marketing Board Film Unit." *Studies in Visual Communication* 9, no. 3 (1983).

Van Bever, L. "The Cinema in the Belgian Congo." *Colonial Review* 13, no. 3 (1952).

"Walt Disney Prepares Health and Educational Films for Africa." *Books for Africa* (April 1944): 424–25.

Weber, Charles W. "British Film, Empire, and Society in the Twenties: The 'Livingstone Film,' 1923–1925." *Historical Journal of Film, Radio, and Television* 9, no. 1 (1989): 3–17.

Woolliams, Gordon F. "Nigerian Nights." *Sight and Sound* 7, no. 25 (1938): 13.

## Official Publications

British Film Institute. *The Film in Colonial Development: A Report of a Conference.* London: British Film Institute, 1948.

Colonial Office Conference. *Summary of Proceedings.* London, 1927.

Commission on Education and Cultural Films. *The Film in National Life: Being the Report of an Enquiry Conducted by the Commission on Educational and Cultural Films into the Service which the Cinematograph May Render to Education and Social Progress.* London: Allen and Unwin, 1932.

*Debates of the Legislative Assembly of Rhodesia.* Salisbury, 1965–80.

*Debates of the Southern Rhodesian Legislative Assembly.* Salisbury, 1923–65.

*Federation of the Rhodesias and Nyasaland Parliamentary Debates.* Salisbury, 1953–63.

*Report of the Chief Information Officer, Southern Rhodesia Information Service (Division of Native Affairs).* Salisbury, 1962.

*Report of the Colonial Films Committee.* London: H.M. Stationery Office, 1927.

*Report of the Secretary for Information, Immigration, and Tourism.* Salisbury, 1966.

*Rhodesia Southern Department of Native Affairs Report.* Salisbury, 1951.

UNESCO. *The Use of Mobile Cinema and Radio Vans in Fundamental Education.* Paris: UNESCO, 1949.

——. *The Cinema and Social Science: A Survey of Ethnographic and Sociological Films.* Paris: UNESCO, 1962.

## Unpublished Manuscripts

Burke, Timothy. "Our Mosquitoes Are Not So Large." Paper presented at Yale Conference on Colonial Representation, January 1997.

Dillon, Roger. "Rhodesian African Cinema Study." Dillon Enterprises, Salisbury, 1976.

Giltrow, David, and Peggy Giltrow. "Cinema with a Purpose: Films for Development in British Colonial Africa." Paper presented at the African Studies Association (U.K.) meeting, University of Kent, 17–19 September 1986.

Hobson, Dick. "The Copperbelt and the Cinema." N.d.

Larkin, Bryan. "Uncertain Consequences: The Social and Religious Life of Media in Northern Nigeria." Ph.D. diss., New York University, 1998.

Mangin, Geoffrey. "Filming Emerging Africa: A Pioneer Cinematographer's Scrapbook—from the 1940s to the 1960s." May 1997.

Smyth, Rosaleen. "The Development of Government Propaganda in Northern Rhodesia up to 1953." Ph.D. diss., University of London, 1983.

Ssali, Mike Hilary. "The Development and Role of an African Film

Industry in East Africa, with Special Reference to Tanzania, 1922–1984." Ph.D. diss., University of California, Los Angeles, 1986.

Taviringana, Silas. "Art and Political Domination: The Case of the Central African Film Unit (CAFU) and the Rhodesia Ministry of Information Entertainment Films." Paper presented at colloquium of Zimbabwe Literal Art, University of Zimbabwe, 10–11 May, 1990.

Zaffiro, James. "Broadcasting and Political Change in Zimbabwe, 1931–1984." Ph.D. diss., University of Wisconsin, 1984.

## Newspapers

*African Daily News.* Salisbury.
*African Eagle.* Salisbury.
*African Home News.* Salisbury.
*African Weekly.* Salisbury.
*African Welfare Bulletin.* Salisbury.
*Bantu Mirror.* Salisbury.
*Bulawayo Chronicle.* Bulawayo, Rhodesia.
*East Africa and Rhodesia.* London, United Kingdom.
*Livingstone Mail.* Livingstone, Northern Rhodesia.
*Nyasaland Herald.* Zomba.
*Rhodesia Herald.* Salisbury.
*Rhodesian Property & Finance.* Salisbury.
*NHUME.* Salisbury.

## Films Viewed

### National Archives of Zimbabwe Audio Visual Library

| Title | Year | Production Company | Director |
|---|---|---|---|
| *We Were Primitive* | 1947 | SRIS | Frank Goodliffe |
| *The Five Messengers* | 1948 | CAFU | Louis Nell |

| | | | |
|---|---|---|---|
| *Mujenje Builds a Bridge* | 1948 | CAFU | Stephen Peet |
| *John Meets Trouble* | 1948 | CAFU | Stephen Peet |
| *Feniasi and Timoti* | 1948 | CAFU | Louis Nell |
| *Game Ranger* | 1948 | CAFU | Louis Nell |
| *The Box* | 1948 | CAFU | Louis Nell |
| *They Left the Plains* | 1948 | CAFU | Louis Nell |
| *The Two Farmers* | 1948 | CAFU | Alan Izod |
| *Africans in Action* | 1949 | CAFU | ? |
| *Bekapi Goes to Nyanyadzi* | 1949 | CAFU | Stephen Peet |
| *Kachesa Farmer* | 1949 | CAFU | Louis Nell |
| *Building Barns, part 1* | 1949 | | |
| *Kilyoni, Peasant Farmer* | 1949 | CAFU | ? |
| *The Thief* | 1949 | CAFU | Stephen Peet |
| *Lusaka Calling* | 1949 | CAFU | Louis Nell |
| *Marimo Finds a New Life* | 1949 | CAFU | ? |
| *Mangwende and the Trees* | 1949 | CAFU | ? |
| *Mattaka Takes Advice* | 1950 | CAFU | Anker Atkinson |
| *Nyoro Gets a Letter* | 1950 | CAFU | Louis Nell |
| *Ncube Cultivates His Land* | 1951 | CAFU | ? |
| *The Story of Mdhlongwa* | 1951 | CAFU | ? |
| *Mattaka Buys a Motor Car* | 1951 | CAFU | ? |
| *Farmers of Mshawasha* | 1953 | CAFU | ? |
| *Philemon the Footballer* | 1953 | CAFU | Stephen Peet |
| *Benzi Comes to Town* | 1958 | CAFU | Anker Atkinson |
| *Jamboree Ruwa Park* | 1959 | CAFU | Roger Fairlie |
| *Copperfists* | 1963 | CAFU | Louis Nell |
| *The Story of Petale* | n.d. | CAFU | Anker Atkinson |
| *Bad Day for Bota* | n.d. | CAFU | Michael Hay |
| *Free from Fear* | n.d. | CAFU | Henry Berriff |
| *Mapolisa* | n.d. | CAFU | Anker Atkinson |
| *Mulenga Wins a Bride* | n.d. | CAFU | Anker Atkinson |
| *Rachael Hlazo* | | | |
| *Home Demonstrator* | n.d. | CAFU | ? |
| *Visit to a Shangaan Village* | n.d. | CAFU | Stephen Peet |
| *Ncube Plows a Slope* | n.d. | CAFU | ? |

| | | | |
|---|---|---|---|
| *Buke's Bicycle* | n.d. | CAFU | ? |
| *A Stake in the Land* | n.d. | CAFU | ? |
| *The See Saw Years* | n.d. | CAFU | Dick Raynor |
| *Two Generations* | n.d. | CAFU | ? |
| *The Two Salisburys* | n.d. | CAFU | ? |
| *Life in The Federation* | n.d. | CAFU | ? |
| *New Acres* | n.d. | CAFU | ? |
| *Farming in the Federation* | n.d. | CAFU | ? |
| *Rhodesia Nyasaland News 1* | | CAFU | |
| *Rhodesia Nyasaland News 2* | | CAFU | |
| *Rhodesia Nyasaland News 3* | | CAFU | |
| *Rhodesia Nyasaland News 4* | | CAFU | |
| *Rhodesia Nyasaland News 47* | | CAFU | |
| *Rhodesia Nyasaland News 63* | | CAFU | |
| *Rhodesia Nyasaland Spotlight 73* | | CAFU | |
| *People on the Move* | n.d. | RIS | ? |
| *Lest We Forget* | n.d. | RIS | ? |
| *Edge of Understanding* | n.d. | RIS | Dick Raynor |
| *Fair Profile* | n.d. | RIS | ? |
| *The Band Leader* | n.d. | Dragon | ? |
| *More Cash for Cattle* | n.d. | Dragon | Geoff Laws |
| *The Good Life* | n.d. | Eagle Films | ? |
| *Pikki Vs. The Gorilla* | n.d. | ? | ? |
| *The Stolen Cigarette* | n.d. | Films of Africa | Blake Darymple |
| *Mary's Lucky Day* | n.d. | Films of Africa | Blake Darymple |
| *Mari Itsva* | 1969 | RIS | ? |
| *Freedom?* | n.d. | RIS | ? |
| *Hurricane* | n.d. | RIS | ? |
| *Contact* | n.d. | RIS | ? |
| *The Saints* | n.d. | RIS | ? |
| *Rhodesian Light Infantry* | n.d. | RIS | ? |
| *Entering a Kraal* | n.d. | RIS | ? |
| *New Initiative* | 1976 | RIS | ? |
| *How to Vote* | 1979 | RIS | ? |

| *Amnesty* | 1979 | RIS | ? |
|---|---|---|---|
| *Age and Mystery* | n.d. | RIS | Roger Fairlie |
| *Batonga Clinic* | n.d. | RIS | ? |
| *A Chief Speaks* | n.d. | RIS | ? |
| *Muhammed Tar Baby* *vs. Kid Power* | n.d. | RIS | ? |

## National Film Archive, London

| *Men of Africa* | 1939 | Strand | ? |
|---|---|---|---|
| *Livingstone* | 1925 | Various | M. A. Wetherell |
| *Riddle of Rhodesia* | 1936? | African Films | J. Albrecht |
| *Veterinary Training* | 1937 | BEKE | L. A. Notcutt |
| *African Peasant Farms:* *The Kilongwira Experiment* | 1937 | BEKE | L. A. Notcutt |
| *Tropical Hookworm* | 1937 | BEKE | L. A. Notcutt |

## Other

| *Rouch in Reverse* | 1995 | Formation Films | Manthia Diawara |
|---|---|---|---|

## *Interviewees and Contributors*

Anker Atkinson

Geoffrey Mangin

Alan Izod

Richard Raynor

Louis Nell

Edward Chiranga

Anthony Kadyevu

[?] Garwe

David Hlazo

Lovermore Mhlala

Ben Musoni

Lawrence Moringay
Sylvester Timuri
Lawrence Vambe

# Index

inability to recognize two-
dimensional images, 39, 51
inability to understand cartoons,
47, 53, 69
reactions of rural Africans to
film shows, 121
reactions to first CAFU shows,
118–19
reactions to kissing on screen,
12, 182
"resistant spectatorship," 107,
157, 163, 202
simplistic sense of humor, 34, 67
tests of film comprehension, 38,
56, 96
undiscriminating nature of, 65
audiences (European), 16, 182

Baëta, A. R., 54
Banda, Hastings, 129, 131
Bantu Educational Kinema Ex-
periment (BEKE), 22, 26, 28,
30, 49, 50, 51, 79, 103
production of films, 27
views on African film literacy, 50
*Bantu Mirror* (newspaper), 143,
163–65
Barkas, Geoffrey, 68
Barotse, 42
Barotseland (Northern Rhodesia),
142
Batonka, 144
Battle of Blood River, 6
Battle of Britain, 63
Bekolo, Jean-Pierre, 209
Belgian Congo, 47, 103, 104, 131,
195
Bell, Oliver, 32, 33, 35
*Benzi Goes to Town*, 88–91, 138
Beriff, Henry, 73, 100
Bilharzia, 33, 96
Bioscope, 1, 8, 14, 17, 20, 162, 164,
208
*Birth of a Nation*, ix
Blantyre (Nyasaland), 99
Bottomore, Stephen, 48, 49
Bowles, J. F., 76

*Box, The*, 77, 125
boxing, 14, 173
Brelsford, Vernon, 100, 131, 133,
147
British Broadcasting Corporation,
157
British Empire, x, 35, 37
British Film Institute, 29, 32, 33,
53
British South African Police
(BSAP), 1, 7, 11, 14, 18, 84, 90
Broken Hill (Northern Rhodesia),
182
Brown, Denys, 70, 79, 126, 134–35
Bulawayo, 7, 8, 132, 135, 144, 150,
165, 176, 183
disturbances in 1929, 14
*Bulawayo Chronicle* (newspaper),
163
Bullock, Charles, 21, 29, 30
Burke, Tim, 46
Bwanausi, E.V., 183

*Cape Times* (newspaper), 148
Cape Town, 11
capitalism, 82
*Captain of the Clouds*, 34
Carnegie Endowment, 22, 27
*Casebook*, 142
cash crops, 79, 133
censorship
arguments against, 21, 183
campaign against during 1950s,
165
of cinema advertisements and
posters, 15, 18
in the Federation of the Rhodesias and Nyasaland, 150–87
of films for Africans, 8, 10, 15,
18, 27–28, 152, 150–87
in India, 35
in Kenya, 28
at mining compounds, 12
of sexually suggestive images, 4,
5, 13, 17, 35, 154, 176
in Southern Rhodesia, 152
support for from educated